The Global Turn

The Global Turn

THEORIES, RESEARCH DESIGNS, AND
METHODS FOR GLOBAL STUDIES

Eve Darian-Smith and
Philip C. McCarty

UNIVERSITY OF CALIFORNIA PRESS

University of California Press, one of the most distinguished university presses in the United States, enriches lives around the world by advancing scholarship in the humanities, social sciences, and natural sciences. Its activities are supported by the UC Press Foundation and by philanthropic contributions from individuals and institutions. For more information, visit www.ucpress.edu.

University of California Press
Oakland, California

Library of Congress Cataloging-in-Publication Data

Names: Darian-Smith, Eve, 1963– author. | McCarty, Philip C., author.
Title: The global turn : theories, research designs, and methods for global
    studies / Eve Darian-Smith and Philip C. McCarty.
Description: Oakland, California : University of California Press, [2017] |
    Includes bibliographical references and index.
Identifiers: LCCN 2016053763 (print) | LCCN 2016056135 (ebook) |
    ISBN 9780520293021 (cloth : alk. paper) | ISBN 9780520293038
    (alk. paper) | ISBN 9780520966307 (epub)
Subjects: LCSH: Globalization—Study and teaching.
Classification: LCC JZ1318 .D366 2017 (print) | LCC JZ1318 (ebook) |
DDC 303.48/2071—dc23
LC record available at https://lccn.loc.gov/2016053763

Manufactured in the United States of America

25   24   23   22   21   20   19   18   17
10   9   8   7   6   5   4   3   2   1

"We have been waiting for a book that would investigate the full impact of globalization on the social sciences and humanities. Here it is."—Boaventura de Sousa Santos, author of *Epistemologies of the South: Justice against Epistemicide*

"More than a manual of methodologies, this innovative book is a reflection on the emerging field of Global Studies—what it is, what it can do, and how it can do it. It's an important book, one that will be widely used and discussed. It provides pathways for research for anyone working on issues related to our increasingly global milieu."—Mark Juergensmeyer, editor of *Thinking Globally: A Global Studies Reader*

"Globalization respects no borders—between countries or between disciplines. This book will be greatly valued by researchers and students for its clear, comprehensive overview of concepts and methods in a field of challenging diversity."—Ulf Hannerz, Professor, Stockholm University, and author of *Writing Future Worlds*

"Sets a new standard for linking theory, case studies, and research design in the study of global processes. The theoretical overview is wide-ranging and accessible, the extended case studies are vivid and timely, and the presentation of research methods and design will be of great value to both teachers and students."—Arjun Appadurai, Paulette Goddard Professor of Media, Culture, and Communication, New York University

"The authors take on the heroic—and ambitious—task of giving definition to an emerging field of inquiry, one whose rise tolls the history of the present in a critically important way. They bring to it an entirely fresh perspective, simultaneously laying out a theoretical framework, a methodological prospectus, and, most of all, a promise to decenter knowledge production from its received, often sterile, hegemonic centers."—John Comaroff, Hugh K. Foster Professor of African and African American Studies and of Anthropology, Harvard University

To Pammie and Ian, mum and dad

To great mentors everywhere who selflessly teach
their students to think creatively and independently,
and to push beyond what they were taught

The world is a sphere, there is no East or West.

—Ai Weiwei (2012)

The image on the cover of the paperback edition, *Iron Ore Landscape* by Fred Williams, confronts the viewer with the vastness of an Australian landscape. Williams upset Western visual conventions by incorporating indigenous aesthetics that include multiple perspectives, visual planes, and a tilted horizon. With no obvious focal point, framing, foreground, or way to measure distance, the viewer is "unmoored" and encouraged to experience being in the landscape with an overwhelming sense of space and an infinite horizon. Scholars encountering global perspectives may experience something similar.

Contents

List of Figures   viii

Foreword   ix

1. Global Studies as a New Field of Inquiry   1

2. Why Is Global Studies Important?   29

3. A Global Theoretical Framework   55

4. Global Research Design   76

5. Global Methods and Methodologies   129

6. A Global Case Study Method   178

7. Examples of Global Studies Research   206

    Conclusion   225

Appendix A. A Global Case Study Outline   231

Appendix B. List of Global Studies Journals   233

References   237

Index   265

Figures

1. Overlapping Assemblages and Relations across Time and Space 5

2. Conceptual Imaginaries 6

3. Unisphere, New York World's Fair, 1964–65 14

4. Disciplines Engaging Globalization 22

5. Global Studies 24

6. Centralized, Decentralized, and Distributed Systems 46

7. Transdisciplinarity 60

8. Joseph Wright of Derby, *A Philosopher Giving a Lecture on the Orrery*, c. 1765 81

9. "Measuring the Width of a River by Triangulation," from Levinus Hulsius's 1605 *Instrumenta Mechanica* 110

10. The Indigenous Research Agenda 172

11. Divergent Dimensions 185

12. Dimensions Intersecting at a Focal Point 186

13. Multidimensional Case-to-Case Comparison 202

14. Multiple Case Comparisons 203

Foreword

We met in 1995 as graduate students and quickly fell in love. Philip had just returned from fieldwork in Mexico and was fascinated with the ways that the arrival of large multinational corporations in small rural communities was dramatically changing the lives of the people in those communities. Eve was finishing up her doctoral thesis on the building of the Channel Tunnel and the transnational impact of the European Union on people living in southern England. We could not clearly articulate it at the time, but both of us were doing field research that engaged with the issues and impacts of globalization. Many different global forces were manifesting within nations and across geopolitical regions, and we were both interested in how new political, economic, cultural, and social processes were changing concepts of nationalism, identity, and people's sense of belonging. We were both beginning to think as interdisciplinary global scholars even though at the time no university had a department of "global studies" and only a few scholars were even talking about globalization.

This book reflects twenty years of conversations between the two of us about what it means to study global processes and how to go about doing such research. Over the decades each of us has been involved in a variety of research projects, many of them not obviously concerned with the "global." But always our work has circled back to the big questions of how to reconceptualize intellectual work so as to better accommodate new forces and processes not contained within the conceptual frame of the nation-state nor easily managed by national governments and state institutions. In what ways do the emerging impacts of globalization push us to develop new theoretical approaches that transcend disciplinary boundaries, and call for the development of new modes of inquiry, analytical tools, research designs, methodological approaches, and forms of data collection?

Driving many of the discussions between us was an earlier discussion Eve had had with Marshall Sahlins, one of the most eminent anthropologists in the United States. Eve was standing in the foyer of Haskell Hall, the home of the Department of Anthropology at the University of Chicago. She had just finished her doctoral defense and was leaning against the wall in limp relief. They were discussing the challenges for anthropological research in the coming decades and what it meant to do ethnographic research in an increasingly complex global age. "But, but . . ." Eve sputtered in protest. "You are making unreasonable demands on students. You are suggesting that in addition to being an anthropologist, we have to be historians and be well versed in law, literature, politics, economics, cultural studies, and so on. You are saying that to study current global issues the researcher has to do it all!" Sahlins looked up at her and smiling in his impish yet commanding way and said, "That's right and you had better get cracking!"

This book is an attempt to help students in new global studies departments, as well as scholars within established disciplines, to think about what it means to do global research. We believe that engaging with global processes need not be a daunting venture. Hence, in this book we are not suggesting that to do global research one has to be deeply versed in multiple disciplines, each with its own literary canons and theories. Even if that were possible, amassing huge bodies of knowledge is not the same thing as innovatively deploying particular knowledge to develop new kinds of research questions and new modes of inquiry. Moreover, we are very much aware that everyone doing global research will have particular challenges relating to their own project. We don't think there is a one-size-fits-all approach to research design and methods. We are suggesting, however, that by engaging in the conversations, insights, ideas, and examples laid out in this book, the reader will come away feeling motivated to think creatively, ask new questions, embrace new knowledge, grapple with new methodological approaches, and write new kinds of research relevant for understanding our increasingly complex world.

While writing global studies research may appear daunting at first, it also presents an enormously exciting challenge. Across the humanities and social sciences, scholars are confronting a range of problems and ideas that could not even be articulated thirty years ago—for example, climate change, postnational identities, social media, electronic surveillance, drones, unending civil wars, and new forms of terrorism and violence. Every one of us is being pushed to reexamine our taken-for-granted assumptions about how the world is organized and functions, and reflect upon new forms of global interdependence and interconnection that bring peoples around the world together but also create new moments of conflict and crisis. The early decades of the twenty-first century present a unique moment and need to rethink mainstream scholarship in order to better engage with and understand a wide range of global issues affecting us all in our everyday lives. We see this as an incredibly exciting time within the academy, offering a range of opportunities to embrace new kinds of research and include new perspectives in the production of more inclusive modes of knowledge. Appreciating the global dimensions in even the most locally based research is vital if scholarship in the Euro-American academy is to maintain its relevance to global contexts in the coming decades. Conventional scholars who are comfortable in their established ways of thinking may balk, but innovative scholars who recognize the urgent need to rethink and retool will rise to the occasion and "get cracking."

Eve Darian-Smith and Philip McCarty, Santa Barbara, California

Acknowledgments

Thanks to our colleagues in the Global Studies Department, University of California Santa Barbara. Special thanks to authors Mark Juergensmeyer, Bishnupriya Ghosh, and Paul Amar whose books feature in Chapter 7. Also special thanks to Sabine Frühstück, Wesley Pue, Todd Sanders, Florence Seow, Katja Siepmann, John Soboslai, Matthew Sparke, and Tim Wedig for reading early drafts of this book. Thanks to Nicholas Buchanan, Ilana Gershon, Isabella Lohr, Matthias Middell, and Margrit Seckelmann for their general support. Eve thanks John Comaroff, Greg Dening, Peter Fitzpatrick, Donna Merwick, and Sally Falk Moore for their mentorship over the years. Philip thanks William Bielby, Denise Bielby, Jon Cruz, Simonetta Falasca-Zamponi, and John Mohr. Finally, thanks to our editor at UC Press, Reed Malcom; to anonymous reviewers; and to Athena Tan for her excellent editing.

Several parts of this book are based on articles that the authors have published in various journals over the last few years. Most notably, these include "Globalizing Legal History," in *Rechtsgeschichte—Legal History* 22 (McCarty 2014b); "Communicating Global Perspectives," in *Global Europe—Basel Papers on Europe in a Global Perspective* 105 (McCarty

2014c); "Mismeasuring Humanity: Examining Indicators through a Critical Global Studies Perspective," in *New Global Studies* 10 (1) (Darian-Smith 2016); and "Beyond Interdisciplinarity: Developing a Global Transdisciplinary Framework," in *Transcience: A Journal of Global Studies* 7 (2) (Darian-Smith and McCarty 2016).

1 Global Studies as a New Field of Inquiry

The impetus for *The Global Turn: Theories, Research Designs, and Methods for Global Studies* stems from our early experiences as young researchers faced with the enormously daunting task of doing research projects that involved global-scale issues. At the time—the early 1990s—only a few scholars were talking about globalization and grappling with its multifaceted implications. Most of them were fixated on the processes, flows, speed, and impacts of new digital communications, new forms of cultural exchange and homogenization, economic market penetrations, McDonaldization, time-space compression, and so on (Harvey 1990; Urry 2003; Appadurai 1996). A few others were beginning to study a range of new global concerns such as climate change, mass migrations, diverse capitalisms, pandemics, regional genocide, religious terrorism, and the worldwide dismantling of the welfare state. Together global processes and global problems raised new challenges and demanded new solutions. Yet at the turn of the century, no single academic discipline seemed to offer sufficient theories, methods, and training to grapple with these complex and interconnected concerns. From the perspective of the individual researcher, how was one to develop appropriate research questions and design a viable research topic? How did one begin the formidable task of doing global research?

Today, in contrast to twenty years ago, many scholars across the humanities and social sciences are engaging with the interdisciplinary challenges presented by the pressing global issues of the twenty-first century. We argue that the collective turn of the disciplines to engage with contemporary and historical processes of globalization, and their related global issues, represents something more than just a substantive concern shared across disciplines. Rather, it is a fundamental shift in analytical perspectives that requires a thorough retooling of our modernist and disciplinary modes of analysis (Appadurai 2000; Bauman 1998). We call this shift the "global turn." Engaging global contexts requires scholars to think globally and to develop new global theories and perspectives on issues that were previously understood as either universal, national, or local (Moraru 2001; Juergensmeyer 2014a). The global turn is also an engagement with scholars beyond the Euro-American academy that transforms the way global scholarship is done (Burawoy 2009; Casid and D'Souza 2014). And beyond this, it is an engagement with diverse societies, other ways of knowing, and the marginalized majorities that are increasingly shaping and reshaping our collective futures (Kupchan 2012: 183). In these aspects and more, the global turn has profound political, economic, sociocultural, historical, legal, and ethical implications that global scholars are just beginning to explore.

This book is designed for scholars who recognize that engaging with the global is vital in order to ensure their work remains relevant and applicable in the coming decades. This book should be useful to a wide range of students and scholars in the humanities and social sciences, as well as those doing research in professional schools such as law or medicine. Specifically, the audience for the book is (1) undergraduate and graduate students that want to study global processes, (2) scholars who are new to the field of global studies and want to design global studies research, and (3) scholars in more conventional disciplines who want to engage with global issues.

We wrote this book because we found that despite the escalating attention being given to globalization, there has been very little conversation within academia to date about how one should go about studying global-scale processes and their myriad forms and ramifications. While scholars increasingly acknowledge that contemporary processes of globalization call for new theoretical and methodological approaches, there is a void in the literature about what these new theories, analytics, methods, and pedagogies would actually entail. As a result, studying global-scale processes and impacts remains a daunting task for most scholars and for the many students that universities seek to train.

We see this book as filling a gap in existing literature and scholarly conversations. It underscores the importance and necessity of global studies research and the exciting opportunities and challenges such work entails. More significantly, this book provides a practical guide for designing and doing this kind of research. It elaborates a coherent approach that we have developed and tested in both the classroom and the field over the past five years. We have found that this approach makes studying complex global issues much more accessible and less intimidating for people new to engaging with the positive and negative impacts of global processes that characterize our contemporary era.

EMBRACING THE GLOBAL

The first point we want to make is that the *global* and a *global imaginary*, however one defines them, favor a holistic approach to understanding contemporary global issues and the deep global histories that shape the present. These holistic approaches can change the way we see the world. For example, embracing deep histories and holistic interconnections make a global imaginary different from *international* and *transnational* imaginaries. The international speaks to the interactions between nation-states—think of the United Nations (UN), for instance—while the transnational speaks to the interactions beyond the nation-state. These interactions may be conducted by states or nonstate actors such as corporations, but the national still frames and anchors the imaginative reach of analysis.

In contrast, a global imaginary includes nation-states, but also a huge array of nonstate actors, organizations, collectivities, processes, relations, ways of knowing, and modes of interaction across, between, and within national and transnational contexts (Steger 2008). The global should thus be thought of as conceptually and epistemologically more encompassing than the *trans*national and the *inter*national, which are anchored to the core concept of the nation-state. A global imaginary exists in uneasy tension with a national imaginary and, in fact, intrinsically challenges the latter's presumptive authority and centrality. A global imaginary offers us alternative ways of thinking about social relations and behaviors that are not limited by state systems and concepts of sovereignty, territoriality, citizenship, and nationalism. This includes non-Western worldviews, cosmologies, religions, aesthetics, ethics, values, ways of being and communicating, and perhaps even different ways of thinking about what it means to be "human" (Tobin 2014; Grusin 2015; Dayan 2011; Smith 2012: 26).

The second point we want to make is that we need to complicate how a global imaginary is typically talked about in mainstream society and media. Most people think of the global in geopolitical terms and correlate it to processes and concepts that transcend the borders of the nation-state. The global is often talked about as involving a global—as in worldwide—spatial reach. It has become synonymous with processes of globalization and economic transnational activities. In contrast to this overarching geographical conceptualization of the global, we suggest that it is not simply a matter of spatial scale or geopolitical reach that makes any issue or process global. "Global" doesn't just mean "big." The local and global are mutually constitutive, creating and recreating each other across conceptual fields in a constant dynamic. This means that the global is found not only in macro processes but also in the full range of human activities. We don't find global processes only in large cosmopolitan cities and multinational corporations, but also in villages and neighborhoods, workplaces and private homes. Our argument is that the global is present where global-scale processes become manifest in real-world contexts, in the lives of ordinary people. Put another way, what makes an issue or process global are the questions one asks that reveal its global dimensions, even if on the surface it appears very small scale and localized (Darian-Smith 2013a; Eslava 2015). One implication of this is that scholars that do not think of their work as "global" can reconceptualize their current projects as global research by asking the kinds of questions that engage a global perspective.

A global perspective involves more than a view of geopolitical scales and jurisdictional levels nested from the local or small scale up through the levels of the national, regional, international, transnational, and global (Sassen 1991; Brenner 2004; Darian-Smith 2013c). The vertical nest-

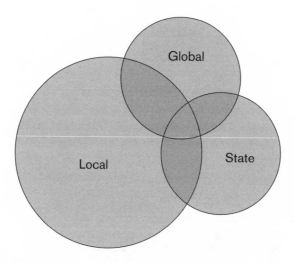

Figure 1. Overlapping Assemblages and Relations across Time and Space.

ing hierarchy of spatial scale has been the dominant way of thinking about political and economic relations between individuals, nation-states, and the international order for decades. This hierarchical way of thinking is often linked with the writings of the American international relations specialist Kenneth N. Waltz, who delineated three levels—systemic/international, national/regional, and individual/local—in his book *Man, the State, and War* (1959).

While this vertical nesting hierarchy provides a neat analytical shorthand for what we are exploring, it is conceptually and materially inadequate (Howitt 1993; Brenner 2001). Rather, a global perspective involves a new conceptualization of practices within a global imaginary. This entails, as global studies scholar Saskia Sassen argues, new assemblages of authority and power that do not privilege one spatial orientation over another (Sassen 2008). Depending on the questions one asks and the issues one is engaged with, the local may occupy the foreground and in fact eclipse the global in terms of analytical and methodological priority and material significance (fig. 1). This recasting of social, economic, political, legal, social, and cultural relations creates opportunities to rethink conventional linear notions of cause and effect since we cannot assume

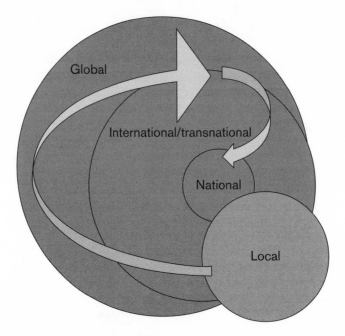

Figure 2. Conceptual Imaginaries.

automatically that the issues with the most encompassing geospatial reach will have the biggest impact. Such rethinking disrupts our instrumentalist view of economic, political, and social processes, which in most scholarship still emanate primarily from the nation-state and are interpreted as making an impact up and down a vertical axis of substate, nation-state, and transstate relations.

As global scholars, we think it is essential to be flexible thinkers and interrogate our taken-for-granted assumptions about the workings of power and related social, legal, economic, and political concepts. In short, we need to decolonize the basic building blocks that have dominated the past three centuries of Western thought (Santos 2007, 2014; Mutua and Swadener 2011). As global scholars, we should be careful not to reify or unduly privilege the nation-state by viewing everything as operating either above or below its framing parameters. In other words, we need to analytically *decenter* the nation-state despite some states remaining very powerful actors. And as global scholars, we want to suggest that it is entirely appropriate, if not imperative, to foreground people living within local and intimate communities. This does not mean that the local is somehow intrinsically good or a more important arena of study, but analyses of global processes should always take into account the people and communities who ultimately feel the impact of those processes even when impacts are unintended or unforeseen. We should be anxious to explore the global dimensions of the local and how local forces may be both resisting and reconstituting national contexts (fig. 2).

Perhaps most important, as global scholars we should embrace a global imaginary without naïvely believing—as was the case in the post–World War II era—in Western industrialized states as the driving force and only source of emancipatory possibility. This means recognizing alternative, non-Western epistemologies and pluralist political, legal, and economic systems, and promoting—as the World Social Forum seeks to do—how another world may be possible (Santos 2007). As Toni Morrison reminded us years ago, embracing the imagination of another can be one way of sharing the world (Morrison 1992). Adopting a global imaginary means appreciating that what happens in one part of the world affects and influences what happens in other parts of the world. Aspirations of global democracy necessarily involve "us" and "them" because another person's insecurity is only a few steps removed from our own. Finally, as global scholars, adopting a global imaginary means understanding the overlapping and intersecting social contexts across times and spaces in which all of our work is situated. This is the case whether one's primary research is engaged with family relations, local communities, global cities, national governments, multinational corporations, international agencies, or global governance institutions. Depending on the research questions one asks, all or some of these dimensions may be in play, in some cases simultaneously.

DECENTERING THE PRODUCTION OF KNOWLEDGE

The current challenges presented by our complex world require global scholars to embrace new ways of thinking. We argue that decentering is an important way of thinking about global challenges. To "decenter" something means to displace it from a primary place, from a central position or role, or from an established center of focus. French philosopher Louis Althusser introduced the idea of a "decentered structure" to structural theory (Althusser 1990: 254–55). Jean Piaget used the idea in his theory of cognitive development. In his work, decentering refers to the stage of cognitive development when a child relinquishes an egocentric world for a more objective world shared with others, and develops the ability to logically consider multiple aspects of a situation (Silverman 1980: 106). In social theory, decentering can mean "to disconnect from practical or theoretical assumptions of origin, priority, or essence" (Merriam-Webster 2015).

The decentering theme will be used in several ways in this book. For example we argue, as others before have argued, that Euro-American scholars need to decenter Western conceptions of history. Further, we argue that to engage with global issues, Western scholars need to decenter the fundamentally modernist and rationalist imperatives to categorize and dichotomize what are essentially decentered social processes. Scholars need to recognize and overcome prevailing logics that put everything into hierarchies, ordered positions, center and periphery models, and developmental progressions with directional flows and linear causalities that start at an origin point and evolve in one direction.

Embracing a decentered world and learning to consider it from multiple perspectives implies a decentering of the production of knowledge that has been, at least for the past four centuries, historically associated with the rise of modernity that emerged out of Western Europe and through processes of colonialism, industrialization, and imperialism spread around the world. Today the Euro-American academy still dominates the production of scholarly knowledge, in part by ignoring longstanding and rapidly growing bodies of non-Western scholarship. There is a pressing need for research dealing with global issues to incorporate knowledge produced outside the Euro-American academy, and to understand this scholarship as a vital source of inspiration and innovation (Comaroff and Comaroff 2012; Grosfoguel 2011; Keim et al, 2014). As Australian and US scholars ourselves, we have to constantly deal with this issue. We have found that there are a number of ways to engage scholarship in other languages and cultures. Scholars can read translated works, have their own work translated, participate in reciprocal scholarly exchanges, copublish, conduct field research, and ideally become conversant in foreign languages. This requires a lot of work, but we find each collaboration is more rewarding than we could have imagined.

Postcolonial scholar Edward Said was an early proponent of the need to create a more inclusive intellectual landscape, one that does not privilege the perspective of industrialized Western societies. Reflecting on the unprecedented escalation of merging systems of knowledge and traditions in the second half of the twentieth century, Said wrote, "We are mixed in with one another in ways that most national systems of education have not dreamed of" (1993: 328). Said went on to say, "To match knowledge in the arts and sciences with these integrative realities is, I believe, the cultural challenge of the moment" (Said 1993: 331; see also Said 1983). Mike Featherstone and Couze Venn add that "as we move into the 21st century, it is clear that the boundaries, limits and classifications of the world are shifting" (Featherstone and Venn 2006: 1). More recently, global scholar Saskia Sassen has argued, "When we confront today's range of transformations—rising inequality, rising poverty, rising government debt—the usual tools to interpret them are out of date" (Sassen 2014: 7). Global scholars, and the emerging field of global studies, should be at the forefront of this engagement and developing new theoretical and conceptual tools for understanding global processes.

In this context, the book *Imagined Globalization* by Néstor García Canclini, a Latin American theorist, is pertinent. He writes:

> In this second decade of the twenty-first century neoliberal thought, normalized on a worldwide scale, has deteriorated, and in several regions it has been seen that not only is another world possible but that many worlds and forms of social organization are possible, as are different relations between men and women, between technology, territory, and investments. This decentered multifocality is what is interesting to me because it changes the terms of explanation and interpretation and discredits the geopolitical predominance. (García Canclini 2014: 209)

A decentered and more inclusive production of knowledge can help scholars everywhere transcend the limitations of existing theories and explanatory paradigms, to more fully grasp the many aspects of global issues, and begin the work of elaborating new, more inclusive, and realistic solutions.

BEYOND MULTIDISCIPLINARY
AND INTERDISCIPLINARY APPROACHES

One way in which universities have addressed the need to develop global modes of inquiry has been to bring together scholars from various disciplines into a single department or research hub for multidisciplinary, perhaps even interdisciplinary, collaborations. Funding agencies have also responded to this need by connecting experts with different specialties to work on specific global projects. For a variety of reasons, however, bringing together disciplinary experts to talk to each other does not necessarily guarantee innovative approaches or theories appropriate for the complexity of our globalizing world. As Eric Wolf noted in his groundbreaking book *Europe and the People without History*: "An [integrated] approach is possible, but only if we can face theoretical possibilities that transcend our specialized disciplines. It is not enough to become multidisciplinary in the hope that an addition of all the disciplines will lead to a new vision" (Wolf 1982: 19).

The Global Turn explores how scholars may overcome the limitations of disciplinary scholarship in order to study global-scale processes and impacts. We argue that moving beyond multidisciplinary and interdisciplinary approaches is necessary: however innovative they are, they are nonetheless bound to the conventional disciplines from which they draw their conceptual differentiation. To be truly global, global scholarship must break free from modernist and Eurocentric concepts and assumptions. This includes moving beyond the prevalent geopolitical state frameworks that are inadequate for examining today's postnational global processes.

In this book we propose a theoretical and methodological synthesis that engages with the multifocal and multidimensional problems of our current times. We propose a *global transdisciplinary framework* that is more than a simple amalgamation or combination of mainstream disciplinary perspectives. Rather, the proposed framework posits a holistic global perspective and teases out new theoretical, analytical, and methodological modes of inquiry that are better suited to understanding evolving processes of globalization and their accompanying reconfigurations of social, cultural, economic, and political relations. We argue that it is not enough for contemporary scholarship to continue to replicate questions embedded within specific disciplines and specialized expertise. What is also needed is to reach beyond the disciplines toward innovative interdisciplinary questions that are relevant to twenty-first-century global research. We suggest that a *global transdisciplinary framework* has the potential to make scholarly knowledge increasingly relevant to pressing global challenges.

The elements of global studies—which we outline in Chapter 2—call for this transdisciplinary framework to include previously marginalized epistemologies and scholarship in the production of new knowledge. What is being forged across the disciplines, we argue, is a new synthesis that has the potential to become applicable and accessible to many scholars, even when their research interests are not explicitly global in nature. In the longer term, it also has the potential to open up Western scholarship to non-Western modes of thinking, knowing, and categorizing. Given the enormity of these potential implications, one of the central objectives in this book is to describe what we mean by a global transdisciplinary framework—which we do in Chapter 3—and explore the ways it may be incorporated into research agendas across the humanities and social sciences.

Building on the notion of a global transdisciplinary framework, we go on to outline a multidimensional methodology that makes it possible to design and implement a viable research agenda that reflects these theoretical developments. We would like to assure researchers that the study of global-scale issues is both an immensely important objective and one that even a beginning scholar can achieve. We are not suggesting that scholars should be deeply conversant in multiple disciplines. We are aware that everyone doing global research will have specific challenges relating to their own project. We believe, however, that by engaging in the conversations, insights, ideas, and examples laid out in this book, the reader will come away feeling motivated to think creatively, ask new questions, embrace new knowledge, grapple with new methodological approaches, and write new kinds of research relevant for understanding our increasingly globalized world.

This book provides novice and advanced scholars with a coherent conceptual, theoretical, and methodological lens through which to better understand unfolding processes of global significance and their impacts. It has been possible to write it because new ways of thinking about globalization in recent years have offered, and continue to offer, us new ways to study it. As we discussed above, for research to be global does not mean that its object of study is necessarily big in a spatial sense or that it must intrinsically have a worldwide reach. Many scholars now appreciate that it is not enough to describe the large-scale forces, processes, and flows that transcend national borders. We must also seek to understand the impact of those forces, processes, and flows on ordinary people in sprawling cities and rural towns, in vast urban slums, permanent refugee camps, border zones, gated communities, detention centers, and so on (Ong and Collier 2004). Many of these sites are subsumed within the national framework, just as many others transcend national borders and underscore the arbitrary and sometimes obsolete nature of nation-states. It is the dynamic, multidimensional interplay of issues along a local-global continuum that provides the unique framing of a global studies approach (see Chapter 2).

Emphasizing the local-global continuum allows scholars across the social sciences and humanities to focus on the ways in which global processes affect small communities and localized social, cultural, economic, legal, and political relations both positively and negatively. Even the largest and most abstract global process becomes tangible and accessible when and where it touches down and is refracted through specific locales and the people who live in them. Being able to see the global through the local and the local through the global is an important way of understanding our globalizing world. This moves scholarly conversations beyond tedious definitional arguments, such as debates on whether the phenomena we study are local, national, regional, international, transnational, or global. Recognizing the entire local-global continuum allows us to see that issues play out at multiple levels simultaneously and thus equips us to take on the interconnected and integrated realities of global processes.

AN EMERGING GLOBAL WORLDVIEW

The field of global studies is typically associated with studies of globalization that began to appear in the 1980s and 1990s. These studies of contemporary globalization were matched with a growing number of studies focusing on globalization in earlier historical periods (Sachsenmaier 2011). According to Manfred Steger's narrative of the history of global studies, "it is no accident that the academic origins of the new field of inquiry [global studies] coincide with the explosion of the keyword [globalization] in both academic and public discourses in the 1990s" (Steger 2016: 238). We contend, however, that the intellectual trajectory that informs the transdisciplinary field of global studies started long before the 1990s. We suggest that the emergence of a new global worldview is linked to the moment of opportunity and optimism that was incongruously opened up by the devastating world wars of the twentieth century (Herren, Rüesch, and Sibille 2012). In this postwar moment, the modern Western understanding of the world was profoundly shaken and concepts such as state sovereignty, citizenship, and nationalism were called into question. An emerging worldview reflected a postwar yearning for peace, stability, and multilateral political cooperation between countries and peoples from a wide range of ethnic, religious, and ideological backgrounds.

Building on the multilateral conversations that surrounded the Paris Peace Conference after World War I, and the first attempt at a League of Nations, the United Nations was successfully established in 1945. The UN played an important role in connecting millions of displaced people after the war, and heralded in the Universal Declaration of Human Rights in 1948. These events ushered in an unprecedented era of global optimism about countries' ability to work together to avoid future wars. Unique to this brief post-WWII period was Western countries' inclusion of the so-called Third World in this global venture. Support for decolonization underscored international efforts to create a more just and equitable world that contributed to decolonization and the "liberation" of many millions of people from Anglo-European control.

An event that encapsulated people's newfound capacity to think in terms of global democracy and freedom was the opening of the New York World's Fair in 1964. The fair billed itself as a "universal and international" exposition. For the 51 million visitors that poured through its gates, the World's Fair represented the promise of technology and advanced communications to link people around the world in new ways. It featured a

Figure 3. Unisphere, New York World's Fair, 1964–65.

new ride by Walt Disney called "It's a Small World"; a rotating "Carousel of Progress" demonstrating new technologies such as televisions, computers, and kitchen appliances; and high-tech trains and architectural wonders that brought to life science fiction's futuristic world (see Samuel 2007; Tirella 2014)

Among these wonders of modern technology, the Unisphere was the fair's key attraction (fig. 3). This was an enormous stainless steel model of Earth that reached twelve stories high and was designed to celebrate "Man's Achievements on a Shrinking Globe in an Expanding Universe." Like the Statue of Liberty, which had been built in France and erected in New York Harbor eighty years earlier, the Unisphere was intended as a symbol of freedom and global democracy (Mitchell 2014). Importantly, the Unisphere also reflected the growing popular excitement associated with a new space age. It foreshadowed the Apollo 8 mission that would take place a few years later, in 1968, and enable its three-man crew to see Earth for the first time from an outer-space perspective. Astronaut William Anders's famous *Earthrise* photograph, and which some have labeled the most influential environmental photo ever taken,[1] invoked a new way of thinking about man's vulnerability in the universe and humankind's common and interlinked future on a single planet.

Events such as the establishment of the UN, the World's Fair, and the success of Apollo 8 and Apollo 11, which put man on the moon, together reflected a remarkable period in which a new global imaginary of mankind's interconnectedness emerged and took on weight in the popular imagination, particularly in the United States. The growing environmental movement furthered this imaginary, spurred on by Rachel Carson's influential 1962 book *Silent Spring* and the 1969 Santa Barbara, California, oil spill. In response to the spill, an estimated 20 million Americans took to the streets in 1970 in defense of the global environment, celebrating the first Earth Day. This mass mobilization forced the US federal government to establish the Environmental Protection Agency (1970) and helped launch Green Party politics in Australia and then Switzerland, the United Kingdom, and Germany (Spretnak and Kapra 1986; Wall 2010).

At the same moment that the UN Charter established a platform upon which to "maintain international peace and security," however, the superpowers of France, the United States, and the United Kingdom were already mobilizing against the Soviet Union and setting up the conditions for the Cold War that posited capitalism against communism. Against the upbeat rhetoric of global inclusion that flourished in the latter half of the twentieth century, it is impossible to ignore the oppressive historical realities that underpinned and perhaps explain the desire for an optimistic global imaginary. The jubilant Unisphere imagery of the World's Fair elided the fact that John F. Kennedy had been assassinated only five months before the world exposition opened. It also obscured the Cold War realities of the 1960s, which witnessed the building of the Berlin Wall (1961), mounting fears of nuclear warfare in incidents such as the Cuban Missile Crisis (1962), looming and ongoing regional wars (Korea and Vietnam), and the USSR's suppression of the liberation movement known as the Prague Spring (1968). In Africa, Latin America, and other parts of the world, the 1960s witnessed extreme violence in response to liberation

---

1. See "That Photograph," ABC in Space, 1999, http://www.abc.net.au/science/moon /earthrise.htm, accessed on August 29, 2106.

movements, deeply tainting the global optimism surrounding decolonization that flourished immediately after World War II. Self-determination was often accompanied by waves of oppression and brutality as ethnic and religious communities were artificially divided and cordoned off into new nation-states across Asia and Africa.

In the wake of genocide and nuclear warfare, or what Eric Hobsbawm has called "total war," the foundations of modern rationality were profoundly shaken within intellectual circles in this postwar era (Hobsbawm 1994). Many societies developed deep-seated anxieties about the failings of modernity's promises of science, development, progress, democracy, and self-determination, which had dominated Euro-American thought since the Enlightenment. These anxieties manifested within twentieth-century European art and literature movements, such as Dadaism and Surrealism, that bridged the post-WWI and WWII periods, as well as in the existentialist, absurdist, and nihilist movements in philosophy and literature. Artists and intellectuals, many of whom had fled Europe for the United States in the late 1930s, grappled with the sensation that nothing was predictable, stable, or fixed in a world turned upside-down that had become in many ways unrecognizable.

Within the Euro-American academy, leading intellectual figures began reaching out beyond the conventions of academic disciplines to explore a turbulent postwar period that had brought women into the labor force, released black and brown societies from colonial rule, and revealed the violence and depravity of ostensibly civilized European societies. As Immanuel Wallerstein notes, this was a period when the "centrist liberal geoculture that was holding the world-system together" was essentially undermined (Wallerstein 2004: x).

Against rapidly shifting social and political contexts, scholars began "deconstructing" or questioning the basic assumptions underpinning modernity. Taken-for-granted categories of nationality, gender, sexuality, race, and ethnicity became sites of controversy, exploration, and experimentation. As a result, new intellectual conversations emerged between scholars from across the disciplines who were drawn together in a quest to understand enduring real-world problems at home and abroad—problems of racism, inequality, development, neocolonialism, and neoimperialism. Opportunities for dialogue among Third- and First-World scholars developed at the fringes of these conversations, introducing new ideas, alternative perspectives, and competing epistemologies into the Western academy that broadened its knowledge base and underscored its Eurocentric bias (Wallerstein 1996: 48).

Pressures mounted for universities to look beyond their national borders as well as to reexamine domestic agendas and respond to the civil rights movements of the 1950s and 1960s. The decades that followed saw a proliferation of interdisciplinary programs on university campuses, including area, ethnic, women, gender, religious, and environmental studies (Ferguson 2012). Cultural, ethnic, and area studies programs ushered new conversations into universities. Some of these programs focused on non-Western regions, issues of race and class, and some on alternative viewpoints and voices of minority peoples. Among these programs, area studies represented an explicit effort to initiate new knowledge about non-Western countries and places.

Within the United States the international studies programs were sponsored in large part by the Ford Foundation, Rockefeller Foundation, and Carnegie Corporation of New York, who worked collectively to support interdisciplinary area studies as a matter of public policy (Lagemann 1989; Chomsky et al. 1998; Ludden 2000; Miyoshi and Harootunian 2002; Szanton 2004; Schäfer 2010). Under the Higher Education Act of 1965 and the introduction of Title VI grants, funding was made available to approximately 125 universities to support area studies, language studies, and education abroad programs, which were known as National Resource Center Programs. This resulted in a diverse number of academic units being developed, such as African Studies, Latin American Studies, Asian Studies, East Asian Studies, European Studies, and Pacific Studies. Together they reflected Cold War tensions and the United States' expanding neocolonial reach and development aspirations into other parts of the world.

In the United Kingdom Richard Hoggart and Stuart Hall established Cultural Studies at the University of Birmingham in 1964 in an explicit attempt to grapple with issues of race, class, and power. Heavily influenced by socialist and Marxist thought, these social theorists and historians began exporting their critical interdisciplinary ideas to the United States, where cultural studies blossomed in the 1980s. At approximately the same time, postcolonial and subaltern studies began to flourish. These fields pushed Western scholars to interrogate their essentialist cultural assumptions and view the history of the world from a bottom-up perspective that foregrounded the experiences of non-European peoples and their often very different readings of the past. While many of these conversations were marginalized on university campuses, they nonetheless opened up intellectual space within the Euro-American academy to develop critical perspectives and foster alternative epistemological positions (see however Spivak 2003; Chow 2006).

The cross-pollination of ideas between these various interdisciplinary programs cultivated a wide range of ideas about subjectivity, identity, governmentality, postcoloniality, and so on. As we discuss in Chapter 3, the concept of *transdisciplinarity*, coined by Jean Piaget in 1970, encapsulates these dynamic theoretical exchanges within and between the global north and the global south in the second half of the twentieth century (Piaget 1972). These exchanges informed a new set of thematics that transcended disciplinary thinking and that have reshaped conventional disciplines within the academy over the past three decades. Transdisciplinarity provides the theoretical platform upon which global studies as a new field of inclusive inquiry is currently building.

DEBATING GLOBALIZATION

The flourishing of new ways to analyze complex social relations between nations and peoples in the postwar period was followed by the emergence of globalization as a focus of study. While there have been many periods of globalization over the centuries, twentieth-century globalization blossomed under geopolitical and technological conditions unique to the current era (Nederveen Pieterse 2012). Global processes in the 1970s took the interconnectedness between nation-states, multinational corporations, nongovernmental organizations, and a host of other nonstate and civil society actors to new levels. Globalization first became topical within the international finance and trade sectors, in new articulations of global capitalism. As markets opened up, new economic theories and policies substantiated what has come to be called the age of neoliberalism. Encapsulating neoliberalism as an economic logic, Milton Friedman,

Nobel Prize winner in economics, declared in 1970 that "there is one and only one social responsibility of business—to use its resources and engage in activities designed to increase its profits" (Friedman 1970).

The United States and United Kingdom led the charge in implementing neoliberal economic policies that favored business interests, maximized private corporate power and profits, and devalued the role of the state in regulating exploitative financial practices that jeopardized labor safeguards and public interests. China began its own push toward market liberalization (Duménil and Lévy 2004; Harvey 2007). New digital technologies heightened the speed and capacities of economic exchange around the world and facilitated a sense—at least in the global north—of a new era of free-market globalization. The financial cycles of the 1980s and 1990s and the formation of international business elites underscored the rise of a new "global imaginary" (Steger 2008). During this period, the United States emerged as the global economic superpower, taking advantage of emerging economies in countries such as Brazil, Russia, India, China and South Africa (collectively referred to as BRICS). Today, of course, the political and economic landscape is very different. The size of China's economy has grown rapidly and the United States is no longer the undisputed world leader. Neoliberalism has come under attack, and it is largely blamed for undermining democratic processes in its promotion of unsustainable greed. The 2008 global economic crisis can be seen as the culmination of a long, slow process of global privatization and deregulation that brought the financial world to its knees, dismantled the middle classes, and created unprecedented levels of global inequality and insecurity (Beck 1992, 2009; Chomsky 1999).

It is important to note that globalization was not entirely driven by transnational economic exchange and international financial practices, as economists, with their determinist theories, are inclined to claim (see Appadurai 1996). In the 1980s and 1990s the world also experienced huge shifts in ideological affiliations with the fall of the Berlin Wall and communism, the rise of postcolonial aspirations through self-determination, and the evolution of new cultural and social networks that were both transnational and subnational in nature. Put differently, in the latter half of the twentieth century new forms of community and subjectivity that transcended standard nationalist ideologies and allegiances emerged. The rise of a global environmental movement and Green Party politics, the dismantling of apartheid in South Africa through global political pressure, the call for a global response to the AIDS epidemic—all of these events highlighted people's global interdependence and affirmed that a global worldview was essential for dealing with issues that could not be managed or contained by any one country. These events, and other global challenges, disrupted the centrality, stability, and ideology of the sovereign nation-state, ushering in what some commentators have labeled our current postnational or "post-Westphalian" age (Falk 2002).

As neoliberal economics picked up traction and dismantled welfarism and regulatory state bureaucracies throughout the 1990s and 2000s, so too did notions of democracy come under attack within both Western and non-Western societies. Ideological and political shifts across the world diminished people's sense of an active public sphere and a strong secular state system that could defend the rights of workers, women, and ordinary people against greedy capitalists and deregulated financial markets. These shifts helped to bolster the rise of religious fundamentalism and extremism around the world among Christians, Hindus, Muslims, and other religious communities. Religious extremism has offered new forms of authority that have attracted millions of people in lieu of the nation-state paradigm, which has proven unable to protect the rights of citizens and in the process diminished many people's sense of national loyalty (Juergensmeyer 2000; Juergensmeyer, Griego, and Soboslai 2015; Yang 2008). This period also saw a return to ultranationalism, racism, xenophobia, and anti-immigrant hysteria (Brown 2014).

In the post–Cold War era, scholars in various disciplines were trying to understand globalization and the "intensification of worldwide social relations" (Giddens 1990: 64; Robertson 1992; Axford 1995; Castells 1996; Friedman 1999; Stiglitz 2002). There were heated debates about the definition of globalization and how best to describe and analyze it (Steger and James 2014). Since the 1990s scholars have split into three main camps: the so-called "hyperglobalists," "skeptics," and "transformationalists" (Held et al. 1999: 2–10; Ferguson and Mansbach 2012:17–26). The diverse opinions about the nature of globalization that characterize each of these camps reflect the expertise and training of individual scholars from across the social sciences and, to a lesser degree, the humanities. In general terms, hyperglobalists focus on the economy, arguing that since the Cold War the world has experienced unprecedented levels of integration and a new form of global capitalism that have profoundly changed its organization and how it is experienced. *Skeptics* argue against this position, stating that economic internationalism occurred to the same degree in the nineteenth century and that contemporary economic expansion does not represent an entirely new era or reflect real historical change. Skeptics also assert that global phenomena do not have a worldwide reach, as hyperglobalists claim, and are in fact only regional—e.g., European, East Asian—in geospatial terms.

Transformationalists, or what Luke Martell calls the "third wave" of globalization theorists, stress the interconnections between economics, politics, society, and culture (Martell 2007). Over the years, tranformationalists have presented more nuanced, multilinear, and multicausal analyses of global processes than the hyperglobalists or skeptics. In part this is a result of the global north now experiencing many of the devastating impacts of neoliberalism that it exacted for decades on the global south, as the plummeting social and political circumstances of Greece, Spain, and other European countries have shown. Transformationalists agree that the world is currently undergoing massive change, but the precise nature of that change is still very much in question.

FROM GLOBALIZATION TO GLOBAL STUDIES

Against the backdrop of scholarly debate about the various meanings and impacts of globalization, global studies emerged as a new field of inquiry that broadened the focus beyond economic forms of globalization. The first global studies programs were established in the late 1990s, and over the last twenty years stand-alone programs and research hubs have flourished in numerous countries including Australia, China, Denmark, Germany, Indonesia, Japan, South Korea, Russia, the United Kingdom, and the United States. Each of these programs developed within specific institutional and cultural contexts and as a consequence has its own unique intellectual profile (Juergensmeyer 2014b; Steger and Wahlrab 2016: 25–52; Loeke and Middell forthcoming). Alongside these interdisciplinary

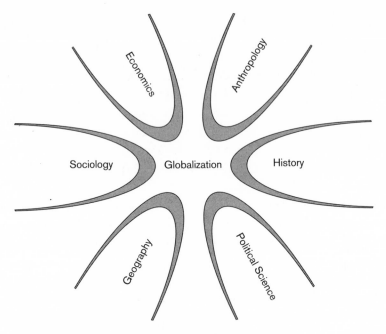

Figure 4. Disciplines Engaging Globalization.

programs dedicated to global studies, subdisciplinary fields that engage specifically with global issues—e.g., global history, global literature, global sociology, and global legal studies—have also emerged within conventional disciplines (see fig. 4). In short, the field of global studies, and its various institutional and disciplinary manifestations, has grown rapidly, and there is now burgeoning institutional support for global scholarship at leading universities.[2]

Many of the early global studies programs, particularly those in the United States and United Kingdom, emphasized macro processes of eco-

2. The Global Studies Consortium, established in 2007, lists approximately thirty institutions that offer undergraduate and graduate programs in global studies. These programs are rapidly growing in number. In the United States, Indiana University established the School of Global and International Studies in 2012; the Department of Global Studies at the University of California, Santa Barbara, launched the first doctoral program at a Tier-1 research university in the country in 2014; and Roberta Buffett gave a gift of over $100 million to support global studies and a new research institute at Northwestern University in 2015.

nomic globalization and international institutions that reflected international relations/international studies scholarship. Alongside this trend, other global studies programs stressed a more humanistic approach and focused on global history, postcolonial studies, cultural diversity, and intercultural exchange. For example, the world and global history approaches at the University of Leipzig laid the groundwork for what is now the Global and European Studies Institute (GESI). Another example is the Globalism Institute (now Centre for Global Research) at RMIT in Melbourne, Australia, which from its inauguration paid particular attention to global political and economic transformations and related political theory (see Steger and Wahlrab 2016: 41–47). One of the pioneering programs was the Department of Global Studies at the University of California, Santa Barbara, founded in 1999. From the start this program included an interdisciplinary curriculum and faculty from both the humanities and social sciences.[3]

Today, among the many global studies programs around the world, there is a concerted effort to develop a more inclusive curriculum that increasingly promotes socially engaged research as well as historical and qualitative methods in an effort to foster culturally informed knowledge production (see, for instance, Appelbaum and Robinson 2005; Khagram and Levitt 2008; Amar 2013). Drawing on a broad range of scholarship, including anthropology, comparative literature, critical race studies, economics, ethnic studies, feminist studies, geography, history, law, linguistics, philosophy, religious studies, sociology, and subaltern studies, a global studies approach highlights the need to rethink our analytical concepts, methods, and approaches to ask new questions about globally integrated processes and dependencies (see fig. 5).

As you would expect, because global scholars borrow elements from conventional disciplines, global studies is impacted by and, over time, may have some impact on those disciplines. But in general interdisciplinary scholars can never entirely satisfy scholars that are deeply entrenched in conventional disciplines. For example, global research often engages with history. Historical context is a necessary dimension to understanding

3. The founding members of UCSB's Global Studies Department reflected this inclusive interdisciplinary approach: Giles Gunn (English), Rich Appelbaum (sociology), Sucheng Chan (Asian American studies and history), and Mark Juergensmeyer (sociology and religious studies). For a history of the department see Steger and Wahlrab 2016: 35–41.

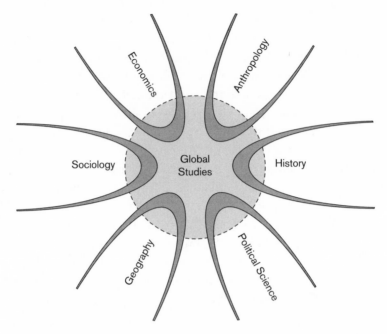

Figure 5. Global Studies.

global issues. For the global scholar, history—or economics, geography, linguistics, or any of the other disciplines—informs one of the many dimensions relevant to global analysis (compare fig. 5 to fig. 12 in Chapter 6). Global scholars draw upon disciplinary perspectives and methods selectively, as needed, to understand multifaceted issues. As an interdisciplinary project, however, global scholarship cannot be entirely contained within disciplines.

Developing a unique interdisciplinary global studies curriculum poses specific challenges that echo the history of the then new women's studies departments of the 1970s. At that time, scholars working in traditional disciplines added feminist content to their regular classes in an attempt to mainstream women, sexuality, and feminist issues more generally. Bonnie Smith, professor of history and women's studies at Rutgers University, recounts, "At the beginning, Women's Studies came to offer a cafeteria-like array of disciplinary investigations of the past and present conditions under which women experienced, acted, and reflected upon the world"

(Smith 2013: 4). Over the decades, however, women's studies converged into a comprehensive field with its own unique curriculum and an expansive array of scholarly inquiries that ranged well beyond the initial scholarly focus on women. Smith notes:

> From the beginning Women's Studies engaged the entire university population. It usually brought in those who were the most intellectually adventurous, whether the course took place in Seoul, South Korea or Los Angeles, US. In short, Women's Studies is a global scholarly enterprise with sparks of energy crossing the disciplines and uniting communities of students and teachers. All this makes Women's Studies a vastly exciting and innovative program of study. (Smith 2013: 4)

Conventional disciplines are mainstreaming the study of global issues within regular courses in a similar fashion. As noted above, today there exist a range of subdisciplinary fields such as global history, global literature, global sociology, and global legal studies. But this cafeteria-like smorgasbord of course offerings that are grounded in specific disciplinary theory and methods is quite different from the distinct interdisciplinary global studies curriculum that leading global studies departments around the world are developing. Like the field of women's studies, global studies is a "global scholarly enterprise" and a "vastly exciting and innovative program of study." And like women's studies, global studies is developing a comprehensive field with its own unique curriculum and theoretical and methodological profile, which may take time to fully mature and coalesce (Campbell, Mackinnon, and Stevens 2010; O'Byrne and Hensby 2011; McCarty 2014a). We view this book as contributing to this process.

Perhaps not surprisingly, a spate of essays asking "What is global studies?" have accompanied the rapid growth in global studies programs, promoting lively debate and commentary (see Juergensmeyer 2011, 2014b; Nederveen Pieterse 2013; Gunn 2013; Duve 2013; Sparke 2013; Darian-Smith 2014; McCarty 2014c; Middell 2014; Steger and Wahlrab 2016). These essays reflect a need to move beyond an earlier preoccupation with defining historical and contemporary phases of globalization to analyzing its many processes, facets, and impacts (Featherstone, Lash, and Robertson 1995; Nederveen Pieterse 2012). As Mark Juergensmeyer argues, there is a need to move from "globalization studies," which studies globalization from various disciplinary perspectives, to "global studies," "the emerging transdisciplinary field that incorporates a variety of disciplinary and new approaches to understanding the transnational features of our global world" (Juergensmeyer 2013a, 2013b). This transition toward what we call a *global transdisciplinary framework* reflects the increasing awareness that global issues, and the theoretical and analytical tools required to study them, are emerging and manifesting within and across local, regional, national, and transnational arenas that require new modes of inquiry and new forms of knowledge production.

It could be argued that global studies programs—at least those interdisciplinary programs that include the humanities and social sciences— have the potential to recast the liberal arts curriculum. In this sense the field has become greater than the sum of its parts. Global studies' interdisciplinary and integrated approach to multiple epistemologies, its holistic understanding of humanity's now-global interconnection and interdependence, and its attention to intercultural understanding and ethical practice suggest a reconfigured liberal arts philosophy (Hutner and Mohamed 2015; Roth 2015; Zakaria 2016).[4] Whether or not one wants to characterize global studies in this way does not detract from the fact that it is one of the fastest growing academic fields in the world. There is a rapidly growing body of academic work that explicitly addresses the processes of globalization, and, more recently, a nascent body of literature has taken up the field of global studies itself (see Steger and Wahlrab 2016; Loeke and Middell forthcoming). Global studies has an increasing number of dedicated peer-reviewed journals, book series, encyclopedias, and professional associations, all producing literature that is explicitly global in orientation (e.g., Anheier and Juergensmeyer 2012, see also appendix B). That being said, we hesitate to label global studies a new discipline. Like the enormously complicated global processes scholars study, conversations describing and analyzing this complex should be messy, dynamic,

4. To foster intercultural understanding and local engagement, the Department of Global Studies at the University of California, Santa Barbara, requires students to study at least two languages and encourages travel overseas for considerable lengths of time, preferably for a year. The department sends more undergraduate students overseas in any one year than any other department in the ten-campus University of California system.

passionate, and constantly open to rethinking. Suggesting that global studies be treated as a discipline runs the risk of closing off intellectual curiosity and stifling its creativity in the urge to establish a literary canon and adopt the trappings of conventional disciplines. In our view, it is essential that global studies remain interdisciplinary and that scholars continue to argue and debate what the field is and could be rather than arriving at a definitive answer in an effort to claim the status of being a cohesive subject of study (Darian-Smith 2014).

The openness to debating and constantly rethinking the field of global studies is also an ethical position. It underscores that Western scholars may not have all the answers to the world's problems and that other people may have new things to say and innovative solutions to offer. As we will discuss more fully in the next chapter, the emerging field of global studies acknowledges the need for new ways of conceptualizing and analyzing global issues. This necessarily entails embracing new forms of knowledge within one's own society as well as beyond from non-Western communities in an effort to think "outside the box." Global studies, perhaps more so than any other arena of inquiry within the Euro-American academy, recognizes that what is happening "over there" in terms of poverty, inequality, exploitation, environmental degradation, and new types of warfare could also happen back home in what David Held calls a world of "overlapping communities of fate" (Held 2002: 57; Roy and Crane 2015). In foregrounding the message that "us" and "them" are intimately interconnected, global studies as a new field of inquiry is both dependent upon and deeply committed to learning from and respecting others. In other words, global studies views intercultural communication as an essential key to better understanding ourselves and our collective futures.

In the next chapter, we outline the significance and characteristics of global studies research. These features have several important theoretical, methodological, and analytical implications. By extracting an integrated global studies approach that builds on the *transdisciplinary theoretical framework* in Chapter 3, we propose a way of asking provocative questions that helps distill research into a unique set of methodological inquiries. In Chapter 4 we walk the reader through the steps of designing a global studies research project; in Chapter 5 we introduce mixed methods and global methodological strategies; and in Chapter 6 we discuss the specific advantages of a global case study, one that enables the researcher to analyze and engage with the complexity of global issues using a manageable research methodology. In Chapter 7 we illustrate our discussion with specific examples of global studies research that successfully deploys what we call a "global case study method."

2 Why Is Global Studies Important?

In recent years a number of scholars have sought to characterize the essential features of global studies scholarship and articulate why the field is so important for understanding our current era (Juergensmeyer 2011, 2014a, 2014b; Duve 2013; Nederveen Pieterse 2013; Gunn 2013; Sparke 2013; McCarty 2014b; Middell 2014; Steger 2015). Building on these conversations, in the first part of this chapter we list the main reasons why we feel global studies as a field of inquiry is important. Some of these reasons may seem obvious but others not so much, and hence we feel that the list below is a necessary exercise in establishing the value of the global studies enterprise. The points are intended to help scholars communicate why the field is important to students as well as to colleagues in other disciplines, university administrators, funding agencies, and so on.

In the second part of the chapter we list the main characteristics associated with a global studies approach that underscore the breadth and depth of what we identify and depict as global studies scholarship. Together these two lists are meant to help the reader quickly grasp the significance of global studies and its signature characteristics that collectively distinguish it as a new field of inquiry. In later chapters we explore how these characteristics feature in designing, implementing and analyzing global studies research projects (Chapters 4, 5, and 6).

WHY IS GLOBAL STUDIES IMPORTANT?

New Solutions to New Problems

A global studies approach offers new ways of thinking that have the potential to generate solutions to the kinds of global-scale problems that our rapidly globalizing world faces. Pressing issues such as climate change, economic development, regional violence, and resource depletion are among the new issues that call for innovative, perhaps previously unthinkable solutions. Global studies scholar Saskia Sassen, echoing many others in the field, argues that we are currently confronted with "limits in our current master categorizations," and as a result fail to see beyond what we already recognize and assume to be important. She argues for the need to look for and "detect *conceptually* subterranean trends that cut across our geopolitical divisions" and open up new ways of seeing, confronting, analyzing, and interpreting the world (Sassen 2014: 8). For example, author and activist Naomi Klein in *This Changes Everything* connects disparate issues such as climate change, neoliberal market fundamentalism, democratization, and global health to argue for fundamental changes in capitalist societies (Klein 2014). Identifying global-scale issues, finding patterns in and connections between them, and proposing new ways to address these issues are some of the core functions of global studies as a field of inquiry.

New Solutions to Old Problems

In some cases a global studies approach can provide new ways of understanding problems that have been overlooked, ignored, or deliberately avoided. For example, global-historical analyses of the international regulatory system indicate that there may be inherent limitations in the modern international treaty system. The inherent limitations are in part the result of imbalances between powerful countries with economic, political, and military clout that can act unilaterally and smaller countries that cannot. These limitations hinder the development of strong multilateral institutions (e.g., International Criminal Court) and treaties (e.g., Kyoto Accord), effectively destabilizing the geopolitical order and increasing the tendency toward both regional conflict and violence by nonstate actors (e.g., ISIS). By shaking up the way we think about international issues, global approaches have the potential to bring new ways of thinking to old and enduring problems, such as immigration and human trafficking, that are notoriously difficult for nation-states to deal with.

One of the most common limitations in our general understanding of how the world is organized and functions is the nation-state's taken-for-granted status as the container of political, economic, and cultural activities. But as Michel-Rolph Trouillot writes so compellingly in his book *Global Transformations* (2003), the nation-state only became accepted as the central political entity around the world in the nineteenth century, with the linguistic spread of languages such as French, English, and German (Anderson 1983; Bhabha 1990). Hence, Trouillot goes on to argue, it is only by appreciating the relatively short history of modern nation-state building that it becomes possible to reconceptualize solutions to old problems:

> We are best equipped to assess the changes that typify our times if we approach these changes with a sober awareness that the national state was never as closed and as unavoidable a container—economically, politically, or culturally—as politicians and academics have claimed since the nineteenth century. Once we see the necessity of the national state as a lived fiction of modernity—indeed, as possibly a short parenthesis in human history—we may be less surprised by the changes we now face and may be able to respond to them with the intellectual imagination they deserve. (Trouillot 2003: 85)

Until scholars break out of the anachronistic international relations paradigm that takes nation-states as the core unit of analysis, they cannot begin to identify, integrate, and analyze global structures, systemic forces, and regulatory issues that operate both above and below the level of the nation-state. This is of course not to suggest that nation-states are no longer relevant in our current times, which is patently incorrect. In the early decades of the twenty-first century, many countries across the global south and global north have taken up aggressive reactionary positions and institutionalized laws and policies specifically intended to shore up a national sense of autonomy and independence. Yet despite conservative political rhetoric, harsh immigration laws, and popular, jingoistic nationalism, the role of the nation-state as the central political entity governing the world is profoundly destabilized in our contemporary, post-Westphalian world (Falk 2002; Brown 2014).

Powerful Analytical Tools

A global studies approach offers unique insights and new, powerful analytical capacities. By situating the local-global continuum in deep historical contexts, global studies has the potential to reveal temporal, spatial, and conceptual connections we could not otherwise have seen or even imagined. For instance, it allows us to begin to trace the connections between empires, colonialism, modern imperialism, and new forms of imperialism in the world today. Global studies suggests that important connections exist between events and processes, even when events appear to be disconnected and separated by time, space, or even our own categories of thought.

A global synthesis supports the development of new analytical concepts. Take, for example, the labor, human rights, environmental, and women's movements. These movements are often studied within the context of a single nation. Even when studied as international social movements, they are typically treated as discrete phenomena. In contrast, a global studies approach would analyze these movements as globally interrelated (Martin 2008). Taking it a step further, a global perspective could link them all together as parts of a larger, *antisystemic* movement that addresses various facets of inequality and injustice in the global political economy. This understanding could in turn support the formation of entirely new levels of *global intersectional solidarity* with the potential for large-scale, worldwide change.

Practical and Policy Applications

A global studies approach is important because it offers unique insights . into real world problems. For example, in *Friction: An Ethnography of*

Global Connection, anthropologist Anna Lowenhaupt Tsing analyzes the processes of cross-cultural communication and miscommunication that contribute to deforestation in the rainforests of Indonesia (Tsing 2005). The actors involved in her study include the indigenous people of the region, relocated peasant farmers, environmental activists, legal and illegal loggers, local politicians, government agencies, international scientists, resource speculators and investors, multinational corporations, and UN funding agencies. The "friction" Tsing describes is the result of their collective interactions, their miscommunications, and all that gets lost in translation. In areas where the government of Indonesia lifted logging bans, intending to allow limited legal access, it also enabled the increasing penetration of illegal logging and property rights violations that it could not monitor. The result was dysfunction at the local and national levels that left the rainforests and indigenous people of Indonesia vulnerable to massive overexploitation by global markets.

The policy implications of this kind of functional/dysfunctional analysis are many. For example, one could use this approach to argue that governments that lack resources should avoid making their natural resources available to unfettered exploitation. Where local governments lack the resources to monitor, enforce, restrict, and benefit from the extraction processes that are detrimental to the environment and local populations, they should rely on types of regulation that are easier to enforce, such as banning all drilling, mining, fishing, and hunting in clearly delineated zones until those activities can be properly monitored and controlled.

Studies such as Tsing's indicate that the insights that result from a global studies approach may be most valuable when deployed at the places where the different political, economic, cultural, and legal elements of global systems interact. By focusing on processes of exchange, and the interactive processes of communication, translation, and interpretation from region to region and from the global to the local, global perspectives can look beyond the nation-state to highlight and interrogate the various functions and dysfunctions within global systems, structures, and institutions. To the degree that geopolitical and economic forces play a part in creating global issues such as mass migration, conflict, climate change, and resource depletion, analyzing larger systems is essential for understanding and acting on these problems.

Global Civics and Citizenship

The field of global studies has the power to transform how both students and more advanced scholars understand current global issues. Every day we are all confronted with headlines that present the world as a dizzying array of apparently disconnected and chaotic events. A global studies approach encourages scholars to identify persistent patterns across time and space. For example, researchers may grapple with the challenge of sustainable economic development. A global studies analysis of economic development may include regional histories of colonization, multinational development policies, national politics, and demographic and environmental changes as well as local institutions, customs, and agricultural practices. In thinking about these multiple elements and perspectives across time and space, scholars are likely to encounter the power and limitations of the modern development paradigm. In a similar way, they can engage with the multiple historical, economic, geopolitical, and cultural factors that shape global issues such as immigration, poverty, regional violence, and ethnic conflict within the context of larger global governance issues such as human rights and global commons. In this way a global studies approach offers scholars a unique, coherent, and more holistic way of understanding ongoing global affairs.

Global perspectives empower scholars and students to understand the world in new ways, as well as to act as citizens of the world (Gaudelli 2016). Teaching the next generation of scholars to reach beyond nationalism to embrace the wider humanity, and encouraging them to think seriously about the possibilities of global citizenship, can transform their fundamental understanding of the individual's role in society and our collective place in the world.

Critical Thinking

In general terms, *critical thinking* means a willingness to think openly, challenge one's own assumptions and concepts, reflect upon the structures of knowledge that guide human actions, and question the implicit bias involved in specific forms of communication. As Michael Scriven and Richard Paul have argued,

Critical thinking is the intellectually disciplined process of actively and skill-fully conceptualizing, applying, analyzing, synthesizing, and/or evaluating information gathered from, or generated by, observation, experience, reflection, reasoning, or communication, as a guide to belief and action. In its exemplary form, it is based on universal intellectual values that transcend subject matter divisions: clarity, accuracy, precision, consistency, relevance, sound evidence, good reasons, depth, breadth, and fairness. (Scriven and Paul 1987)

Being a critical thinker is not about being negative or trying to disman-tle everything, as some unsophisticated scholars are apt to claim. Rather, being a critical thinker is about refusing to be complacent in the surety of one's understanding of a problem or concept, and asking new questions in order to both test one's ideas and seek new ways of knowing and explain-ing. Critical thinking is taught in many national curricula at the high school level and is viewed as essential to fostering engaged intellectual exchange and reflective contextualization. At the university level, critical thinking lies at the core of pioneering and progressive scholarship, be it in the social sciences, humanities, or physical sciences.

The term *critical thinking* has its roots in the second half of the nine-teenth century and is typically associated with neo-Marxist thought and its criticism of the rational actor model fundamental to modern liberal eco-nomics. In the twentieth century, critical thinking is associated with the Annales School and Frankfurt School of the interwar period. Members of the Annales School included Lucien Febvre, Marc Bloch, and Fernand Braudel. Together, these scholars introduced a new historiography that took a more holistic approach in its serious engagement with cultural and social historical analyses of all classes of society, including peasants, farmers, and the poor. The Frankfurt School's members included Max Horkheimer, Theodor Adorno, Herbert Marcuse, Erich Fromm, and Walter Benjamin. Other important critical thinkers include Antonio Gramsci, György Lukács, and Jürgen Habermas, to name a few of the more well known. Many of the members moved to Columbia University in New York to escape the persecu-tion of Nazi Germany. These intellectuals were disillusioned with the ide-ologies of capitalism, socialism, communism, and fascism and sought to understand the structures and mechanisms of class conflict and social ine-quality. In theoretical terms, they strove to overcome the limitations of established positivist and observation-based thinking, which, they argued, constrained innovative political thought and action.

Today critical theory informs a vast array of theoretical perspectives across the humanities and social sciences, including literary criticism, hermeneutics, semiotics, cultural studies, subaltern studies, world-systems theory, critical race theory, feminist theory, queer theory, and postcolonial theory (Collins 1990). These critical perspectives differ to the degree that they explicitly seek social transformation. That being said, each shares in the quest to interpret social meaning, to expose underlying forms of consciousness and narratives of subjectivity, and to reflect upon the power dynamics between structure and agency (Mulnix 2012). In all of these scholarly endeavors, it is important not to equate critical thinking with moral virtues or some set of predetermined objectives. As Jennifer Wilson Mulnix argues,

> Critical thinking, as an intellectual virtue, is not directed at any specific moral ends. That is, it does not intrinsically contain a set of beliefs that are the natural outcomes of applying the method. For instance, two critical thinkers can come to hold contrary beliefs, despite each applying the skills associated with critical thinking well and honestly. As such, critical thinking has little to do with what we think, but everything to do with how we think. (Mulnix 2012: 466)

Within the field of global studies, critical thinking is recognized as an essential element in fostering new questions and new kinds of research applicable to global-scale issues and processes (Appelbaum and Robinson 2005; Juergensmeyer 2011; Lim 2017; Steger and Wahlrab 2016: 147–81). Critical thinking is present in the ways global studies scholarship interrogates the logics, categories, ideologies, and assumptions that reinforce hierarchies of power and the status quo. It surfaces in global studies' commitment to interdisciplinarity and its intrinsic challenge to established disciplinary forms of knowledge. For example, global studies probes the limits of the nation-state and the international relations paradigm, problematizing nationalism and monolithic national identities (Anderson 1983). Global studies also critiques mainstream economics, free-market ideologies, and the assumptions behind economic modernization and development models that center Europe and relegate everyone else to the periphery (Escobar

1995). Critical thinking is further evident in the field's questioning of new forms of imperialism and structural and institutional modes of discrimination, exploitation, and violence. Global studies hence interrogates concepts such as rationalism, nationalism, secularism, modernity, individualism, liberalism, development, and democracy as well as naturalized categories of race, gender, class, religion, and ethnicity.

Being critical should not be understood as a destructive or negative impulse, but rather as a constructive and inclusive impulse. Unpacking dominant paradigms is often analytically productive. So while opening up scholarship to multiple and alternative viewpoints can be threatening in that it challenges established truths and ways of understanding, it can also be a creative process, producing new avenues of inquiry and pointing toward new syntheses and solutions (Nederveen Pieterse 2013: 7). Finally, and perhaps most importantly, critical thinking highlights the need for inclusivity in global studies scholarship through promoting the voices of the oppressed, recognizing non-Western epistemologies, and incorporating the global south in the production of new forms of knowledge.

Non-Western Epistemologies and Multiple Voices

The field of global studies reflects a growing scholarly appreciation for the fact that our contemporary world calls for new theoretical, analytical, methodological, and pedagogical approaches. More profoundly, some scholars are now acknowledging that the Euro-American academy may not have all the answers to comprehending and dealing with our increasingly interconnected world. There is a growing recognition that Western paradigms of knowledge may not be able to solve the problems the West has created.

According to ethnic studies scholar George Lipsitz, "New social relations around the world are rapidly producing new social subjects with their own particular archives, imaginaries, epistemologies, and ontologies . . . . epistemic upheavals require us to rethink fundamental categories about place, time, and knowledge" (Lipsitz 2010: 12–13). Taking a cue from ethnic studies, a global studies approach requires us to reconsider dominant forms of knowledge production and engage with critical voices and plural epistemologies that are not typically represented in Western scholarship and pedagogy (see Freire 2000; Ngũgĩ 1986). Global analyses should include marginalized experiences and voices speaking in non-English vernaculars, many of which may bear witness to the injustices in a global system that includes gross inequality, extreme poverty, human rights abuses, exploitation of human and natural resources, environmental degradation, regionalized violence, and genocide (Lim 2017; McCarty 2014b). Reciprocal intellectual exchanges, bilingual translations, and joint research projects provide avenues for inclusion of different perspectives. It is only by deliberately making room for critical voices and alternative epistemologies, as well as sharing editorial power with non-Western scholars in the production of new knowledge (Smith 2012), that global studies gains the potential to recognize and engage with the many facets of the most serious global issues facing the world today (Featherstone and Venn 2006; Darian-Smith 2014).

Valorizing and legitimating non-Western epistemologies, however, involves much more than either passive moral support or active material support. Western scholars must overcome their ethnocentrism and be prepared to have their own worldviews changed by pluralistic ways of knowing (Santos 2007, 2014). This is very difficult for some scholars in the global north, who remain convinced of their own intellectual superiority. Yet unpacking dominant paradigms should be considered positively, as a creative, constructive, and inclusive process and an opportunity to overcome the "provincial, arrogant, and silly" posturing of Western scholars who assume their work applies to the entire world (Rehbein 2014: 217). More significantly, it is the surest path to surmounting the inherent limitations of Western scholarship, making new, productive avenues of inquiry possible, uncovering new ways of looking at global issues, and leading to more just and sustainable outcomes.

This recognition of the fundamental need to promote, embrace, and learn from people outside the Euro-American worldview builds upon the sociology of knowledge literature, which points to the need to think beyond the nation-state. Michael Burawoy notes that this new interdisciplinary approach "has to be distinguished from economics that is primarily concerned with the advance of market society and political science that is concerned with the state and political order—Northern disciplines ever more preoccupied with modeling a world ever more remote from reality"

(Burawoy 2014: xvii). Adding to this conversation, Nour Dados and Raewyn Connell argue that "the *epistemological* case for a remaking of the social sciences has been firmly established. The great need now is to develop *substantive* fields of knowledge in a new way, using perspectives from the South and what might be called a postcolonial theoretical sensibility" (Dados and Connell 2014: 195). This requires, declares Boike Rehbein, "not more and not less than a critical theory for the globalized world" (Rehbein 2014: 221).

As critical global studies scholars, we must be highly attuned to the dominance and exclusivity of knowledge produced in the global north. Refusing to embrace and learn from non-Western knowledge aligns us perilously with former colonial eras of oppression and discrimination, where ignorance, arrogance, and the silencing of others ruled the day. We must remain vigilant and curb our universalistic presumptions if we are to avoid replicating, albeit in different ways, the colonial and imperial violence of our Western intellectual forebears (Darian-Smith 2016; Smith 2012; Kovach 2009).

Developing Global Ethics

Kwame Anthony Appiah has written extensively about the idea of a shared global ethic in his influential book *Cosmopolitanism: Ethics in a World of Strangers* (2006). As the world becomes ever more complex and interconnected, there is a commensurate need to take global ethics very seriously. Appiah urges us to "learn about people in other places, take an interest in their civilizations, their arguments, their errors, their achievements, not because that will bring us to agreement, but because it will help us get used to one another" (Appiah 2006: 78; see also Beck 2006; Beck and Sznaider 2006).

In the context of global studies, getting used to one another necessarily entails making room at the table for people normally excluded from the processes of knowledge production. It means actively fostering new forms of agency, participation, and expression within the wider contexts of our rapidly shifting geopolitical landscape (Falk 2014). It may even require, as revolutionary black feminist Audre Lorde wrote decades ago, learning how "to make common cause with those identified as outside the structures in order to define and seek a world in which we can all flourish. It is learning how to take our differences and make them strengths" (Lorde 1984: 113). This means explicitly acknowledging that any global process, event, problem, or issue involves a plurality of ethics, and that respecting, learning, and engaging with others from different ethical perspectives is essential in striving to live in a world of peace and mutual support.

CHARACTERISTICS OF GLOBAL STUDIES RESEARCH

There are certain characteristics associated with a global studies approach, some that are unique to the newly emerging field and some that are adapted from various disciplines. We argue that these elements are important for understanding global issues, as well as making the field more coherent, applicable, and accessible to a wide range of scholars irrespective of their intellectual training.

Holistic Approaches

Global studies seeks to recover a holistic approach to analyzing societies and the peoples that constitute them. This means approaching one's research with the big picture in mind, consciously integrating the political, economic, and sociocultural elements that may not be immediately obvious within a conventional nation-state framing and modernist analytical paradigm. Unfortunately, a holistic approach to studying societies has been in decline within the academy for several decades. It has largely been overwhelmed by the modern rush toward specialization and discrete categories of expert knowledge. The impulse toward holism can still be found within in certain disciplines, such as anthropology, and some interdisciplinary fields, such as social psychology. These disciplines and interdisciplinary fields have long sought to reintegrate that which has been disintegrated by the ever-increasing rationalization of Western society and its educational institutions.

Modern scholars typically approach topics such as economics, politics, culture, and law as singular fields of analysis. Global studies scholars, in contrast, seek to thread apparently discrete phenomena back into the fabric of relations—social, political, economic, historical, and geographic—

from which they have been artificially extracted and abstracted (Wolf 1982). What can appear as discrete institutions and realms of productive activity in society are necessarily functioning parts of a whole. Treating such elements as separate, independent units fundamentally misrepresents the interdependence of their functions within the entire social system.

Social structures and functions are not fixed or morally neutral. They endure and provide some level of historical continuity, but they do not entirely prevent change and transformation. They produce and reproduce society, but they also reproduce discrimination and inequality. It is essential to remember that fields like law and health care may seem like distinct areas of value-neutral activity, but in fact they are contested social constructs that cannot be removed from their sociocultural contexts and must always be situated within the fabric of social, political, and economic relations that inevitably involve conflicts over power and self-interest.

The preference for a holistic approach shapes many aspects of global studies scholarship and is the conceptual platform upon which the approach that we present here is built. The drive to present a more holistic picture, or what others have called a "big picture," can be found in nearly every chapter of this book and in most global studies literature. This holistic impulse is a core principle of the global case study method that we describe in detail in Chapter 6.

Transgressive and Integrative

Thinking holistically, we further argue that global processes and the tools we use to analyze them are essentially *transgressive* and *integrative*. By *transgressive* we mean breaking down boundaries, in the spatial sense of crossing geopolitical boundaries (north/south, south/south, south/east) and in the temporal sense of crossing what are often presented as discrete historical periods (Sachsenmaier 2006; Nederveen Pieterse 2012). This transgressive impulse seeks to go beyond conventional, Eurocentric modes of thinking and violate scholarly conventions that obstruct or reign in attempts to think more inclusively about the world and its complex processes. Transgressing conventional modes of thought and related sensibilities—when done with sensitivity—blurs disciplinary boundaries and many fundamental categories of Enlightenment thinking, presenting opportunities for new modes of intercultural conversation.

By *integrative* we mean more than an interdisciplinary synthesis: recognizing multiple connections between what are often thought of as discrete social, political, and economic processes, as well as the fundamental interdependence of apparently autonomous phenomena. Combining and coordinating diverse elements into an aggregated whole is not meant to replace one monolithic vision with another monolithic vision. Rather, it is a way of teasing out the synergies, connections, and networks that inform our understanding of any global issue. It means rejecting any dogmatic or singular perspective and deliberately seeking a multiperspectival lens.

Interconnection and Interdependence

Modern Western scholarship seeks to rationalize the study of society and social practices, breaking units of analysis down into ever-finer categories and discrete areas of specialization. In contrast, global studies reintegrates our understanding of the world. It proceeds from the assumption that studying society's components separately may obscure the massive interconnectivity of all of its parts. Historical and archaeological records indicate that human civilizations have always been interconnected and that it rarely makes sense to separate human history into distinct geographical regions or specific time periods. The ingrained habit of dividing up the study of society into distinct units is one of the main reasons that scholars find it difficult to see the myriad interconnections between the economic, political, legal, and cultural realms of social activity. In an increasingly globalized world, whenever and wherever we look for connections we find that apparently discrete elements are interdependent and mutually constitutive.

Analyzing interconnections and interdependence is not a purely theoretical exercise and has important practical applications. For example, global studies shows us that the more policy makers underestimate the structural interconnectedness of related global issues, the more likely it is that their policies and programs will have fewer predictable outcomes and more unintended consequences. The multiplication of unintended consequences has real-world implications for international development programs and many other public policies.

Engaging the holistic, transgressive, and interdependent qualities of global issues may at first make the world appear disorganized and chaotic. Disrupting established ways of knowing, however, has the potential to yield new understandings and analyses. Take, for example, global issues such as poverty, growing urban slums, and terrorism. Recent increases in all three indicate that these apparently discrete phenomena may be interactive elements in a larger global system (Kaldor 2006; Davis 2006).

Global-Scale Issues and the Local-Global Continuum

At first glance, global studies may seem to focus on large economic, political, and social processes that are truly global in scale. Issues such as economic development, climate change, resource depletion, regional conflict, human rights, and immigration all have at least one thing in common: they reach beyond the limits of the nation-state even when they are articulated primarily as nationalist projects or concerns. These issues are global in scale in the sense that they ignore political boundaries and have an impact on all nations, albeit to varying degrees. Up until relatively recently the largest unit of analysis was the nation-state, which made it difficult for scholars to see the larger, integrated world system within which various state and nonstate actors operate. As a starting point, global perspectives enable global systemic analyses that are not limited to a national/international frame.

As we discuss in Chapter 1, "global-scale" doesn't simply mean "big." It does not mean that global scholars only study macroscale processes or that they need to "study everything and everywhere" (Duve 2013: 23). Building on the work of human geographers in the 1980s and 1990s, global scholars see local places as historically contingent and embedded within and refracted through global processes (Pred 1984; Massey 1994; Swyngedouw 1997; see Giddens 1984 on structuration). So while global-scale issues may have macroscale dimensions, they also have localized manifestations. For global studies scholars, global-scale issues require a shift of focus not just from the national to the global, but from the national to the entire local-global continuum (Nederveen Pieterse 2013; Darian-Smith 2014). Further, global studies scholars argue that these kinds of global-scale issues can manifest *simultaneously* at multiple levels and that they often manifest differently at regional, national, and local levels. In this sense the local, national, regional, and global are better understood as embedded sets of relations: inseparable and continually creating and re-creating each other.

Global studies scholars see the local and the global as two sides of the same coin, but without essentializing these two faces or viewing them as static or fixed. Global studies scholars are thus attentive to the ways in which global-scale processes become manifest in the lives of ordinary people and across the full range of human activities. Writes Dominic Sachsenmaier, "Any kind of research with a decidedly global perspective will also have to find ways to balance the universal and the particular. It has to be sensitive to both the inner diversity of global structures and the global dimension of many local forces" (Sachsenmaier 2006: 455). Hence, depending on the questions a researcher asks, the global can be found in large cities, but also in villages and neighborhoods. The global can be found in multinational corporations, but also in the workplace. It can be found in mass cultural icons and the symbolic rituals of daily life, in grand historical narratives and individual life stories (McCarty 2014b; Sassen 2011; Roy and Ong 2011; Juergensmeyer, Griego, and Soboslai 2015). The ability to grasp global-scale issues, to integrate larger global systems analysis into a multilevel analysis of the entire local-global spectrum, and to see the global through the local and vice versa give global studies a unique spatial and conceptually relational framing.

Built into this understanding of global-scale issues is the recognition that new geopolitical spatial dynamics are not restrained by a conventional nation-state framing. Importantly, this does not mean that global studies only engages with social, cultural, political, economic, and legal issues "beyond the state," as introductory texts to global studies commonly argue. We think this is a rather simplistic understanding of what characterizes an issue or process as "global," and it bogs down conversations in definitional technicalities about geospatial reach. In contrast, we suggest that a more productive line of inquiry results from perceiving global-scale issues across a local-global continuum. A local-global continuum is not a series of spatial containers vertically nested from the local, through the national, up to the global. Rather, it is a more distributed, decentralized,

and deterritorialized understanding of overlapping and mutually constitutive geopolitical and conceptual sites and arenas.

One conceptual difficulty in dealing with global-scale issues is that in
some cases they vary so greatly across local cultural contexts that it may
challenge the definition of abstract Western concepts such as human rights,
development, and justice and their assumed universality (Chakrabarty
2000: 9; Merry 2006). Nonetheless, global-scale issues necessarily link
large analytical abstractions to their varied local manifestations. This ability
to integrate larger global systems analysis into a multilevel and multidimensional analysis of the entire local-global spectrum and to identify
impulses of influence in this mutually constitutive network is a new way of
understanding the world. And it raises new research questions and a conceptually accessible methodology that is not grounded in any one particular
discipline (which we discuss in more detail in Chapter 5).

We argue that what makes any subject matter global is for the researcher
to ask questions and employ methods that explore interconnections across
past and present, across disciplines and analytical frames, and across substantive issues that have been limited in their conceptualization by a focus
on the nation-state (Darian-Smith 2013a, 2013b). Hence, across the social
sciences and humanities more and more scholars are becoming attuned to
the global dimensions present in their research, dimensions that are
refracted through a global imaginary, even when their research is on the
surface nationally or locally framed. The more scholars in different disciplines look for global dimensions in their work, the more they find. As we
discuss more fully in Chapter 6 with respect to a global case study, this is
because processes of globalization do not just occur beyond the nation-
state but manifest at various spatial, temporal, and conceptual scales
within, across, and between conventional national orientations.

Decentered, Distributed, and Deterritorialized Processes

Global issues are not only large and complex, but, like the Internet, they
can also be decentralized and distributed across times and spaces. They
tend to have a deterritorialized quality: they are everywhere and nowhere,
or at least not neatly contained within established political borders and
natural boundaries in the ways to which we are accustomed (fig. 6). They

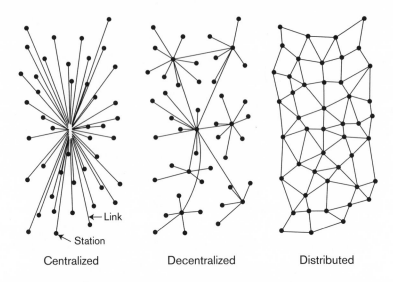

Centralized   Decentralized   Distributed

Figure 6. Centralized, Decentralized, and Distributed Systems.

may have more than one center or no center at all (Baran 1964; Nederveen Pieterse 2013; McCarty 2014a).

Global issues may also have no hierarchy, directional flow, or even clear linear causality (McCarty 2014b: 3). As a result global processes may have multiple centers and peripheries within, beyond, and across national lines. As Jan Nederveen Pieterse argues in his article "What Is Global Studies?," we need a "multicentric" approach that more closely examines new hubs of power, connectivity, and exchange and takes into account "concerns not just from New York, London, Paris or Tokyo, but also from the viewpoint of New Delhi, Sao Paulo, Beijing or Nairobi" (Nederveen Pieterse 2013: 10). Boike Rehbein adds that in a multicentric world, "the peripheries have entered the centers (and vice versa), while dominant and dominated are not homogenous groups" (Rehbein 2014: 217).

The issue of immigration provides a pertinent example of distributed and deterritorialized processes. Immigration, transmigration, and return migration have become so widespread and complex that immigration can no longer be said to have a clear directional flow from one point to another—from the global south to the global north or vice versa. The sense of violation that accompanies the massive dislocation and cross-migration of people fleeing poverty and war is not limited to one nation or another. This problem affects the borders of all nations, and the crisis is felt simultaneously—although to different degrees—all over the world. The Third World is no longer somewhere "out there," safely far off, as it may once have seemed to those living in the First World. Of course, this is also true for the global south, which has had to deal with both the positive and negative impacts of Western capitalism's infiltration (see Prashad 2012).

The point-to-point model of immigration fails to adequately describe the complex flow of people around the world. From a global perspective, the ebb and flow of immigrants over the last two hundred years has been closely tied to the flow of global capital through a global economy. Where global-scale issues such as immigration are driven by global-scale economic and political processes, these issues tend to defy geographic and political boundaries. This makes it difficult to study global-scale issues using territorial categories such as the nation-state. It follows that the data sets that nation-states collect are also territorially bound and essentially flawed for a global analysis. If immigration is a distributed issue driven by decentralized global-scale processes, then it is no wonder that national immigration policies based on flawed, nation-bound understandings of immigration fail to adequately deal with the issue.

Historical Contextualization

Global studies scholars recognize that history matters and that what went before explains a great deal about the world today (Mintz 1985; Hobsbawm 1997). It is impossible to understand the current geopolitical map and multiple conflicts without some understanding of the colonial and imperial histories that established modern national boundaries and set up enduring ethnic and territorial tensions. In short, a complex, interconnected, and globalizing present can only be understood in the context of a complex, interconnected, and globalizing past.

Take, for example, terrorism. In some ways the kinds of terrorism we see today are completely new, yet terrorism as a political tool has existed for centuries. By inserting contemporary terrorism into historical contexts, we can see that while terrorists might claim religious motivations, acts of terrorism are also political and cultural acts (Juergensmeyer 2000, 2001). Reinserting global processes into historical contexts allows us to reconnect the dots and make sense of what may otherwise appear to be discrete phenomena and random events. Global analyses look for patterns of both change and continuity, highlighting the deep historical continuities between the past and ongoing global processes (McCarty 2014b).

It is important to note, moreover, that histories are always plural. Global histories should be decentralized and not privilege one historical narrative over another. One community's understanding of the past must be situated against other peoples' narratives and historical memories, which may be contradictory or even oppositional (Trouillot 1995). It is not sufficient to tell a singular or dominant Eurocentric understanding of history. Further, it is not sufficient for us in the Euro-American academy to tell the histories of others as if we knew better or had a more sophisticated understanding of what really took place. A global historical perspective recognizes that each society and people has its own unique understanding of the past, and that these various social understandings inform each other in dynamic interplay across time and geopolitical space.

Sachsenmaier writes that new directions in global history suggest that history as a discipline "can contribute significantly to the study of globalization and to the struggles to establish global paradigms of thinking" (Sachsenmaier 2006: 465).[1] He goes on to remark:

> Now that scholars have begun to pursue global agendas while remaining sensitive to the full complexity of the local, the devil is in the detail. Or, seen from another perspective, the treasure trove is in the detail. In lieu of a detached macro-theoretical synthesis, the relationship between the global and the local will need to be explored through a myriad of detailed studies . . . Global and transcultural history can be at the very forefront of such an endeavor. (Sachsenmaier 2006: 461)

---

1. For some scholars global history differs from world history in that it specifically engages with historical analysis in the so-called global age (Mazlish 1993). The distinctions between world and global history, however, are becoming more difficult to identify; see Pernau and Sachsenmaier 2016).

For global scholars the historical/temporal dimension includes historical narratives as well as different conceptions of time itself. Not only do
different cultures have different understandings of time (Ogle 2015), but
global processes often occur on time horizons that are not recognized by
fast-paced modern societies and the dominant global political framework
(Hutchings 2008; Lundborg 2012). For example, some forms of environmental damage, such as leaching of toxins into water catchment areas, can
be lethal to local residents. This kind of *ecocide*, however, is not classified
as criminal violence in modern legal systems in part because the damage
may occur over decades and generations (Nixon 2013). The slow pace of
processes such as climate change, ocean pollution, and habitat destruction
present unique regulatory challenges. The short time cycles associated
with media, politics, and public attention make it difficult to develop
multidecade strategies and implement long-term policies.

Global Social Structures

It is not an exaggeration to say that the concept of social structure was the
cornerstone on which the modern social and behavioral disciplines were
built. The founding fathers of social theory, including Auguste Comte,
Karl Marx, Émile Durkheim, Max Weber, W. E. B. Du Bois, and Sigmund
Freud, each contributed their own systemic or structural theories of society. This is one of the main reasons their contributions remain influential
to this day.

The ability to see beyond individual behavior to identify enduring patterns in society that constrain this behavior is perhaps the singular skill of
a social scientist. This skill is analogous to what C. Wright Mills called the
"sociological imagination" (Mills 1959). It is the ability to see that the individual's free choices, called *individual agency*, are actually constrained or
influenced by a myriad of preexisting conditions, norms, values, institutions, and structural relations. How an individual acts is hugely influenced
by language, culture, nationality, legal system, age, gender, socioeconomic
status, religion, family, education, geographic region, and so on. These
social factors thoroughly shape individual "free" choices—choices such as
whom to marry, what job to take, or what kind of transportation to use.
The influence of social structures is such that the outcomes of individual

"free" choices become overwhelmingly, statistically, and distressingly predictable.

Recognizing that individual agency is constrained by social structures also almost inevitably leads to the recognition that social systems are not value neutral. Social and economic systems function, but the existing systems function better for some people than for others. With the recognition of social structure comes the realization that inequality is not a natural or random occurrence. Inequality is socially structured, determined by pre-existing patterns, norms, and institutions of society. Structural and critical thinking are hence very closely linked.

The concept of social structure remains crucial to understanding global issues. We argue, however, that there is a need to revisit the notion of social structure and expand it beyond the modern nation-state and single-society paradigm in which it was developed. We need to rework the concept of social structure so that it can be applied to larger geopolitical economic structures and their varied impacts around the world. This kind of global political economic approach focuses our attention on the structural features of the current world order, highlighting the enduring political and economic inequalities within and between states and a variety of non-state actors.

Breaking Down Binaries

Increasing levels of communication, integration, and interdependence in the global system require us to complicate simple binaries such as East/West, colonizer/colonized, First World/Third World, and developed/developing. Such binaries can be used effectively to emphasize inequality and injustices between continents and regions of the world. These same binaries, however, also obscure the complexity of global issues. We may talk of rich and poor countries, but only a handful of countries are unequivocally rich or poor; the large majority of them fall somewhere in between. Dichotomies such as rich/poor obscure variations between countries, as well as internal variations within each country. Even the poorest countries have wealthy elite, middle, and working classes. Conversely, even the richest regions have poverty and inequality. Moreover, assuming the conventions of a global north/global south divide may preclude us from recognizing a multitude of relations that can be characterized as south/south or south/east (Roy and Crane 2015). These new binaries are themselves problematic in their monolithic essentializing of human difference, yet they are important for shaking up modernist conventions of how to view the world in which "the West versus the rest" has prevailed for centuries.

Immanuel Wallerstein's world-systems approach is a good example of systemic thinking that moved beyond nation-states and simplified binaries (Wallerstein 1974). Even though Wallerstein's core/semiperiphery/periphery model is often used as if it were a simple triad, this is not an accurate portrayal of his work. Wallerstein described a complex global system made up of distributed systemic processes that are deterritorialized in the sense that they can exist side-by-side in the same place. In his approach, core and periphery are the two ends of a spectrum. Along this spectrum some nations have more diversified economies and more total core processes than other nations. It is important to note that in his model this spectrum could also be applied to subnational regions. Within every nation there are subregions made up of predominantly core, semiperipheral, or peripheral processes. "Global cities," for example, can be understood as core areas containing many diverse core, semiperipheral, and peripheral processes, and these cities are in some ways more closely linked to each other than to the peripheral, rural areas that surround them (Sassen 1991).

One must always be careful when applying Western binary logics and abstractions to non-Western regions. As the world becomes more globalized, the lines between East and West, First World and Third World, and global north and global south are increasingly blurred. These analytical conventions should be treated with care so as to avoid replicating categories of thought associated with modern imperialism and colonialism. The people and issues that Europeans historically positioned "out there" at the margins are now right next door, and vice versa. At the same time, while it has always been appropriate, only recently have scholars recognized the need to apply developmental and human rights paradigms to postindustrial societies. In global studies and across the humanities and social sciences more generally, scholars should avoid using binary logics that oversimplify and obscure variation and inadvertently perpetuate a singular worldview. We should continually work to develop new terminology that more accurately reflects a wider range of diversity and variation across a continuum.

Hybridity and Fluidity

In addition to a strong preference for binaries, Western scholarship has a particular fondness for fixed categorical distinctions. It assumes that categories such as race, ethnicity, class, gender, or nationality accurately describe people's identities and how people classify themselves. The implicit assumption behind these kinds of schemas is that they are both *comprehensive* and *mutually exclusive*. But such categories have many overlapping variations and are never truly fixed, stable, or complete.

Categories are assumed to be mutually exclusive when a person cannot fit into more than one category. With increasing immigration and a better understanding of the deep histories of human movement, it is clear that our tidy racial and ethnic categories are overly simplistic and essentializing. Similarly, national identities have become complex, hyphenated, and multiple. There have always been groups that don't fit neatly into the available categories, and globalization is making it increasingly difficult to ignore the limitations of nation-states' categorical schemata. As Nederveen Pieterse argues, "We have been so trained and indoctrinated to think of culture in territorial packages of assorted 'imagined communities' that to seriously address the windows opened and questions raised by hybridization in effect requires a decolonization of imagination" (Nederveen Pieterse 2009: 57).

Developing new terminology that more accurately reflects the range of possible identities in a globalized world is not sufficient. Any new understanding of hybrid identities also needs to take into account the transient nature of identity production itself. People have the ability to take on different identities in different social settings. People in hybrid racial, ethnic, and national categories can shift back and forth between categories, or occupy their hybrid identities, depending on the context. According to Zygmunt Bauman, "if the *modern* 'problem of identity' is how to construct an identity and keep it solid and stable, the *postmodern* 'problem of identity' is primarily how to avoid fixation and keep the options open" (Bauman 1996: 18; see

Darian-Smith 2015). This kind of fluidity indicates that scholars need to increase the range of variation of their conceptual frames, making allowances for overlapping categories as well as movement between categories that in turn may alter the essentialized construct of the category itself.

GLOBAL STUDIES AS OPPORTUNITY

The inclusive nature of global studies as a field enables scholars to be interested in a wide range of substantive topics. These include, but are not limited to, human rights and global governance; human trafficking, sex trade, and slavery; conflict, violence, terrorism, and genocide; crime, security, and policing; poverty and inequality; economic and community development; global cities and urban slums; global markets and regional trade agreements; fair trade and supply chain issues; labor, sweatshops, and workers' rights; the environment, natural resources, and the global commons; energy and sustainability; global social movements, women's movements, and microfinance; food systems, food security, and traditional agriculture; humanitarian aid and disaster relief; philanthropy; immigration, diaspora, refugees, and asylum; global health, pandemics, nutrition, and epidemiology; education and transnational knowledge production; religions and religious nationalisms; and science, technology, and media (see Anheier and Juergensmeyer 2012).

In addition to engaging with their own substantive research, many global scholars are active on their campuses developing exciting new curricula, making connections with scholars in other disciplines, and building institutional support for innovative interdisciplinary collaborations. Beyond the campus, they engage with their communities as global citizens, public intellectuals, and activist scholars. They often have enduring interests in world affairs, intercultural exchanges, and the promotion of intercultural understanding. Many also nurture this kind of global citizenship among their students by mentoring students and encouraging them to participate in study abroad, language programs, and field research, and to respect other cultures and historical traditions.

The point is that as a global scholar you can take your research in nearly any direction and engage with nearly any combination of global issues.

Moreover, each global topic is deeply complex and no one scholar, or even group of scholars, can possibly hope to master any one of them fully. So we end up with the question with which we began Chapter 1: How does one begin the formidable task of doing global research? Our argument in this chapter and throughout this book is that rather than going in infinite directions and being totally overwhelmed, it is possible to do global studies research in an orderly and manageable way. Our overall goal is to convince the reader that doing global research can be enormously rewarding and well worth the time, energy, and challenge. More profoundly, contemporary researchers cannot afford to sit back and fail to engage with historical and contemporary global processes if their work is to remain relevant and applicable to the academy.

As a critical new field of inquiry, global studies stands poised to help dislodge the global north's epistemological universalism. To put it another way, global studies has the potential to become the intellectual platform upon which scholars forge theoretical and methodological contributions that decolonize Western expertise. Global research may seem formidable, but we view it as an extraordinary opportunity to shape new modes of inquiry that are of the utmost imperative to every one of us living in an increasingly interconnected world.

3 A Global Theoretical Framework

In this chapter we argue that the Euro-American academy is entering a new integrative paradigm that is moving scholarly practice beyond the disciplinary/interdisciplinary divide. Drawing on the development of interdisciplinary approaches over the past four decades, we suggest that the theoretical and analytical boundaries between conventional disciplines are becoming less relevant in the creation of lines of inquiry and production of knowledge that expressly seek to explore today's complex global world.

This chapter links the reasons why global studies is important (Chapter 2) to wider theoretical developments in the social sciences and humanities. We trace the historical development of innovative intellectual conversations within the Euro-American academy, focusing on interdisciplinary approaches that have developed across the humanities and social science disciplines since World War II. Referring to Jean Piaget's 1970 concept of *transdisciplinarity* as emblematic of these developments (Piaget 1972), we argue that combining transdisciplinary theoretical innovations with the unique perspectives emerging within the field of global studies creates the groundwork for a new coherent, accessible, and inclusive paradigm that we call a *global transdisciplinary framework*. The framework makes it possible to study multifaceted, global-scale issues in a holistic fashion, deploying various perspectives at multiple levels and across spatial and temporal dimensions. The framework also intentionally includes previously marginalized perspectives and epistemologies in the production of new forms of knowledge. What is being forged, we conclude, is a new paradigm that is applicable and accessible to many scholars even when their research interests are not explicitly global in nature. In the longer term, it also has the potential to open up Western scholarship to non-Western modes of thinking and foster inclusive, productive, and relevant globally informed scholarship.

To be clear, we are not suggesting that traditional disciplines and their specialized knowledge and methods are becoming obsolete or less important. Nor are we suggesting that transdisciplinary scholarship is widespread in the academy—we recognize that some scholars resist any efforts toward it. Still, we argue that leading intellectuals are—and have been for many decades—actively engaged in integrative scholarship that seeks to transcend disciplinary distinctions. By building on these intellectuals' lead, and layering on global studies' additional insights, we can begin to develop new ways of theorizing and designing research projects that speak to the world's current complexities.

THE DISCIPLINARY/INTERDISCIPLINARY DEBATE

The Euro-American academy continues to be plagued by well-rehearsed debates over the relative value of interdisciplinary scholarship. These debates consume a great deal of time and energy and tend to rehash disciplinary antagonisms that have remained unresolved for decades. Scholars who defend the traditional disciplines imply that interdisciplinary scholars are dilettantes or argue that interdisciplinary research makes only superficial connections across theoretical approaches and bodies of literature. Moreover, interdisciplinary scholarship is often seen as unwieldy, unaccountable, fragmented, and difficult to assess for the purposes of merits and promotions (Jacobs and Frickel 2009; see also Strathern 2005). On the other side, the champions of interdisciplinary scholarship portray the disciplines as self-marginalizing dinosaurs on the verge of extinction.

These debates can get bitter as communities of scholars fight over funding and limited resources within their institutions. In the United States, this has been very much the case in recent years as university administrators have tried to deal with the impact of the economic recession. As a result, support for interdisciplinary scholarship has generally declined across many university campuses in the Euro-American academy.[1]

Whether one is a supporter or a critic of interdisciplinary scholarship, one of the central problems in debates about its relative value is that these debates are entrenched in modernist concepts and logics such as individualism, nationalism, rationalism, and secularism (Ludden 2000). Just as international studies implicitly reaffirms the national, interdisciplinarity implicitly reaffirms the modern disciplines. Interdisciplinary approaches can only extend so far beyond the disciplines against which their innovation and purpose are measured. In an effort to move past disciplinary/ interdisciplinary debates and "today's arid rhetoric of 'interdisciplinarity'" (Fitzgerald and Callard 2014: 4), this chapter focuses on broader trends affecting not one discipline, or the interactive space between any two disciplines, but many disciplines concurrently.

As the intellectual debate over interdisciplinarity has raged unabated over the past four decades, fundamental changes have overtaken academic practice. Leading intellectual contributions have emerged at the intersections between established disciplines, including the contributions of Michel Foucault, Pierre Bourdieu, and more recent scholars such as Bruno Latour, Amartya Sen, Martha Nussbaum, and Kwame Anthony Appiah. As we discuss in Chapter 1, these changes reflect a new worldview that began to emerge following World War I and reached a peak in the aftermath of World War II.

In the postwar period, the Euro-American academy questioned its belief in stability and fixity of accepted knowledge. Building on the social and legal changes wrought by the civil rights movements in North America, Europe, and Latin America, many of the ways of thinking that had dominated

---

1. It is important to note that this reduction of support for interdisciplinary work has not been matched by leading funding agencies. For instance, in the United States the National Science Foundation and National Institutes of Health have increased their budgets over the past five years for interdisciplinary and collaborative research and are on the whole embracing innovative research theories and methods.

nineteenth- and twentieth-century academia began to be challenged. Interdisciplinary programs emerged throughout the 1970s and 1980s, and included area, environmental, ethnic, feminist, gender, religious, and science and technology studies (Ferguson 2012). Interdisciplinary scholarly innovations jumped again in the 1990s with the end of the Cold War, increasing awareness of international processes, and new, integrative forms of political, economic, and cultural globalization. To meet these emerging challenges, scholars forged new, previously unimaginable connections across disciplines. These divergent academic endeavors have more recently coalesced into a transdisciplinary framework that in some ways makes both disciplinary boundaries and the concept of interdisciplinarity itself less relevant.

Interdisciplinarity is long established in the physical sciences, engineering, and medicine. Neuroscience is a salient example of transdisciplinarity. As a burgeoning field of inquiry, neuroscience "has become a combination of anatomy, physiology, chemistry, biology, pharmacology, and genetics with a profound concern for culture, ethics, and social context . . . To survive in the twenty-first century the neurosciences will have to link all of their parts even further and bring genetics, the environment, and the sociocultural context together in order to develop more complex models of [the] mind" (Burnett 2008: 252; see also Fitzgerald and Callard 2014). Within the social sciences and humanities disciplinary boundaries have similarly been blurred, though, as we discuss below, this has often gone unacknowledged and even unrecognized.

Our objective in this chapter is to demonstrate the presence of transdisciplinarity within existing scholarship and call for all scholars to embrace it, whether one self-identifies with its innovative research agendas or not. We feel that such an embrace is absolutely essential given the prevalence of corporate pressures within universities to "dice disciplines, faculty, and students, and finally experts into tiny, specialized fragments" that prevent scholars from thinking holistically and creatively, and engaging with "the most pressing moral, political and cultural questions" of our times (Hedges 2008: 89–90). Embracing transdisciplinarity offers a way to overcome what has been called the "balkanization of the academy into narrow enclaves" (Hall 2010: 27). Embracing transdisciplinarity is one way scholars can explicitly "engage in and generate deep critical thinking" that seeks to better understand our complex present (Hall 2010: 27).

DISTINGUISHING INTERDISCIPLINARITY
FROM TRANSDISCIPLINARITY

Though lesser known, transdisciplinary scholarship developed concurrently with that of interdisciplinary scholarship. It was Swiss development psychologist Jean Piaget who formally introduced the concept of *transdisciplinarity* in 1970. In his writings he used the term to refer to scholarship that "would not only cover interactions or reciprocities between specialized research projects, but would place these relationships within a total system without any firm boundaries between disciplines" (Piaget 1972: 138).[2] As Basarab Nicolescu notes, this description did not mean that Piaget advocated dismantling conventional disciplines in favor of a new super- or hyperdiscipline. Rather, Piaget was interested in "contemplating the possibility of a space of knowledge *beyond* the disciplines" (Nicolescu 2008: 1).

According to the International Center for Transdisciplinary Research, which was founded in Paris in 1987, transdisciplinary research complements interdisciplinary and multidisciplinary research but is nonetheless distinct (fig. 7). Multidisciplinary approaches use the perspectives of a number of different disciplines with no necessary overlap, while interdisciplinary approaches use the methods and theories of one discipline to inform other disciplines. In contrast, the goal of transdisciplinarity is to move beyond the limits of both the disciplines and interdisciplinary approaches to provide new ways of organizing knowledge and modes of thinking (Blassnigg and Punt 2012; also Gasper 2010).

One of the important elements of transdisciplinary work is that it is problem based and thus concerned with the practical applications of knowledge in the real world, where issues tend to be multifaceted and call for multiple analytical perspectives. Transdisciplinary scholarship also explores how knowledge is constituted in the first place as a reflection and product of particular worldviews, ideologies, and cultural biases. According to

2. Following Piaget, Erich Jantsch and André Lichnerowicz adopted the term at a 1970 international workshop on interdisciplinary research and teaching in Nice, France, organized by the Organization for Economic Cooperation and Development in collaboration with the French Ministry of National Education and the University of Nice (see Apostel et al. 1972).

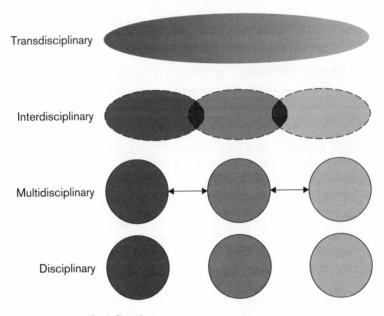

Figure 7. Transdisciplinarity.

Rosemary Johnston, transdisciplinarity "overtly seeks ways to open up thinking to 'maps of unlimited possibilities'... to create mindscapes that are unfettered by traditional patterns and procedures" (Johnston 2008: 229–30). Transdisciplinary scholarship is potentially emancipatory in that it explicitly seeks to free up modernist ways of thinking and our organization of knowledge in the academy by incorporating Western and non-Western knowledge into a more holistic approach to pressing contemporary issues. Adds Patricia Leavy, "Transdisciplinarity produces new knowledge-building practices... that [are] vital for making academic research an authentic part of the globalized world it claims to study" (Leavy 2011: 14).

While transdisciplinarity is relatively new as a named scholarly approach, we suggest that its primary concern, to open up the production of knowledge to multiple perspectives and worldviews, finds resonance in the more encompassing approaches of intellectual generalists that were so influential before the modern disciplines were established and became entrenched. The great figures of the Scientific Revolution, including Francis Bacon, Nicolaus Copernicus, Johannes Kepler, René Descartes, and Isaac Newton, along with many others, were not bound by modern disciplines if for no reason other than that the disciplines had not yet been established.

Similarly, early Enlightenment thinkers such as John Locke, David Hume, Montesquieu, Voltaire, and Thomas Jefferson pushed the boundaries of conventional thought by drawing upon a vast array of literature, philosophies, theories, and methods. These predisciplinary scientists and philosophers influenced the great social thinkers of the nineteenth century such as Jeremy Bentham, Auguste Comte, John Stuart Mill, Karl Marx, Émile Durkheim, Max Weber, and W. E. B. Du Bois, who were almost entirely unfettered by the disciplines. These classic modern thinkers drew upon many areas of learning, including history, science, economics, politics, and philosophy to think about the complex social issues surrounding colonialism, the rise of the nation-state and nationalism, and accompanying calls for democracy, industrialization, and modern imperialism that marked the turbulent times in which they lived. In many ways these earlier intellectuals, now often considered founders of their various disciplines, were remarkable for their open and flexible embrace of transdisciplinary approaches.

Not until later in the nineteenth and early twentieth centuries did the modern disciplines began to crystallize knowledge into discrete areas of expertise. Disciplines such as political science, sociology, history, anthropology, economics, and law became institutionalized in universities and through professional associations, funding networks, journals, and conferences, all endeavors that were for the most part sponsored by nation-states. At the same time that knowledge production was being nationalized, earlier integrated and holistic scholarly approaches went out of favor. Each of the disciplines developed their own norms and criteria for what counted as authoritative knowledge and functioned as clubs of knowledge production that excluded nonmembers (Pierce 1991; Stichweh 2001). While disciplines such as law and economics claimed to be more rational and scientific than others, the disciplines were all framed by the logics of modernity and all ultimately depended on Western concepts such as individualism, rationalism, secularism, positivism, private property, and the nation-state (Foucault 1975). Yet while the production of knowledge was being cordoned off into discrete academic disciplines, the influence of thinkers such as Marx, Durkheim, and Weber never declined. Even today we find that these predisciplinary scholars provide new ways to identify and engage with the interconnected challenges of our contemporary age.

Since Piaget's founding publication on transdisciplinarity in 1970, a number of scholars from various intellectual backgrounds have taken up the approach (Fam et al. 2016). Unfortunately, in the social sciences and humanities transdisciplinarity has been overshadowed by the disciplinary/interdisciplinary debate and has not gained widespread recognition in the academy. The disciplines are too often focused on defending their boundaries and resources to fully engage in cooperative efforts. For instance, one of the key strategies the established disciplines have used to resist interdisciplinarity is to co-opt emergent interdisciplinary fields. A case in point is the field of political economy, which can be traced back to at least 1615, two hundred years before the word "economic" took its current meaning in English (1835) and nearly three hundred years before the development of the modern disciplines. This history has not prevented disciplines such as economics, political science, and sociology from laying claim to political economy at different times. Another example is international relations (IR), an interdisciplinary field established around the League of Nations in 1919. When it was founded, IR explicitly included the disciplines of philosophy, economics, history, geography, law, policy, sociology, anthropology, criminology, and psychology, among others. Yet political science has more or less successfully claimed IR as its exclusive domain, possibly salvaging its own relevance but ultimately diminishing the value of its prize (see Cohen 2014 ; Yetiv and James 2017). Similarly, the once exciting and productive interdisciplinary field of social psychology has turned into two markedly less productive subfields, one in psychology and the other in sociology. Patterns of limited and wholesale appropriation are repeated with respect to cultural studies, media studies, and dozens of other emerging interdisciplinary programs. In this sense the disciplines are subtly converging as they struggle to overcome their own limitations by co-opting what were once interdisciplinary approaches (Gass 1972). One result of this co-optation is that many hardcore disciplinary scholars in fact already do work that takes them beyond the disciplinary paradigm.

Even though academia has consistently resisted, undervalued, and co-opted both interdisciplinary and transdisciplinary approaches, in practice these approaches have influenced mainstream disciplines in many ways. In other words, there have been developments internal to all the disciplines, even within those most resistant to change, that suggest a range of commonalities and connections between them. These developments are cumulatively creating what we call a transdisciplinary framework, which is increasingly evident in leading intellectual contributions from scholars across the disciplines. This common framework includes shared thematics, theories, and approaches that, we argue, many disciplines—irrespective of training strategies and substantive research focus—are engaging to varying degrees. In short, despite the recent retrenchment of the conventional disciplines, in practice a blurring of disciplinary boundaries and formation of common intellectual ground has already occurred.[3]

AN EMERGING TRANSDISCIPLINARY FRAMEWORK

The development of a shared transdisciplinary framework points to the possibility that many disciplines now have more analytical concepts in common than they may be willing to admit. The following is a brief outline of the major transdisciplinary themes that have been emerging within the academy in the decades since World War II. Not all of the scholars mentioned would identify their approaches as transdisciplinary or even interdisciplinary. Nonetheless, their work and insights have had an impact on scholarship across the humanities and social sciences and contributed to the formation of a common framework for dialogue between the disciplines. In Leavy's words, "entirely new research pathways" that "produce new knowledge-building practices" have been developing (Leavy 2011: 14). Below we identify eight transdisciplinary thematics that together

3. In the United States this development can be seen in the university teaching curriculum. Despite institutional barriers to advancement for interdisciplinary scholars, since 1985 the number of interdisciplinary degrees awarded to students has increased sharply. Between 1985 and 2010 the number of multi- and interdisciplinary bachelor's degrees awarded increased by 307 percent (from 13,754 to 42,228). Source: Table 313 of the Digest of Education Statistics 2013, US Department of Education National Center of Educational Statistics (NECS). http://nces.ed.gov/programs/digest/d12/tables/dt12_313.asp.

represent an intellectual sea-change across the Euro-American academy. These thematics are not comprehensive by any means, but they do highlight the most obvious areas of collective engagement across all social sciences and humanities disciplines over the past forty years. Each of these themes have implications for global research design and methodology (see Chapters 4 and 5).

Race and Ethnicity

W. E. B. Du Bois's work, though not widely read until after World War II, laid the groundwork for theories of race and the psychology of racial domination. The "color line" that Du Bois described was global in scope and worked across a local-global continuum—dividing the consciousness of former slaves from that of their masters, the northern United States from the South, white Europeans from black Africans, and the colonizer from the colonized (Du Bois 1986). Du Bois built on early developments in psychology, including Sigmund Freud's psychoanalytic approaches, which delved into the murky waters of the subconscious and emphasized the subjective nature of experience and understanding. Leading scholars who have been deeply involved in the politics of race and its subjective and geopolitical manifestations include Frantz Fanon, Patricia Hill Collins, Stuart Hall, Cedric Robinson, Paul Gilroy, Eric Williams, Patricia Williams, Henry Louis Gates Jr., William Julius Wilson, Cornel West, Ann Stoler, Audrey Smedley, and Howard Winant. Together the work of these and many other scholars has helped establish a wide variety of ethnic studies programs that examine the complex cultural politics of such topics as multiculturalism, immigration, and diaspora. Today, whether scholars study race or not, everyone works in an intellectual milieu that recognizes race and ethnicity as salient dimensions of social power.

Class and Inequality

The post-WWII period saw the disciplines open up to new conversations about socioeconomic class systems and structures. Antonio Gramsci, a prisoner of war under Benito Mussolini's fascist regime, developed the concept of *cultural hegemony* to explain how powerful elites could manipulate the values and perceptions of the working classes. Frankfurt School theorists examined the symbols and rituals of class behavior, and scholars such as Michel Foucault, Jürgen Habermas, and Pierre Bourdieu presented a new emphasis on the linguistic and cultural capital that informed social class struggles. Following a European reengagement with Marxist class analyses, there was a wider materialist turn as the Euro-American academy adopted political economic approaches in the 1960s and 1970s. These analyses and approaches are now commonplace, and they continue to generate new fields of influence in disciplines such as geography, communications, media studies, literature, and history, with the notable exception of certain economics departments.

Gender and Sexuality

The academic engagement with gender and sexuality continues to fundamentally challenge the traditional patriarchal underpinnings of Western culture that are deeply embedded in its religions, philosophies, politics, and jurisprudence. These patriarchal assumptions have permeated capitalism, nationalism, modern society, and imperialism, and still contribute to the ongoing domination and exploitation of women. Feminist thinkers from Sojourner Truth in the 1850s to Betty Friedan in the 1950s championed women's rights. In the latter half of the twentieth century, radical and essentialist feminism were transformed by the poststructural turn along with other areas of study. In the 1970s feminist theorist Dorothy Smith developed standpoint theory, which underscored that women's knowledge was different to men's, that women had different truths, and that alternative ways of knowing and being were socially constructed and based upon women's lived experiences (see "Feminist Methodologies," Chapter 5). The idea that different groups could have different ways of knowing based on their own lived experiences found wide resonance in race, ethnic, and gender and sexuality studies. Gender theorists such as Judith Butler explored the social construction of gender and sexuality. Scholars such as Kimberlé Crenshaw, Patricia Hill Collins, and Marlee Kline developed the theory of intersectionality by expanding standpoint theory to include race, ethnicity, class, and sexuality. Intersectionality assumes that the effects of discrimination based on minority statuses are cumulative and form a matrix of domination that overdetermines minority status (Collins and Bilge 2016: 2; Hancock 2016). The idea that minorities are cumulatively disadvantaged by their various statuses is now accepted in a wide range of disciplines and public policies. Whether or not an individual scholar studies gender and sexuality, we all work in an intellectual milieu that recognizes gender and sexuality as salient dimensions of social power that could be relevant dimensions in nearly any line of historical or contemporary research (Amar 2013; Lowe 2015).

Poststructural Theory and Social Constructionism

The philosophical movement known as poststructuralism emerged in the 1960s and fundamentally challenged modern schools of thought, particularly functionalism, structuralism, and phenomenology. This movement shared certain elements with the French Annales School and the work of British Marxist historians such as E. P. Thompson, which introduced a new historiographical approach that featured the perspectives of ordinary people rather than focusing on kings, wars, battles, and public events. Poststructuralist theorists engaged with advances in linguistics, semiotics, Marxism, discourse analysis, and psychoanalysis. Poststructuralists were also influenced by the work of Thomas Kuhn, a physicist, historian, and philosopher of science whose work drew attention to the aspects of scientific practices that are socially constructed and consequently relativistic. His work on the production of knowledge popularized the concept of a *paradigm shift* that still applies to pioneering intellectual movements including, we would argue, the emerging field of global studies (Kuhn 1962).

Scholars often associated with poststructuralism include Jacques Derrida, Michel Foucault, Roland Barthes, Gilles Deleuze, Judith Butler, Jacques Lacan, Jean Baudrillard, and Julia Kristeva, though not all of them identified with the term. That being said, all were interested in the social power of semiotics—signs, symbols, language, sounds—introduced most famously by Ferdinand de Saussure, but also developed by figures such as Ludwig Wittgenstein and J. L. Austin (Saussure [1916] 1983). Poststructuralism's focus on the production of knowledge and how knowledge in turn constitutes the social construction of values and beliefs opened up new interpretive frameworks, including an increasing focus on individual subjectivity.

Today, social constructionism has become the dominant framework for exploring how people define themselves and others, and how people construct, contest, and make meaning within the social structures in which they live (Berger and Luckmann 1966; Rose 1990). To put this differently, poststructuralism offers ways for understanding how societies—and individuals within societies—create networks of social relations that construct social realities as well as create the mechanisms for change over time. This inclusion of individual agency in a more dynamic theory of social change was a tectonic shift within the academy that is now largely taken for granted. But that is our point: these multiplex changes happened across the disciplines, not just in one, and are now considered constituent parts of all the impacted disciplines. Whether or not scholars today acknowledge the influence of poststructuralism in their own research, we all work in an intellectual milieu that recognizes that identity, history, authority, and social power are socially constructed and contested.

The Cultural Turn

Within the context of poststructuralism and the linguistic turn, the fields of literary criticism, media studies, cultural studies, and interpretive anthropology all contributed to a wider "cultural turn" that shifted attention across the disciplines to the causal and socially constitutive role that culture plays in society, as well as to the subjective interpretation of meaning. The humanistic and subjective elements of culture continue to provide an important counterweight to the objective, positivistic, and scientific impulses that historically have dominated the social sciences. Following the earlier neo-Marxist Frankfurt School, the interdisciplinary fields of media studies and cultural studies focused attention on the political dynamics of culture, something previously regarded as apolitical (Lazarsfeld and Merton 1948; McLuhan 1964; Douglas [1970] 2003). Literary critic Raymond Williams (1958) argued that the modern notion of culture developed as a result of the social and political changes that accompanied the Industrial Revolution. Williams's work at the intersection of class and culture contributed to the foundation of the Birmingham

School of Cultural Studies, where Stuart Hall (1980) and others drew on Gramsci's concept of hegemony to analyze cultural domination—the ways in which the ruling classes manipulate the production of mass culture, including language, literature, arts, and media, to reflect their own beliefs, ideologies, and values, thereby maintaining the dominant culture's hegemony over the lower classes and various subcultures. Cultural studies tied the production of culture to the production of social power, demonstrating that different forms of economic and political capital could be exchanged for cultural capital, and vice versa. In a similar vein, anthropologist Clifford Geertz (1973) pointed the way on the interpretation of culture and systems of meaning in non-Western contexts. The cultural turn added the concepts of hegemony, domination, and subculture to our collective vocabulary, and from that point forward cultural identity and the processes of cultural production, representation, criticism, reception, interpretation, consumption, appropriation, and self-representation were all understood to be contested political processes.

Postcolonialism, Orientalism, and Cultural Imperialism

Postcolonial scholarship over the last forty years has provided enormous insights on contemporary cultural flows and tensions within state and transstate contexts. These insights have been deeply informed by the theoretical contributions of Frantz Fanon and Edward Said, who established a long trajectory of critical thinking about the subjugation of non-Western peoples (Fanon 1961; Said 1979). Specifically, postcolonial theory reveals the violence and technologies of domination involved in modernity and capitalism as well as contemporary state, substate, and transstate nationalisms. Moreover, postcolonial theory provides the intellectual bridge linking historical colonial injustices to contemporary global asymmetries of economic, political, and social power between the global north and global south.

Postcolonial studies, and postcolonial theory in general, are largely associated with a rethinking of a dominant European historiography that places the West at the center of the world (Guha and Spivak 1988; Loomba 2005; Amin 2009). Postcolonial studies posits a plurality of cultural perspectives and systems of meaning that do not correlate to a hierarchy dominated by Western values and scientific rationality. As an intellectual movement, postcolonialism is associated with South Asian scholarship, subaltern and literary studies, as well as analyses of resistance. It emerged out of the global south in the 1970s and gained an increasing presence in European and American universities (Darian-Smith 2013b). Theorists whose work is often associated with postcolonialism include Dipesh Chakrabarty, Homi K. Bhabha, Arjun Appadurai, Jean Comaroff, John L. Comaroff, Achille Mbembe, Upendra Baxi, Peter Fitzpatrick, Paulo Freire, Boaventura de Sousa Santos, and Gayatri Chakravorty Spivak. Postcolonial theory acknowledges and recovers the ongoing significance of colonized peoples in shaping the epistemologies, philosophies, practices, and shifting identities of dominant Western knowledge and subjectivities (Freire [1970] 2000; Santos 2007, 2014). According to these scholars, colonial assumptions of Western superiority endure across time and undermine contemporary attempts to build more inclusive multicultural societies. Today, despite state policies that ostensibly embrace multiculturalism and cultural diversity, racial categories and racialized differences continue to exist in all societies. Whether or not scholars engage with the consequences of racism, colonialism, and imperialism in their own research, we all work in an intellectual milieu that can no longer discount these violent histories that still shape a racialized and neoimperial present.

Nationalisms and Identities

The near-global spread of nationalism via democratic revolutions, modern imperialism, socialism, fascism, and decolonization makes nationalism one of the most successful political ideologies in history. Over the course of the modern era the nation-state became the cornerstone of the international regulatory system. The poststructuralist idea that individual and collective identities are socially constructed had a significant impact across the academic disciplines in part because it undermines modern national identities as natural or taken-for-granted categories. As Benedict Anderson argued in *Imagined Communities* (1983), nationalism is a collective form of identity that is socially constructed and contested.

Nationalism also operates internally within the state to categorize and authorize citizens and to manage the divide between legitimate citizens and people who are considered illegitimate outsiders or aliens. Citizenship gives access to the resources, rights, and protections of the state. Hence, defining the criteria for citizenship has been a source of constant conflict and tension. In the 1960s, the label "identity politics" first appeared in feminist and black social movements in the United States, the United Kingdom, and other Western democracies calling for the recognition of minority political and civil rights (Harris 2001). Over the subsequent decades, identity politics have framed bitter national debates over issues such as immigration, terrorism, abortion, health care, and labor rights, as well as state policies of multiculturalism (see Schwartz, Luyckx, and Vignoles 2011; McGarry and Jasper 2015).

Decentering the Nation-State

Scholars in many disciplines are aware that nation-states are being reconfigured in light of new economic, political and cultural dynamics of globalization that operate beyond, within, and between countries. The sovereignty of the nation-state is being challenged by the onset of global forces such as market integration, regional trade agreements, deregulation, underdevelopment, new regionalized and deterritorialized forms of conflict, global warming, the proliferation of NGOs and other nonstate actors, as well as growing global social movements around human rights, women's issues, and the environment, among others (Beck and Willms 2004; Brown 2015). Together these forces profoundly weaken the capacities of nation-states to act as autonomous political and economic units. The resulting general sense of insecurity is matched by deepening state militarization and hypersecurity.

Global forces in turn contribute to the displacement of millions of immigrants and refugees fleeing poverty, violence, and environmental degradation, further destabilizing neighboring countries. In the current regulatory system displaced persons go largely underrepresented and unprotected. The displaced may find that they are stateless and no longer have a homeland, a national identity, or the protection of citizenship, leaving them extremely vulnerable to ethnic persecution, economic exploitation, slavery, and sex trafficking (Bales 2016; Brettell and Hollifield 2014). The long-term displacement of millions of people can form racial and ethnic diasporas that further complicate singular national identities. These forces call into question state-bound concepts of nationalism, identity, citizenship, economy, politics, governance, law and so on. This is what scholars mean when they say we are living in a postnational age (Darian-Smith 2015; Balibar 2015).

At the same time, the nation-state is also challenged from within by rising separatist movements, religious fundamentalists, as well as ethnic and indigenous nationalisms. Many of these movements are linked to history of colonization and decolonization. These challenges are contributing to an ongoing crisis of legitimacy within nations, and there is a measurable disenchantment with democracy, loss of faith in governments that appear ineffectual, and a growing sense that governments represent multinational corporations and the ultrawealthy rather than the average working-class citizen. These sentiments are reflected in voter dissatisfaction, xenophobia, islamophobia, as well as the return to religious fundamentalisms, ultranationalist right-wing politics, and in some cases neofascism. The nativist anti-immigrant backlash is showing up in far-right movements around the world including the Brexit vote and in Donald Trump's wall to keep immigrants out.

Scholars across the disciplines are studying the various impacts of the nation-state's decentering or destabilization, including rethinking the concepts of sovereignty (Hardt and Negri 2001) and global governance (Falk 2014; Gill 2015). As the sociologist Ulrick Beck argues, conventional scholarship assumes that "humankind is split up into a large but finite number of nations, each of which supposedly develops its own unified culture, secure behind the dike of its state-container . . . It structures our entire way of seeing. Methodological nationalism is the unquestioned framework that determines the limits of relevance" (Beck and Willms 2004: 13). Decentering scholarship challenges the assumption that nation-states are the primary unit of analysis and social organization (Khagram and Levitt 2008). Transcending the limitations of "methodological nationalism" that have constrained Western political thought opens up new ways of making sense of complex transnational and translocal relations that have been eclipsed by its limited theoretical and conceptual horizons (see methodological nationalism in Chapter 5).

TRANSDISCIPLINARITY AND FUTURE SCHOLARSHIP

What does a shared transdisciplinary framework mean for future scholarship? We argue that acknowledging the presence of this framework may help us move beyond disciplinary-versus- interdisciplinary debates by allowing us to recognize the interrelated dimensions of any issue (Lim 2017). Of course, the common transdisciplinary thematics we described above are by no means comprehensive. For instance, systems theory seems to operate across the disciplines in a similar way (Bertalanffy 1969; Baran 1964; Luhmann 2013). Nonetheless, given the quantity and importance of these shared analytical approaches it is hard to deny that together they have had an enormous impact on a wide range of academic disciplines over the decades. Their effects are evident in multiple scholarly approaches and social theories and have shaped concepts such as intersectionality, orientalism, postnationalism, biopolitics, racial formation, and governmentality. Moreover, they have given rise to intellectual movements, referred to as the "cultural turn," the "linguistic turn," the "spatial turn," and more recently the "global turn," that have swept across a broad range of disciplines within the humanities and social sciences (Arias and Warf 2008; Tally 2013). Together these various theoretical concepts and intellectual movements have crisscrossed cultures, continents, and ideologies and brought widespread scholarly attention to the sociocultural dimensions of political and economic power that have become central to many intellectual communities around the world.

A number of scholars currently publishing in the Euro-American academy, including Jürgen Habermas, Bruno Latour, Judith Butler, Amartya Sen, Dipesh Chakrabarty, Kwame Appiah, Saskia Sassen, David Harvey, Mike Davis, Joseph Stiglitz, Paul Farmer, Talal Asad, Noam Chomsky, and many more, stand out for making contributions that are influential across numerous disciplines. Such scholars can be controversial, but they all have the ability to reach beyond their theoretical or methodological training and make their specialized knowledge speak to wider audiences. In many ways, these scholars represent the kind of flexible and innovative thinking that moves beyond conventional disciplines and posits new ways of producing and organizing knowledge.

The transdisciplinary framework has progressed to the point that it is hard to imagine any discipline in the social sciences or humanities today entirely ignoring issues of class, race, ethnicity, gender, and religion and the critiques that fields focused on these issues deliver. Similarly, most disciplines cannot ignore the intersections of economic, political, legal, and social power dimensions across, within, and beyond nation-states. Increasing numbers of scholars are problematizing the centrality of the nation-state as the container and horizon of relevant knowledge and analysis. In other words, no academic discipline has remained entirely untouched by the deep legacies of poststructuralist, constructivist, linguistic, and interpretivist theories. Whether or not they have read the works of Gramsci, Foucault, Said, or Collins, scholars across the social sciences and humanities doing innovative and cutting edge scholarship must directly and indirectly grapple with their legacies and contributions.

We are not suggesting that every scholar in every discipline is consciously embracing the critical social theories and perspectives that characterize the transdisciplinary framework. There will always be scholars in the disciplines and subdisciplines who for various reasons remain uninterested in engaging with interdisciplinary approaches. Specialization and the production of specialized knowledge is still a proper and necessary function in the academy. In fact, the continued production of specialized kinds of knowledge is necessary for developing the new interdisciplinary approaches and more encompassing frameworks that we need to analyze global issues and shifting geopolitical realities. Both specialization and generalization are necessary, just as quantitative and qualitative approaches are necessary. In fact, it is precisely the communication between specialized and general knowledge and between quantitative and qualitative knowledge that innovative scholarship needs.

ARTICULATING A GLOBAL TRANSDISCIPLINARY FRAMEWORK

Research that brings together the global studies characteristics that we outlined in Chapter 2 with the transdisciplinary framework outlined in this chapter is resulting in the formation of a new analytical paradigm. The hallmark of this new paradigm is that it shifts scholarly focus to the entire local-global continuum as an object of study and wider context of analysis (McCarty 2014c). We call this new paradigm a *global transdisciplinary framework*. This framework is both *postdisciplinary* and *postinterdisciplinary* in that it moves past the inherent limits of conventional academic disciplines, making it possible to engage holistically with the kinds of multifaceted global-scale challenges the world faces today. We argue that a global transdisciplinary framework is applicable to research in both mainstream disciplines and new fields of inquiry, whether or not research foci are obviously global in scale.

The challenge in conveying a global transdisciplinary framework is made easier by the fact that many of our students understand that the academy needs to develop new approaches to contemporary problems. Young people tend to be less invested than established scholars in a worldview that privileges nation-states and the disciplinary-bound production of knowledge. In short, globalization isn't new to them, and adopting a global transdisciplinary framework to understand their highly integrated world simply makes sense. Moreover, the students find that the framework can be liberating and empowering given that they are confronted every day with headlines that present the world as a dizzying array of apparently disconnected and chaotic events. A global transdisciplinary framework encourages students to identify persistent patterns across time and space that make it possible for them to connect the dots. In this way the framework can transform our students' understanding of a wide range of current global issues. And in the process, it encourages students to reach beyond the boundaries of their own cultural values to embrace humanity more widely in ways that could potentially transform their fundamental understanding of the individual's role in society and our collective place in the world.

Our experience in research and in the classroom leads us to argue, somewhat counterintuitively, that a global transdisciplinary framework makes analyzing global issues more accessible. This framework enables an integrated approach to addressing global issues that involves selectively analyzing relevant historical, spatial, economic, political, and social dimensions and engaging with a range of theories and methods driven by one's research questions rather than one's disciplinary training. It allows the deployment of micro, midrange, and macro theories and qualitative and quantitative methods at different levels of analysis as needed. We argue that this holistic framework is productive, analytically flexible, and surprisingly practical to implement with the limited resources scholars typically have at their disposal. The ability of our students to grasp this integrated paradigm, use it to understand current events, and apply it in their own real-world research is evidence that it can be communicated effectively and applied productively. Its success in our classrooms also suggests that its value can be conveyed to wider audiences, including university administrators, funding agencies, policy makers, and, ultimately, the general public.

In the next chapter, we explicitly talk about how to design a global research project that is informed by and makes concrete what we mean by a global transdisciplinary framework. Linking theory to design and selecting methodological approaches that best address one's core research questions raise a number of challenges to conventional ways of designing a research project. We are keen to help junior and senior scholars think through some of these challenges and more effectively design a research plan that foregrounds the global dimensions in their work and makes it more applicable to understanding our contemporary moment.

4 Global Research Design

In the preceding chapter we outlined what we mean by a global transdisciplinary framework and explicitly discussed its theoretical approaches, which draw from across the social sciences and humanities, from scholars working within and across the global south and global north. In this chapter, we move on to a more nuts-and-bolts discussion that links theory to research design—a necessary next step toward engaging in global studies research. This chapter addresses the challenges a global studies approach raises for conventional research design, and it lays out some of the concerns that may come into play when attempting a research plan for scholarship with global dimensions and applications.

As we discussed in Chapter 3, a global transdisciplinary framework requires us to recognize that global issues are nearly always transected by social, political, economic, spatial, and temporal dimensions and issues of race, ethnicity, class, gender, and religion. All of these elements can manifest simultaneously and in different ways at local, national, regional, and global levels. For the individual scholar, designing a theoretical and methodological approach to studying today's complex global processes can appear overwhelming. Fortunately, adopting a global transdisciplinary framework offers a way forward in studying and producing new knowledge that speaks to the interconnected complexities of the twenty-first century. Evidence to support this claim comes from our own research and teaching experience. We find that applying a global transdisciplinary framework helps students design viable research projects. Students don't need to analyze every dimension of a particular global issue, but they do need to recognize the presence of various dimensions that may or may not be relevant, depending on the objectives of their study. Likewise, students don't need to analyze all the conceptual and spatial levels from local to global, but they should recognize that the issue they are dealing with may be operating at any one or all of those levels and that the interaction between levels may be the issue's most fascinating and important aspect.

Depending on your research subject, objectives, and questions, you will have to make various decisions to lay out a viable and accessible global research design. There already exists much literature in the social sciences and humanities about research design for qualitative, quantitative, and mixed-method approaches (Creswell 2007, 2014). Each discipline has its own standard texts on how to do research that speaks to its dominant concerns.[1] We do not intend to replicate these discussions in this chapter. Instead, we problematize the standard methodological approaches that have developed over the past hundred years within a Euro-American academy bound by state-centric framing, and we adapt those modernist approaches to global studies scholarship. Our point is that the theoretical transdisciplinary framework that we discussed in Chapter 3 has emerged concurrently with a multidimensional methodological framework that deliberately engages with mixed methods and integrates multiple forms of data so as to better engage with global research questions. The goal of such a holistic approach is to position the researcher to more fully understand the big picture that contextualizes and constitutes the global issue they are investigating.

---

1. There is a great deal of overlap between the disciplines. For a general text, see Creswell 2014. For sociology, see Berg and Lune 2011; Fowler 2014; for history, see Tosh 2015; Bombaro 2012; for anthropology, see Bernard 2011; DeWalt and DeWalt 2011; for communication, see Merrigan and Huston 2014; for political science, see Gerring 2012; Ragin 2008; Brady and Collier 2010; and for international relations, see Jackson 2010; Lamont 2015; Klotz and Prakash 2009.

THE FOUNDATIONS OF EMPIRICAL RESEARCH

Doing primary research is an academic endeavor that differs in several important ways from other academic endeavors such as teaching, learning, writing, and grading papers. As every graduate student discovers, conducting your own primary research is very different from what we do in the classroom. While effective teaching involves a dynamic relationship between teacher and student, it helps to think of teaching in simplistic terms as the passing of existing knowledge on to the next generation. In contrast, the goal of conducting research is to create new knowledge that doesn't necessarily already exist. Ideally researchers produce the kinds of knowledge that could change our understanding of an important issue. Being a researcher—an explorer, if you will—and finding out things about the world that are not already known is a unique and exhilarating challenge.

The logic behind academic research in global studies, as in most modern fields of study, is the empiricism that developed with the Enlightenment and remains common to many modern academic disciplines. Put simply, empirical research is based on recording one's direct observations or experiences, which in turn can be analyzed and interpreted through qualitative and/or quantitative methods. In the social sciences and humanities, scholars usually combine a variety of methods to better answer questions that cannot be answered through experiments in a laboratory setting. This is because unlike chemical experiments, which are conducted in controlled settings, social scientific and humanistic research typically involves examining people and seeks to understand how they think and behave across a variety of historical periods and cultural settings. Since people are not robots and act differently in different political and social contexts that change over time, their actions are typically not reducible to replicable experiments and static, objective data.

The so-called scientific method has a very long history; historians often locate its initial development with Greek physicians who established a school of anatomical research in Alexandria. Physicians such as Herophilos (335–280 BCE) and Erasistratus of Chios (304–250 BCE) rejected medical traditions such as bloodletting in favor of observing phenomena directly, believing that medical practice based on experimentation and observing how patients responded to certain treatments was more effective. Erasistratus was a very skilled surgeon who contributed greatly to anatomical understanding about the role of the heart as a pump necessary for the circulation of blood, laying the groundwork for William Harvey and his thesis on the circulatory system in the seventeenth century. Erasistratus's detailed observations informed his exploratory expansion of medical understanding of the human body and paved the way for new modes of understanding and knowledge (Lloyd 1999).

A range of inductive-deductive methods developed around the quest for experimental evidence. The Greek philosophers Plato and his student Aristotle, who worked in the fourth and fifth centuries BCE, and later scientists such as the Arab physicist Ibn al-Haytham (known as Alhazen) and the Persian scientist Abū al-Rayhān al-Bīrūnī (known as Al-Bīrūnī), who worked in the tenth and eleventh centuries, grappled with developing a scientific method that could produce replicable experiments and independently verifiable universal laws. Alhazen and Al-Bīrūnī were both extraordinary scholars of the medieval Islamic era. Alhazen was widely hailed for his research on optics, mirrors, and light. He was one of the earliest scholars to talk about the idea of a hypothesis, which would have to be proven by experiments and replicable results. Al-Bīrūnī was celebrated for his expertise in physics, mathematics, astronomy, the natural sciences, and linguistics, and his work underscored the desirability of a multiperspectival approach to understanding complex phenomena. These Islamic scholars promoted what would come to be known as the scientific method in fundamental ways approximately two hundred years before it was further developed by scientists of the Renaissance such as Leonardo Da Vinci, Galileo Galilei, Descartes, and Johannes Kepler (see Dear 2001; Grafton, Shelford, and Siraisi 1992).

Ancient Greek and Arabic classical texts, translated into Latin, enabled an emerging scientific method to be recovered and introduced in Europe in the twelfth and thirteenth centuries. There it was taught in new universities such as the University of Bologna (established in 1088) and the University of Paris (established c. 1160–70). But not until the Renaissance period did truly new scientific thought flourish in Europe. This was prompted in part by the rise of humanism, which included new knowledge about perspective in art and architecture, and in part by the discovery of the New World in the late fifteenth century, which challenged many classical notions about the natural and physical world (see Hall 1994; Grafton, Shelford, and Siraisi 1992). The notion that universities were not just the conservers and depositories of knowledge to be handed down to the next generation, that in fact they should produce new thought and actively advance knowledge for its own intrinsic worth, led universities to proliferate across Europe. These new institutions of learning nurtured and encouraged research, and the standard curriculum included a range of fields: the arts, law, medicine, mathematics, engineering, and astronomy (Rudy 1984; Ridder-Symoens 1992). In these flourishing hubs of intellectual activity the scientific method, as first proposed in classical times, was hotly discussed and debated.

Descartes's "Cogito ergo sum" (I think, therefore I am) is one of the foundations of modern Western philosophy and science. Other famous contributors to the debates over scientific method and the role of logic and reason within it were philosophers, scientists, and mathematicians such as Francis Bacon (1561–1626), Galileo (1564–1642), and Sir Isaac Newton (1643–1727), who is famously remembered for his discovery of the laws of motion and the theory of gravity. Together these scholars and the new knowledge they produced helped establish the modern sciences, which were thought of as a system of universal truths. Throughout the Enlightenment, the field of scientific inquiry opened up even further. Inventions such as the chronometer, which helped ships navigate the high seas, and the steam engine, which drove mechanized equipment and railways, helped to usher in European colonialism, the Atlantic slave trade, and the Industrial Revolution (Uglow 2002; Sobel [1995] 2007). Figure 8 depicts a demonstration of an orrery, a mechanical model of the solar system that was used to demonstrate the motions of the planets around the sun—making the universe seem almost like a clock (see Uglow 2002: 122–24).

More recently, Karl Popper (1902–94) and Thomas Kuhn (1922–96) have argued over whether there is a single scientific method that applies to all scientific knowledge. Kuhn proposed in his very influential book *The Structure of Scientific Revolutions* (1962) that scientific breakthroughs occur when there is what he called a "paradigm shift," which allows for new ways of thinking that may have been overlooked or dismissed before. Moreover, he argued that the idea that there is a scientific truth depends

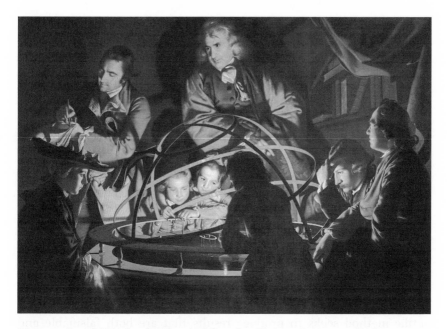

Figure 8. Joseph Wright of Derby, *A Philosopher Giving a Lecture on* the Orrery, c. 1765.

upon the consensus of the scientific community at the time, and that one generation's "truth" can be denounced by the next generation entirely (Kuhn 1962; Shapin 1994; Jasanoff 2004). Hence, our understanding of science cannot depend on "objective" truths, since all researchers exist within a scholarly community and bring to their findings their own subjectively informed social worldview. As a result, we can see in the world competing and often inconsistent notions of what constitutes scientific knowledge. This revelation finds increasing resonance today with a growing appreciation in the global north of non-Western perspectives and alternative understandings of the world.

Debates over what constitutes science and the most appropriate scientific method to elucidate knowledge have continued over the centuries and underscore that neither concepts of science and methods are not fixed. For instance, deep divisions lie between rationalists and empiricists: the former claim that new knowledge can be gained through reason and so may be independent of sense experience, while the latter claim that sensory experience is the primary source of our concepts and efforts to gain new understanding. Fortunately for most researchers designing global studies projects, these debates—while fascinating in their own right—are not of central concern. Still, ongoing conversations over what constitutes appropriate methods of inquiry should function as a constant reminder that we need to (1) constantly question our taken-for-granted assumptions and categories of thought, (2) think carefully about what we recognize as appropriate data or evidence and ask if we are overlooking something that may, perhaps counterintuitively, be significant, and (3) appreciate that what we collect and how we organize data to substantiate a credible argument relies on logic and relational values that are deeply culturally informed.

In the natural sciences, the empirical model assumes a necessary relationship between theory, methodological observation, logical analysis, and reliable evidence or data. In oversimplified terms the empirical methods used in the natural sciences rely on direct observation, experimentation, data collection, careful documentation, and logical analysis. The scientific method seeks to produce results that are both falsifiable and reliable in that they can be replicated by independent researchers (Latour 1988). The humanities and social sciences have adapted the empirical methods used in the natural sciences to study human society. In the process they had to make accommodations for the fact that the object of their study, humans, don't act in entirely predictable ways. Social behaviors and thinking cannot always be replicable in the manner of a chemical experiment (see Flyvbjerg 2001).

The legacy of the empirical method means that in most academic disciplines the authority of the field to some degree still rests on this empirical foundation. The empirical credibility of a field derives from a number of sources, including the relevance of the substantive issues that the field engages with, the explanatory power of its theoretical frameworks, the reliability of its empirical methods and analytical procedures, and the significance of its findings. So despite differences in their capacity to replicate evidence, the humanities and social sciences have in common with the physical sciences a reliance on observable evidence that informs a theory, which is then tested and analyzed so a conclusion can be drawn. The conclusion in turn informs a new theoretical framing for which researchers may or may not find evidence to back up. In other words, theory informs research design and methods, and conclusions reinform theoretical propositions in a constant dynamic interrelationship between theory, design, methods, and findings. This is how researchers forge new understandings and produce new knowledge.

Though there is now quite a lot of variation, the basic outline of this empirical method is still recognizable in most disciplines. In any given field of study the existing body of academic literature provides the core vocabulary, including the conceptual, theoretical, and analytical frameworks for analyzing certain kinds of issues. A researcher draws on the existing literature to develop a central research question that addresses one or more of the relevant issues. The research question then acts as a guide for designing a research strategy that is capable of producing the kinds of reliable evidence that are needed to answer the question. Ideally, this empirical approach not only develops out of the existing literature in a particular field but also produces findings and conclusions that contribute something back to literature in that field. Stated simply, the theories drive the research question, the research question drives the research design, the methodology produces the evidence, and the analysis of the evidence leads to findings that contribute new knowledge to existing literatures.

Most disciplines have a limited set of accepted data collection methods and analytical procedures that have proven to provide reliable empirical evidence over time. Some disciplines use methods that are more quantitatively oriented in that they rely primarily on direct observation or the systemic analysis of quantitative data (experiment, survey, statistical analysis). Other disciplines include methods that are more qualitative in that they rely more on subjective observations, emphasizing the researcher's own insight and interpretation (interviews, participant observation). What constitutes an appropriate research design differs across fields and disciplines that foreground some research questions over others. This is not to imply that one research design is more empirical or scientific than another, only that certain disciplines regard some evidence as more significant than other kinds of evidence. This claim to being more scientific is often based on the argument that the evidence used is more *objective* than other kinds of evidence. But it is important to remember that all data sets are limited by the research methodology that produced the data (Stiglitz, Sen, and Fitoussi 2010; Darian-Smith 2016).

In a similar way, some disciplines are more conscious of the role of theory in shaping their research questions and research design than other disciplines, which may cling to the idea that they are impartial observers and doing "objective" scholarship. The latter disciplines claim that data drives theoretical advances rather than theory driving what kind of data is collected in the first place. But most researchers understand that what is really going on is a dynamic interaction between new theories, appropriate designs, rigorous methods, and empirical findings, and that one scholarly approach is not more empirical or intellectually superior than another.

Despite the differences between more quantitative and more qualitative methodological approaches, it is very important to recognize that both types of research rely on empirical observations and logical analysis of evidence to support their central arguments and conclusions. Global studies as a field recognizes the valuable contributions of both quantitative and qualitative scholarship from across the humanities and the social and behavioral sciences.

EXISTING LITERATURE AS CONTEXT

In order to be considered credible, a research design and resulting findings must withstand the criticism of peers and should ultimately be replicable, or at least able to be substantiated by independent research. For students, faculty advisors often act as the reviewing peers. For faculty, their peers are other professionals trained in the field. The peer-review imperative is why researchers should present their results at professional conferences and publish them in peer-reviewed journals. If the research is carried out properly and survives the scrutiny of peers, it may contribute something to the existing body of knowledge in its field. That, in a nutshell, is the goal of global research—to study important global issues, to have one's findings published and contribute to existing literature, and ultimately to open up new ways of thinking about global issues that may have an impact or provide a solution.

It is important to recognize the role that existing bodies of literature play in the research design process. Academic research *by definition* develops out of and speaks back to existing bodies of scholarly literature. This means that existing literature in a given field is the necessary context within which scholars identify academic issues, form questions, and design research projects. Since the goal of research is to contribute to existing knowledge, research is not typically something that springs fully formed from one's own thought processes. The literature in any given field identifies relevant issues, defines basic concepts and theoretical frameworks that can be used to understand the issues, and provides data collection and analytical methods that can be used to study those issues. The grand ideas in one's head matter to the degree that those ideas can be made to engage with existing bodies of academic literature. This means that aspiring researchers must have some familiarity with the relevant literature in the field. *It also means that every stage of a research project, from its design, to its implementation and analysis, to the discussion of the conclusions and their significance, should explicitly reference relevant literature.* This is one important reason why papers, research proposals, dissertations, and publications are required to have pertinent citations throughout.

The field of global studies, like any other academic field, engages with an existing body of literature on global themes. There is a rapidly growing body of work that explicitly addresses the processes of globalization and, more recently, a nascent body of literature about the field of global studies itself. A significant portion of research on global issues, however, is still produced within the frameworks of conventional disciplines such as anthropology, economics, geography, comparative literature, history, political science, law, and sociology. A great deal of literature relevant to global issues can also be found in interdisciplinary fields such as development, postcolonial, environmental, ethnic, feminist, and religious studies. Scholars interested in global issues should be familiar with literature that is explicitly anchored in global studies but can also draw freely from relevant literature in other fields.

THEORETICAL AND CONCEPTUAL FRAMEWORKS

Because theory, research design, methods, and data are all necessarily linked, designing a research project in global studies typically involves global theoretical approaches and concepts. Existing global studies literature provides researchers with a variety of theoretical approaches and conceptual frameworks, many of which we mentioned in Chapter 3.

Theory is not meant to be static. The process by which theories are proposed, tested, rejected, and revised is dynamic. Existing theoretical approaches and concepts are meant to inform research design and implementation, but at the same time research findings are meant to transform existing theories that themselves pose new kinds of questions. Because global studies is a relatively new field, this dynamic process of producing and rejecting new theories and methods is heightened. And because part of the objective of global studies is to increase the engagement between Western and non-Western scholarship, the dynamic process of new theory production should be further accelerated by intercultural exchanges.

Even though global studies scholars draw on literatures from across disciplinary boundaries, it is important to remember that the substantive issues, theories, and methods in each discipline are shaped and in some ways limited by the fundamental assumptions and concepts underlying that discipline. Conventional disciplines all represent powerful but very different ways of knowing and producing new knowledge. Disciplinary approaches enable certain kinds of analyses and disable other kinds of analyses. Interdisciplinary and transdisciplinary scholars should keep in mind that the theories, concepts, and data that one discipline uses may not translate perfectly into other disciplines. For example, many of the taken-for-granted concepts we use in our classrooms every day, concepts such as culture, development, and sustainability, can and do have very different meanings in disciplines such as anthropology, economics, political science, psychology, and sociology. This is because concepts and vocabularies are socially constructed and embody and reflect the cultural contexts in which they are constituted, articulated, implemented, affirmed, and contested.

When academic concepts do travel between disciplines, it is probably because they represent common Western academic concepts such as the autonomous individual, the rational actor, market logics, and a monolithic understanding of the nation-state. Global studies scholars should not be surprised to find that modern Western academic literatures embody the hyperrational logics and assumptions that characterize the Euro-American societies that spawned the modern disciplines in the first place.

While these logics enable certain kinds of analyses, they simultaneously disable other ways of knowing (see Chapter 2). For many scholars, engaging with non-Western concepts may seem daunting. But we can begin by recognizing that bodies of non-Western academic literature exist and that they have valuable contributions to make in the form of new working vocabularies, concepts, and analytical frameworks.

THE RESEARCH QUESTION

A research question or thesis is the central inquiry that drives a particular research project and determines its overall design. The importance of the thesis to the research design process cannot be overstated given that at the most basic level research is the process of answering a specific research question. The research question should ultimately determine the entire structure of the research design, including the conceptual framework and related methodological and analytical approaches. Stated plainly, *if you don't have a research question, then you aren't doing research*. You might be reviewing the literature or summarizing your observations, but without a research question you aren't really seeking to answer anything.

This may seem obvious, but in practice we find that many students do not recognize the importance of having a clear researchable question. Students are typically interested in broad issues such as inequality, development, gender, or the environment. The average student has a set of abstract interests and has written papers on those broad topics. Our interests in broad topics are necessary for motivating research, but they are not sufficient for carrying out a viable research project. What many students do not adequately understand is the difference between these kinds of general interests and the more tangible kinds of questions that can provide the basis for a viable research project. A focused research question is the kind of question that can be answered within a specific time period and with the resources and data that are likely to be available. For most researchers, these resources are in short supply. The scope of the project should be scaled back to reflect those limitations.

Students' difficulty with identifying researchable projects may be due in part to the fact that secondary schools and colleges devote little attention to research training. Students are frequently trained to read a given set of articles and then make logical arguments about an issue using the assigned articles as evidence. Or they may be given a particular experiment to conduct. Such exercises help students become familiar with the literature, identify their interests, and develop their analytical skills. These exercises, however, are not the same as designing and carrying out your own primary research. Learning to design and carry out primary research is a much more involved endeavor that requires a grasp of existing literature in the field and substantial methodological training. It also requires a significant investment of time on the part of the student as well as their faculty mentor. As class sizes grow and resources are reduced, teaching institutions are finding it increasingly difficult to provide the kind of intensive methods training and close research mentorship that students need in order to learn how to do their own primary research. As a result, many students entering graduate programs have never really been taught to develop a researchable question, never mind design and carry out their own primary research projects.

Most researchable questions share certain necessary characteristics. A researchable question is one that

- reflects the researcher's wider interests while carving out a feasible project
- emerges out of, builds upon, and addresses existing literature in some way
- is not impossible to answer (How many angels can dance on the head of a pin?)
- does not already have an obvious answer (Do the poor wish they had more opportunities?)
- can be answered with information that is obtainable via appropriate research methods
- can be answered within the time and with the resources available to the researcher

In short, a researchable question is a question that is relevant to the academic literature on a given topic and can be answered with information produced by the researcher. Finding a good research question that is both engaging and productive can be difficult, but there is a knack for it that can be learned. It gets easier once you start looking for and thinking explicitly about what makes a good question. As proof, most experienced researchers are able to recognize a good research question as soon as they hear it. The best research questions imply new connections and tend to spawn subquestions and hypotheses. Thinking creatively about how one might go about answering a good question is itself a productive exercise.

DEVELOPING A GLOBAL RESEARCH QUESTION

The central research question should drive the entire research design, from the conceptual framework to the methodology and analytical approach. Further, an effectively contained research question leads to a research design that is feasible given limited time and resources. This characteristic makes finding the right question even more important in global studies, where topics span the local-global continuum and are often interconnected in complex ways. Having a contained, researchable question is of paramount importance when a researcher is dealing with extremely complex global issues. Without a clear focus, global studies researchers can easily become lost in a sea of endless connections and possibilities.

The best research questions in global studies often take into account what we refer to as the local-global continuum (see Chapter 2). This means locating very abstract global concepts where they touch down in the real world, in the lives of ordinary people. These large abstract concepts often look very different from the perspective of the local or from related micro/ macro, inside/outside, or emic/etic angles. For example, the way nonacademics understand global-scale issues such as climate change or migration is often very different from the way academics understand them. The differences between these various perspectives are almost always interesting and offer a good starting point for thinking through a strong research question. This attention to multiple perspectives also raises a number of characteristics that are commonly found in global studies research.

The first characteristic of most good research questions is that they have a critical edge. Critical questions bring into question the status quo, the unquestioned assumptions that make things appear the way they are (on criticality, see Chapter 2). By approaching things from a variety of perspectives, a good research question often points to a contradiction or implies connections between things we don't think of as related. For example, a good question might highlight the connections between economic production and sexual reproduction, or the exchange between financial capital and cultural capital. You might not at first be able to answer definitively what those connections are in a specific context, but exploring the connections is likely to generate more focused research questions that are answerable.

The best research questions are also reflexive in that they recognize that the researcher is not an impartial observer who somehow creates neutral or objective knowledge. Researchers should recognize that their own assumptions, abilities, and limitations play a role in shaping the outcome of the research. They should recognize the epistemological chasm between researcher and subject, East and West, and global north and global south. As we discussed with respect to Kuhn's insights and his notion of a paradigm shift, our understanding of science does not comprise objective truths. All researchers exist within scholarly communities and bring to their findings their own subjective worldview.

All researchers, and particularly those in global studies, should also recognize the ethical dimensions of their research. The knowledge that academics produce can and often does have an impact on the people we study. We should ask ourselves: What kinds of knowledge are we producing, and why are we producing it? How might that knowledge be used and misused? What impact might the research have in the world? Much research in global studies involves studying asymmetries of power between rich and poor countries, regions, and continents and the impacts of these power dynamics on vulnerable communities. Thinking about how one's research findings may be used inadvertently to further oppressive forces and put marginalized people at risk is a very necessary component of research design.

Research questions that include critical, reflexive, and ethical characteristics tend to have a kind of timeless quality. This is true whether the research is conducted under the banner of global studies or in any discipline or interdisciplinary field. The best research questions can be asked almost anywhere and at almost any time in human history. They raise a number of subquestions that can be addressed explicitly or implicitly, such as

- As a researcher, what are my assumptions? In what ways are they built into my theory, method, practice, and project?
- What assumptions are built into the terminology of my topic (e.g., aid, development, civil society, democratization)?
- What do the people involved think the issues are, and how do they make sense of them?
- What assumptions do everyone involved in the issue share?
- How is consensus built, maintained, challenged, and changed?
- What is hidden in the assumptions that make consensus possible?
- Who are the actors? Why are they involved? Who has power and who doesn't?
- Who are the agents and the opponents of change and what do they stand to gain or lose?
- Who is telling the story? Who benefits from different versions of it?
- How is history being exploited and reinterpreted, and for what purpose?
- How do processes of interpretation, translation, appropriation, and miscommunication play into the issue? Where is there continuity in change and vice versa?
- What points of view are silenced or excluded from the discourse?
- How are processes of domination and exploitation being justified?
- If there is conflict, do some aspects of the conflict go unresolved?
- How do people make sense of, adapt to, or cope with conditions they don't control?
- What alternatives are being proposed or are implied, and why?
- Are some alternatives rejected or accommodated, and is the status quo maintained?

One reason why defining a good research question is difficult is that it is as much about the reaction of the researcher to the question as it is about the question itself. If a research project is to have a chance of being interesting to others, it first has to be interesting to you. Do you find the question intellectually engaging and stimulating? Does it make you reorganize your thoughts and rethink what have read? Is it productive for guiding and organizing your writing? Does the question make you want to jump up and get to work to answer it? Know why your project is exciting and interesting. When you are deep in the process of elaborating your research project, it is easy to lose sight of your original motivation.

It is very important to note that research questions do not spring from the mind fully formed. Researchers often start with a simple question that evolves and becomes more refined as the research project develops and a researcher becomes more knowledgeable about the subject. Evolving research questions tend to wander about a bit and do sometimes circle back, usually becoming sharper and more subtle in the process. It is a good idea to keep track of the various versions of their central research question and subquestions. The overall thesis or central research question may not reach its final form until the project is done, and then may morph into the next research project. Even though the research question may evolve during the research process, it nonetheless, and somewhat para-doxically, serves as the foundation for the entire research design.

RESEARCH DESIGN

Research design is a necessary component of most research proposals, including research proposals for master's and PhD degrees as well as for faculty and researchers seeking funding. Typically student proposals are vet-ted by faculty at the home institution. Faculty research proposals are vetted by a panel of peers made up of other faculty and professional researchers.

The research design process in global studies follows the same general contours of the research design process in other fields of study. The schol-arly authority of global research rests on the same kinds of empirical assumptions, research designs, data collection methods, and analytical approaches that are used in conventional disciplines. The fundamental assumptions about the relationship between theory, data, and analysis remain the same. A research design in global studies should include a clear conceptual framework and a clearly stated central research question or the-sis. It should also include a well-defined methodology and explanation of the specific methods to be used. Basic data collection and analysis methods in global studies, such as archival research, observation, interviews, surveys, and statistical analysis, are the same as in other disciplines (see "Basic Data Collection Methods," Chapter 5). The statistical methods used to analyze quantitative data are the same as well. Your proposal should explain any specific analytical techniques you will use. Additionally, research proposals often require a discussion of possible findings and how they address your original research question. And finally, most proposals include a section about the kinds of conclusions that you might be able to draw from your research and their potential significance to the field. In other words, you need to be able to say what your research will produce and why it matters.

Researchers in global studies must take into account an unusually wide array of issues that could impact the design and implementation of their research project. Some disciplines have relatively straightforward goals and expectations for research design and implementation. These disciplines may have clear theoretical assumptions and limited and clearly defined procedures for data collection and analysis. This is not the case in an interdisciplinary field such as global studies, where research can be conducted anywhere in the world and conceivably draw on any number of methodologies from disciplines across the humanities and the social, behavioral, and natural sciences. Researchers interested in global issues face not only a wide range of substantive issues and possible theoretical frameworks but also an array of methodological options.

Depending on the nature of your central question and the kinds of evidence you seek, you must develop a research design that is capable of providing the kinds of evidence you need to address the question. All research designs and methodologies must strike an imperfect balance between empirical and interpretive, deductive and inductive, and exploratory and explanatory approaches. Even "raw data" collected under the most rigorous quantitative methodologies involves numerous value-laden and subjective assumptions, priorities, and interpretations. Similarly, even the most interpretive methodologies and analyses include empirical and quantitative elements. How a particular research design balances these elements depends on a number of factors, including the expectations common in the field, your interests and goals, your central research question, the kinds of evidence and answers you seek, and the data collection and analytical methods you employ.

Researchers interested in global issues should be ready to explicitly address several fundamental research design issues that may not routinely be addressed in conventional disciplines. For example, in a new interdisciplinary field where theoretical paradigms are still developing, it is not unusual to design research projects that are much more exploratory than explanatory. Or it may be necessary to explain why it makes sense to use any given quantitative, qualitative, or mix of methods in a multimethod research design, or why it makes sense to look for information in certain parts of the world and not others. There may also be concerns about the availability of archival materials or even the reliability of official statistics, depending on where those statistics come from and how they were collected. For example, in many societies certain kinds of crimes are routinely underreported by both victims and governments, skewing the official statistics. In global studies it is also common have to deal with ethical issues that are unique to international and intercultural contexts. In some cases a research design may need to consider whether it is practical or advisable to carry out research in politically unstable or otherwise unsafe regions of the world.

TYPES OF RESEARCH DESIGNS

In broad terms, most research designs fall into one or more of several major categories: explanatory, exploratory, descriptive, or applied. In practice, these approaches can look very similar. Nearly any substantive topic can be studied using any one or more of them, and they can involve the same basic data collection and analytical methods. One reason for this is that these approaches differ primarily in intent, end goals, and the conclusions that the researcher wishes to be able to draw. Even though the approaches are in some ways similar, it is important for the researcher to know the key differences between them and how the research project fits into this schema.

Explanatory Research

As the name suggests, explanatory research occurs when a researcher seeks to explain something that is going on in the world by applying existing theories. The primary assumption behind explanatory research is that existing theory can explain outcomes as causes and effects, associations and interactions. The explanatory approach develops in fields where the factors influencing observed outcomes are understood well enough that outcomes can be predicted with some reliability. Take, for example, the impact that education has been shown to have on individual income. In most cases education comes before income, so education is assumed to be the independent or causal variable that impacts the dependent variable, income. An explanatory research project might test the hypothesis that variations in levels of education explain variation in incomes within a given population.

By definition, then, explanatory research is at some level theory driven. When too much weight is given to theory, however, it can become a problem. No one theory can be used to explain everything. When researchers cling too tightly to one particular theoretical explanation, it can make them reluctant to consider other theoretical approaches that could help explain different aspects of the study. A very strong affinity to one theory also makes a researcher dogmatic and ultimately more likely to reject important evidence that doesn't fit the theory. In psychology this is called *confirmation bias.*

Another difficulty associated with explanatory research lies in developing the kinds of evidence that can be used to confirm theories about causal relationship or association. For example, while it may be relatively easy to show *how* a group of people acted in a given situation, it can be much more difficult to establish with any level of confidence *why* it acted as it did. The individual actors in the group may all have different explanations for what happened and why they were involved. Ask a dozen strikers why they chose to walk the picket line, and their answers could include, "It beats working, don't it?" and "Joe here is my ride." You aren't likely to get a detailed recounting of your favorite labor theory because individuals don't always verbalize their motives in terms that fit academic theories. An individual's self-reported explanation about their own behavior may also change over time, particularly when unfolding events alter the situation. Unless a researcher has a solid research design and very deliberately collects the necessary data, it can be difficult to support causal explanations or show definitive associations.

The difficulty of collecting data that conclusively demonstrates causality or association can impose severe restrictions on the kinds of research questions that can be asked and the kinds of relationships that can be explained. Researchers can be motivated to ask only questions that can be answered with available data. Unfortunately, the result can be a rather narrowly focused hypothesis testing that ignores the larger context or simply confirms existing theory. Going back to the example of the impact of education on income, the basic question about whether education impacts income has been answered time and again.

Explanatory research should not just explain what is already known, with an end result that simply confirms existing explanatory paradigms. The higher goal should be to explain what has not already been explained, to challenge existing theory, to push the boundaries of our basic assumptions, to refine and ultimately improve our theoretical paradigms.

Exploratory Research

In contrast to explanatory research, exploratory research is necessary where theoretical paradigms do not exist or have not developed sufficiently to provide causal explanations with predictive power. Some areas of inquiry may not have existing conceptual frameworks within which to develop an easily testable hypothesis. In this situation, exploratory research is needed to identify agents, forces, variables, impacts, and outcomes. Implied in the exploratory approach is the purpose of developing a set of working theories and accounts of what may be going on. Typically, the result of exploratory research should be a basic framework for understanding the issue that will encourage further research and aid the development of new theories and explanations.

Exploratory research is called for when the researcher encounters topics that she or he finds interesting but does not understand. For example, many years ago a colleague of ours was doing research on transsexual subjects when he encountered a sex worker who did not fit his gender paradigm. This person was transsexual in that they had had sex reassignment surgery. They had stopped transitioning, however, when they reached the point where they had female breasts and male genitalia. Our colleague found that this person had been "between" sexes for years and was happy with things as they were. They had consciously decided not to transition any further in either direction. The problem was that the person was no longer "trans," at least not in the sense that they were transitioning from one defined sex to another. At that time in the mid-1990s, gender theory did not have the conceptual tools and vocabulary to deal with transsexuality except as such a mode of transition. Scholars were not yet thinking of transition itself as a desirable sexual identity in its own right. This caused our colleague's previously explanatory research to take a much more exploratory turn. Subsequent research on gender has established a rich vocabulary for this kind of work, including terms such as androgynous, agender, nonbinary, genderqueer, genderfluid, and pangender.

Exploratory research applies to entirely new substantive topics, but it can also apply to new theoretical approaches and perspectives. Established topics can be explored from new angles, and new connections and conclusions can result. In this sense, much of global studies has an exploratory element. Global scholars often use an exploratory approach when they apply global perspectives to established issues and reexamine conventional approaches.

To do exploratory research, it is not enough to pursue a topic that you know little about. The example of transsexuality above demonstrates that exploratory research, much like explanatory research, comes not from ignorance but from one's familiarity with a relevant body of academic literature. You must become familiar enough with a given body of literature to know when you have encountered something for which there isn't already a sufficient explanatory paradigm.

Avoid the temptation to use the phrase "exploratory research" as a free pass not to develop a proper research design. Experience has shown that clever students go off to exotic locales with very little forethought or planning, intending to do exploratory research on trendy-sounding topics. This kind of research ends up looking a lot like tourism and can include more drinking and flirting than anything else. Students that do not take exploratory research seriously enough often end up dropping out of graduate school when they realize that they have nothing worth writing up.

One of the chief difficulties of exploratory research is that it is all too easy to do a great deal of unfocused exploration and end up with nothing worthwhile. You can find yourself in a pile of notes and memorabilia, but with no data that you can analyze in any systemic fashion. This is because data is not as random and interchangeable as one might think. Information, evidence, or data is typically collected for a specific purpose. If carefully and intentionally collected, the information discovered may end up being useful for its intended purpose, though even that is not a guarantee. But data that was collected for a specific purpose is not easily adapted for other uses. For example, political polling data cannot be retasked for social science research as easily as one might expect. In short, information collected in an unsystematic fashion with no clear design can end up being useless.

In many ways, designing and executing exploratory research that successfully produces useful knowledge is every bit as demanding as any other kind of research. If anything, developing a viable research project in areas that are not well covered by the literature requires *more* forethought and planning. Moreover, researchers engaged in exploratory research may need to adjust the design of their research as they go along based on what they encounter, and this may in turn change the goals of the project. Exploratory research is risky, and for even the most seasoned researcher it holds the prospect of their doing a large amount of work and ending up empty handed. On the other hand, exploratory research is how one can make the most astounding contributions to the production of new knowledge. Exploratory research can open up new conversations and create spaces for reimagining what is going on in the world. Its charting of new intellectual landscapes can be an extraordinarily creative and exciting process. Nonetheless, in order for exploratory research to contribute something useful, it must be thoughtfully planned and carefully executed.

Descriptive Research

Descriptive research is very different from explanatory and exploratory research in that it is not primarily focused on either applying existing theories or developing new theories. The goal of descriptive research is to accurately describe a topic in some detail, and to provide data without theory or analysis. This area of research is sometimes accused of not being scientific or empirical enough. The main concern is that descriptive research is not driven by a specific research question, so it can be argued that it is not really research. This criticism could apply to purely descriptive writing, though purely descriptive writing is very rare in the academy. This is because all researchers—in fact, all humans—operate with an extensive, if unspoken, set of theoretical assumptions about how the world works and why people act the way they do. We carry within our consciousness a range of theories about gravity, psychology, and social and economic behavior, and our implicit theories and assumptions end up shaping our research whether we acknowledge it or not. Even when researchers try to be entirely untheoretical, they typically fail. It is almost impossible to do research that is devoid of personal, institutional, or political motivations that take the work well beyond the purely descriptive.

Despite these limitations, it is important to recognize that descriptive research can serve a variety of important purposes. One example is the preservation ethnography that anthropologists practiced in the early 1900s. As more people around the world came into contact with industrialization and urbanization, it became apparent that many indigenous communities were being severely challenged by disease, genocide, forced migration, and so on. Colonialists often argued that native peoples would inevitably become "extinct" and many native languages, cultures, and histories would die with them. In response to what came to be known as the "vanishing race theory," some anthropologists sought to preserve native culture by collecting artifacts, interviewing elders, and making audio and visual recordings of indigenous languages, music, and myths (Gould 1996; Cole 1985). The motivation was not to spend time analyzing and theorizing the materials that were gathered, but simply to record and collect before it was too late.

Detailed descriptive work may not technically be research, but certain types of descriptive research can provide researchers with data and other important information that can improve our understanding of various topics. One can still find contemporary descriptive ethnographic studies that are almost completely free of explicit analysis. These studies can provide useful material and at a minimum can be helpful for teaching students how to analyze and apply different theoretical frameworks (e.g., Sikes 1997). That being said, researchers interested in doing global studies research should not plan on carrying out purely descriptive work without first checking with their advisors. Most major research institutions and funding agencies require a clear research thesis along with an elaboration of theory, method, and data.

Policy and Applied Research

Policy and applied research differ from most other kinds of research in that they are designed to have a practical outcome—in most cases, improving a specific practice or policy that will have an impact on an identified group of people. This kind of research produces knowledge with a specific application in mind. It includes research intended to improve existing educational practices or social services, and it is frequently found in fields such as social policy, social work, public health, juvenile and adult corrections, and criminology.

The line between general research and applied research can get very fuzzy. The findings of general research can end up having practical applications. Similarly, the findings of applied research can contribute to general research conducted without such instrumental objectives in mind. So it is not so much research findings that distinguish these different approaches but rather the intent of the researcher. In applied research the objectives, desired findings, and research outcomes can end up driving the research agenda to varying degrees in ways that violate the empirical research paradigm.

The intent of the researcher is also one of the most problematic ethical areas for applied and policy research. The stated goal, to provide research for a specific purpose, can put the researcher in ethically dicey situations depending on who is seeking what outcome and which sector of society it is meant to benefit. Few policies and practices are politically neutral; most are the result of political agendas. Consider applied research that is intended to improve standardized tests in elementary education, or policy research that supports "three-strikes" laws (habitual offender laws). These kinds of applied research can very easily end up serving the political agendas that were responsible for the original policies and practices in the first place. To state this differently, applied research that is implemented uncritically can support ideology-driven policies without bringing into question the assumptions behind these policies and their impacts on society.

This problem is further exacerbated by the decline in funding and resource opportunities, and the tendency among some scholars to "follow the money" with little regard for the political agendas behind some rather questionable private and public funding agencies. History has repeatedly shown that when we put the production of knowledge into the service of something other than the acquisition of knowledge, we put core academic values at risk. Remember that reactionary, racist, neo-Nazi, and other hate groups have think tanks and sponsor their own brands of applied and policy research. It is important to think critically about political and social motivations behind applied or policy research and consider carefully who will benefit from the expected findings.

SAMPLING LOGIC

Sampling is a very powerful tool that makes it possible to conduct research on large populations without directly studying every individual in the population (Henry 1990). Understanding sampling logic is an important part of understanding selection and representation in empirical research. The logic of selection and representation impacts nearly all empirical research across the social sciences and humanities in one way or another.

One of the basic assumptions behind empirical research is that our research findings should accurately reflect something that is going on in the world. By "world" we mean the human social world, and by "social" we are referring to groups of people. If the group of people being studied is very small, it may be possible to study everyone in the group directly. Most research, however, is done on a larger scale. Interviewing every member of a group is very labor intensive, time consuming, and expensive. When group size reaches into the thousands, the time and effort required becomes prohibitive. When researchers try to study national populations it becomes impossible for one researcher to directly study every individual. Fortunately, it isn't necessary to study every individual in a group to represent the whole group. That is where sampling logic comes in. Using sampling logic it is possible to carefully select a subset of individuals to represent what is going on in the larger population. The following are terms used in sampling.

Sample: The sample is a subset that is systematically selected so that it can be said to accurately represent the larger population.

Sample Size or *n*: To properly represent a population requires a sample size large enough to overcome any nonrandom variations in selection process. The sample size needed to represent a larger population is determined by statistical probabilities. Let's assume that that the sample size needed to study the population of the United States is n=1500 individuals. A sample of 1500 people would be large enough to represent the population accurately without being biased toward one group or another within the sample. A sample size that is significantly smaller would likely overrepresent some groups and underrepresent other groups. A sample size much larger would only increase the cost of doing the survey without significantly increasing the accuracy of the results.

Population: This is the total number of the people in the population being studied. Importantly, we can rarely know the exact population of a country. Because people are constantly being born and dying, coming and going, changing their names, and so on, even the most rigorous national census is only an estimation of the current population. The exact population is never known with absolute certainty. In fact, just trying to identify the size and characteristics of a particular population is one of the most common and important forms of demographic research.

Sampling Frame: A sampling frame is a list that approximates the total population to be studied. Ideally, a sampling frame is large enough that the excluded portion of the population is statistically insignificant. The sampling frame can vary depending on the population being represented, but common examples include census data, the phone book, and the voter registry.

Random or Probability Sample: This is a randomly (purely by chance, with no predictability) selected subset of a population (Henry 1990: 96). For the sample to be random, each member of the population should have an equal and independent chance of being chosen. The resulting random sample is assumed to be an unbiased representation of the sampling frame. For example, for a phone survey a researcher could select every fifth phone number out of the phone book. Assuming that the sampling frame represents the population, the sample size is large enough, and the sampling method is random, then the sample can be said to be a probability sample that represents the population without bias.

Nonrandom Sample: This type of sample results from sampling methods where the selection process is not random, or where the probability of selection cannot be determined. Snowball sampling is an example of a nonrandom sampling method. Snowball sampling uses people in the sample group to identify additional members to be included in the group (Henry 1990: 14). This kind of approach can be used to gain access to networks of people in hard-to-identify populations (Emmel 2013: 37). The results of nonrandom selection methods are nonprobability samples. These nonrandom sampling methods can be used effectively to explore the characteristics of specific groups, but they cannot be said to represent a population in the same unbiased way as random samples (Emmel 2013: 134).

Selection and Representation

The topic of sampling logic is most often discussed in relation to the survey method and statistical analyses of that data. The fundamental logic of selection and representation, however, applies to nearly all empirical research, qualitative and quantitative, micro and macro (Emmel 2013). For example, when scholars conduct studies of individuals, or ethnographic studies of small groups, they most often do so because they are trying to say something about (or represent) processes that impact larger groups of people. The selection of the individual may not be random and probabilistic, but it can still be used to represent something about the larger context. Individuals are selected because their individual stories say something about the real world. Similarly, the study of the life of one woman, one immigrant, or one employee almost always says something relevant about larger groups of women, immigrants, or employees. This is why this kind of research is done: to represent. Nearly all empirical research has some element of this selection and representation dynamic to it.

Researchers may not always recognize the sampling logics in their own work because their sampling logics are implicit rather than explicit. Take, for example, a study of baroque Portuguese literature. A literary scholar might select certain works from the period and use them to represent the wider body of literature. Depending on the requirements of the academic field, the scholar may or may not need to elaborate their selection criteria or justify why they chose certain literary works over others. They may not need to discuss how well the chosen works actually represent the wider literature of that period. Nonetheless, there was probably some logic behind the selection of those specific literary works. Perhaps they were the most famous works of the period. Or perhaps they were examples of a particular genre that the researcher was interested in. What if it turned out that all the works selected came from Portugal? Then it could be argued that the study does not represent the wider body of Portuguese literature because it did not include literature from Brazil and other Portuguese-speaking regions of the world. In any case, explicit or not, there is almost always a sampling logic behind the selection of data to analyzed. It is usually better to be explicit about your sampling criteria and the group you are trying to represent. In addition to being methodologically transparent about your sampling parameters, this reflexivity represents an ethical stance—a consciousness about who is doing the representing and who is being represented.

Limitations of Sampling Logic

There are a number of limitations that constrain sampling logic, one of the most obvious being that sampling logic itself is a product of modern Western thinking. Sampling logic developed in the nineteenth and twentieth centuries alongside the growing modern bureaucracies of nation-states, and as a mode of statistical calculation it is very much part of defining national citizens, public policies, and nationalist agendas (Desrosières 1998; Darian-Smith 2016; Lepore 2015).

Even if it can be argued that a survey is a neutral statistical instrument that can fairly represent a target population, implementing such a survey has become increasingly difficult. Take the modern phone book, which polling organizations have used for decades, as the classic example of a sampling frame. Due to recent demographic and technological changes, the names it lists may no longer represent the general population as accurately as phone books once did. Fewer people own their homes, and non-owners are less likely to be listed in the phone book. Also, the advent of cell phones and the Internet means fewer and fewer people have the kinds of numbers that are listed. Minorities, immigrants, poor people, young people, students, and prisoners are among the growing groups of people that are not equally represented in the phone book for various reasons. Using the phone book as a sampling source, at least in the United States, now tends to yield a disproportionate number of older, wealthy, and white home owners (Lepore 2015).

Technologies and demographics are changing so much that even large survey organizations are finding it increasingly difficult to find reliable sampling frames. The problem has become so severe that sampling frames became an issue in the US presidential election in 2012. As they have for decades, polling organizations used the list of registered voters as their sampling frame. They focused on the listed voters that were most likely to vote. It turned out, however, that the list of likely voters is one of the sampling frames that has become less representative of the general population over time. Relying on this list skewed the poll results so that it was difficult for either party to predict the outcome of the election. When Election Day came, it was clear that several political polls had seriously underestimated the impact that young people and minorities would have on that election.

When talking about sampling and representation, we must acknowledge that a number of populations have never been well represented by modern scientific sampling techniques. Indigenous populations have always been, and remain to this day, difficult to reach with standard research methods. LGBTQ communities and other groups that may be stigmatized and reluctant to self-identify are also difficult to identify using standard research methods. Similarly, immigrants have long been underrepresented, more so when they are criminalized and called "illegal immigrants." Generally speaking, poor, criminalized, and stigmatized populations tend to remain underrepresented. Even in wealthy countries modern research methods nearly always leave some portion of the population undercounted.

Global Sampling Logics

The problem of finding a reliable sampling frame to accurately represent an entire population is magnified when we carry sampling logic out of the national context and into the global sphere. While finding a reliable sampling frame in the national context is becoming increasingly difficult, finding a reliable sampling frame for the global population is impossible. The global population is already larger than seven billion. Recent efforts have standardized various national data sets, and these sets are providing unprecedented access to certain kinds of data. At the same time, ongoing global issues such as poverty, corruption, immigration, civil war, international conflict, and growing numbers of refugees make it increasingly difficult to find sampling frames in the areas affected by these issues.

As far as we know, a scientifically valid survey on the entire population of the world is impossible at the present time. But even if it isn't possible to find a sampling frame for the entire global population, it is still possible to identify appropriate sampling frames for specific populations and issues and use them to conduct probabilistic or scientific surveys. We can also use the various nonprobabilistic sampling methods to study these populations and issues. The key is to recognize that sampling frames limit the claims to representations that we can make. In fact, this has always been the case. We have always been working with subsets of populations that are significantly less than the whole population.

When we shift sampling logic into the global context, the number of underrepresented people, those out of reach of scientific methods, jumps into the billions. Underrepresented minorities become the underrepresented majority of the world. For those of us who practice global studies in Europe and the United States, it becomes clear that we cannot press on statistically overrepresenting ourselves—typically white, privileged educators—while ignoring the underrepresented masses of people populating the globe.

We will touch on the challenges associated with using a limited number of cases to represent larger global processes again in Chapter 6, "A Global Case Study Method."

RELIABILITY AND VALIDITY

In considering various possible research designs, it is helpful to understand the concepts of reliability and validity and the tension between the two. *Reliability* refers to how well a research method produces stable and consistent results. If a method produces substantially similar results when repeated by the researcher or replicated by other researchers, it can be deemed reliable. For example, quantitative analyses of data sets tend to be reliable in the sense that if another researcher properly applies the same analytical procedure, they will reliably get the same results. *Validity* refers to how well a research method measures what the researcher wants to measure. If a method produces results that can be verifiable by other means, we can consider the results to be valid. For example, a survey about voter response to political candidates would be considered valid if other indicators such as event attendance, early ballots, and exit polls confirm its results.

So which do you want in your research design—reliability or validity? Clearly we would like to have both. The problem is that the reliability and validity of any particular method are situational. By this we mean that these qualities are not fixed features of a given method and can change in different situations and applications. No one method produces reliable results in every application. Similarly, no one method produces valid results in every application. Further, in certain situations methods achieve one of these qualities at the expense of the other.

To better understand the tension between reliability and validity in research, consider yourself doing a nationwide survey on the frequency of child abuse. Imagine designing and sending out thousands of surveys to a randomly selected set of households across the country. The survey could directly ask parents, "Do you physically beat or otherwise abuse your children?" How do you think most parents would answer that question? We imagine that most would say they do not abuse their children. This would include parents who are by any legal standard abusing their children. However, because people answer surveys subjectively, the results of this huge and very expensive survey would probably support the conclusion that child abuse simply does not happen. Given enough funds it would be possible to have several independent researchers repeat the survey to verify the results. Suppose follow-up surveys proved that the results were entirely reliable, at least in the sense that other researchers could repeatedly reproduce the results. Would we then be able to say that child abuse does not happen? The results might be "reliable," but do they have any meaning? Would they be valid in the sense that they accurately reflect what is going on in the world? In this case, the findings would not be meaningful. Talk to child protective services or spend the night in the emergency room of any hospital and you will likely see cases of child abuse that completely invalidate the findings of this very reliable survey. The reliability of findings is not the same thing as their validity.

Let's look at a different example: the classic ethnography. To do an ethnographic study, a trained cultural anthropologist conducts extensive fieldwork in a particular culture. They typically learn the local language and then live among the people they are studying for a year or more. The anthropologist then writes a narrative description of the people and culture they observed. Given that ethnographies are written by trained observers, it should not be a surprise that most have very high validity—they accurately reflect some aspect of what was going on in that place at that time. But are ethnographies reliable in the sense that they can be replicated and verified by other researchers? For a number of reasons, ethnographies are not reliable in this sense. In fact, they are notoriously unreproducible. Two ethnographers can go to the same site, follow the exact same methodology, and produce completely different ethnographies. This is in part because the experiences of any two ethnographers will likely be different. Ethnographers have different skill levels, personalities, appearances, races, genders, classes, analytical approaches, and writing styles. The characteristics of the researcher will invariably influence their social interactions and ultimately their field experience. Each ethnographer will take a different path, experience different chance events, meet different people, notice different things, and have different reactions. Because ethnographers and their experiences are different, the ethnographic descriptions they produce are also likely to vary. In this example, the method could be said to have high validity but very low reliability.

Do the forgoing examples imply that one method is better than the other? Or that some methods are good and some bad? No; our point is that methods are just tools. No one research method is the right tool for every kind of research. In any given situation, different research methods have different strengths and weaknesses. All research designs must strike an imperfect balance between reliability and validity. In order to produce significant results researchers should employ only those methods that are appropriate to the situation and are likely to produce the kinds of evidence needed to address the central research question.

Global Validity

The issue of validity takes on new meaning in global contexts. Different cultures have different understandings of what is valid. Recognizing these intercultural dimensions means that we cannot simply define the validity of our research in our own terms. If we do, we run the risk of replicating the intellectual imperialisms of the past.

Further, if validity is a measure of how much our research findings reflect what is actually going on in the world, then we have to recognize that our reality is rapidly changing. The world is becoming increasingly interconnected and globalized. As a result the issues we all engage with have become increasingly interconnected and global. To the degree that other academic fields fail to recognize this transformation, they are becoming less relevant to in a rapidly globalizing world. By adapting our methodologies to better accommodate new complexities, the field of global studies gains a real-world relevance that is rapidly declining in many conventional disciplines and fields that cling to the past and their modernist roots.

TRIANGULATION

When considering the issues of reliability and validity in research design, it is helpful to understand the concept of *triangulation*. This technique, which was used by ancient civilizations, involves measuring the angles from two known positions or landmarks on a baseline to find the location of a third point. For example, one can use the Pythagorean theorem—the square of the hypotenuse is equal to the sum of the squares of the other two sides—to find the distance between two points (fig. 9).

When attempting to triangulate a location, the farther apart the known reference points on the base line, the more accurately one can measure the angles and fix the position of the third unknown point. Triangulation techniques are still used in modern geometry, astronomy, land surveying, cartography, and navigation. Researchers use triangulation to increase confidence in the accuracy of research findings by applying more than one type of measurement or method.

Figure 9. "Measuring the Width of a River by Triangulation," from Levinus Hulsius's 1605 *Instrumenta Mechanica.*

Methodological Triangulation

As we described above in our hypothetical example of a self-report survey on child abuse, research conducted using only one method can provide results that do not accurately reflect the real world. While we intentionally exaggerated the details of that example, it highlights the fact that all of the available social research methods, qualitative and quantitative, have inherent limitations. Triangulating results by using two or more methods is one of the most effective ways to overcome the limitations of reliability and validity that are built into social research methods.

In many research designs, simply adding a second data source can greatly increase overall accuracy and validity. Going back to the hypothetical child abuse survey, a researcher could spend enormous amounts of time and energy trying to increase the validity of the survey method. For example, they could survey thousands of people, include any number of open-ended questions about the respondent's attitudes toward parenting, or create an index of questions that measures the severity of discipline in the home. Even with an enormous investment of time and money, however, it is unlikely that anyone could design a self-report survey that would yield good results on child abuse. A more efficient way to increase the validity of the overall research design would be to simply try a different data collection method. A handful of qualitative interviews with social workers, for example, would dramatically increase the accuracy of this study.

Triangulating one set of results with qualitative interviews or secondary data analysis is often easy and cost effective. It also requires less methodological flexibility than you might think. Academics too often learn one research method and thereafter design all their research projects around it. By doing this, they may needlessly sacrifice the reliability, validity, accuracy, and even relevance of their findings. Unfortunately, the academic disciplines, academic institutions, and even funding agencies that are meant to support academic research often reinforce the bias in favor of monomethod research designs.

Conceptual Triangulation

Research factors other than methods can limit the accuracy of findings in social research. These factors can include theories, disciplines, and epistemologies. As with methods, each theoretical approach has its own strengths and limitations. A single-theory study is very likely to perpetuate the limitations of its analytical paradigm. Think of it like trying to judge distance with one eye closed. Depth perception relies on two observation points that are spaced apart. A researcher capable of approaching a subject with more than one theoretical framework can provide a kind of *theoretical triangulation* that enables new perspectives and understandings. The result is often a more rounded analysis.

The concept of triangulation can also be applied to academic disciplines. The perspective of a single observer is inherently limited. It follows that the perspective of a single discipline is limited by its theoretical approaches and assumptions. Interdisciplinary research that incorporates scholars and approaches from two or more disciplines can provide global researchers with a strong form of *interdisciplinary triangulation* that has the potential to transcend the limitations of the disciplines themselves.

Taking the argument a step further, we can also apply the concept of triangulation to epistemologies. The academic theories developed within a society are likely to be limited by its ways of knowing, because scholarly communities within that society will hold its underlying epistemological concerns and assumptions. Collaborating with independent researchers with very different perspectives from around the world is one way to actively seek *epistemological triangulation*. Collaborating with and learning from others is one of the most effective ways we know to triangulate global research, produce knowledge that better encompasses alternative understandings of the world, and ultimately improve the validity of the research process and its findings in a rapidly globalizing world.

ETHICAL DIMENSIONS OF GLOBAL RESEARCH

There are a number of important ethical concerns that apply to academic research (Flynn and Goldsmith 2013). These ethical issues can generally be grouped into three main categories: (1) academic honesty or integrity, (2) the protection of individual research subjects, and (3) the impact of research on society.

Academic Integrity

For researchers and their institutions, the ability to conduct research rests squarely on issues of trust, honesty, and integrity. As with other professions, academics must have credibility to do their work. If academics could not trust the integrity of each other's research, they would hardly be able to function. This is why codes of conduct in most professions touch on the following topics:

- honesty
- integrity
- transparency
- accountability

- confidentiality
- objectivity
- respectfulness
- obedience to the law

Beyond the academy, the public's implicit trust in academics, academic institutions, and the importance of academic research in general is vital to public support for research. Without the public's trust and support, researchers would not have access to willing research subjects, research institutions would not receive public funding, individual grants would not be funded, research articles would not be published, and research findings would have no impact on the relevant field of knowledge. Unprofessional behaviors such as theft, plagiarism, falsifying findings, and exploitative or harmful treatment of research subjects undermine the integrity of individual researchers and their research institutions and can ultimately undermine public support for academic research.

Protecting Research Subjects

One of the primary ethical concerns in doing research is to avoid doing harm to people. Unfortunately, academic research can cause harm to its direct participants as well as to social groups who are not directly involved. In most cases the harm is not intentional. It is more often an unforeseen and unintended consequence of research done with the best intentions. Researchers can, however, anticipate and avoid even unintentional harm. In most cases, we find that the risks researchers take and the harm these risks cause to subjects are *entirely avoidable*. Most guidelines require researchers to get the informed consent of their research subjects. But securing informed consent is just the starting point of the researcher's responsibility. Researchers need to learn about research ethics, consider the ethical implications of their research very carefully, and make every effort to anticipate and avoid causing any harm to people.

ETHICS REVIEW BOARD

Most major research institutions have oversight committees for academic research that involves human subjects. They are sometimes called Ethics

Review Boards (ERBs) in Europe and Institutional Review Boards (IRBs) in North America. In general, ethics boards are charged with defining the rules, procedures, and guidelines that help reduce potential harm to research subjects. They also oversee individual and institutional compliance with those rules. Most ethics boards require

- a description of the proposed research project, research methods, and expected outcomes
- the informed written consent of every subject participating in the research
- notice that consent can be revoked at any time during the study
- appropriate procedures for protecting the subject's privacy

By encouraging ethical research, ERBs serve to protect human subjects from harm while simultaneously protecting the integrity of the research institution. They also prevent one careless researcher from "poisoning the well" and making it more difficult for other researchers to access subjects and gain the informed consent they need to do their research. And it probably doesn't hurt that protecting research subjects also tends to reduce the legal liability of both the researcher and the research institution.

Ethics committees may require scholars to protect the privacy of their research subjects. But again, the scholar's responsibility does not end with consent and confidentiality. At every stage of the research process, from design to publication and beyond, scholars should diligently work to anticipate and minimize any possible harm that their research might cause to human subjects.

TYPES OF HARM

Academic research can cause several different types of harm to individual human subjects. Researchers should be aware of different types of harm and think through the ways that their research might contribute to one or more of them. Types of harm to human subjects can include, but are not limited to

- loss of trust (misleading the subject about the aims of your research)
- public exposure, loss of privacy (sexual orientation, infidelity, drug use)

- social harm (loss of social status or membership, damage to relationships)
- emotional distress (Milgram Shock Experiment, inflicted insight)
- psychological harm (Stanford Prison Experiment, humiliation)
- physical harm (injury, heart attack, Tuskegee Syphilis Experiment)
- economic loss (cost of participating in study, loss of employment, cost of medical treatment)
- legal harm (civil or criminal charges, arrest, detention, deportation)

Before human subjects guidelines were common, some researchers conducted experiments that caused subjects to experience physical or emotional stress, and some subjects even risked illness and injury. Contemporary research guidelines prohibit these kinds of studies. Today the most common forms of harm that researchers cause to subjects are probably those that result from the public exposure and loss of privacy. While the loss of privacy might not seem as serious as physical harm, it can lead to stigmatization, unemployment, emotional distress, arrest, deportation, rights violations, and in certain situations, violent reprisals. For example, employees who talk about unfair working conditions, such as women who report workplace harassment, could conceivably be fired from their jobs if their identities were disclosed or discovered. Even more horrifying, research exploring warring factions in conflict zones can easily end up putting research participants at risk.

Most research institutions have rules and guidelines about doing research on vulnerable individuals. For example, while countries may differ on details, there are usually strict rules on using children as subjects of research precisely because children are considered very susceptible to manipulation and harm. Children may not understand the purpose of the research or the possible consequences of participating, and therefore cannot legally give their consent to participate. This applies even if they are child soldiers and engaging in forms of violence usually associated with adults. Similarly there are strict rules about doing research on medical patients, prisoners, refugees, undocumented migrants, and anyone else that is in some way confined or restrained. This is in part because these captive audiences may be emotionally vulnerable, more susceptible to the influence of authority, and often not physically free to walk away from the researcher and their research.

Researchers are required to protect the privacy of their research subjects throughout the entire research process, from the selection of subjects to the publication of their findings and beyond. Most research institutions have guidelines and protocols in place to protect the privacy of research subjects and the security of research data. Researchers should establish protocols for privacy and data security early in the process and maintain them throughout.

It is important to recognize that true anonymity of research subjects is very difficult to establish and maintain. Even if the researcher decides never to know the names of his or her subjects, someone probably does know who they are. It might be other research subjects, other researchers in the organization, members of the subject's family, or other community members. Someone may have recognized them entering or leaving the research facility. In this era of hypersurveillance, the subject's comings and goings were probably recorded and their license plate photographed. Surveillance technologies and practices are introducing many challenges to protecting subjects' privacy.

Even if the researcher does not publish the full names of their research subjects, there are still many other ways that subjects can be identified and lose their privacy. Different kinds of personal information can be used to do this, such as

- first names, nicknames, usernames, avatars
- photographs (Facebook, facial recognition software)
- email, street address, area of residence
- place or type of employment
- age or date of birth
- race, ethnicity, gender, class, religion
- physical appearance
- distinguishing features, clothes, and mannerisms
- personal history, place of birth, education

In most cases it is quite easy to use these kinds of information and process of elimination to determine a research participant's identity. The smaller the community or pool of subjects, the easier it is to identify the participants. Over time, the probability of individual identification increases. The more media attention a study draws, the more likely it is that someone will identify its subjects. For these reasons, researchers should avoid publishing any identifying information.

In practice, researchers cannot actually guarantee confidentiality or anonymity. Even when researchers follow privacy protocols from the start, establish and maintain data security, and refrain from identifying their subjects in publications, privacy can still be breached in any number of ways. Research notebooks, computers, and files have been lost, stolen, and hacked. Identities have been published without the researcher's knowledge or consent. Research documents and data have been subpoenaed for civil and criminal cases. Research documents have also been confiscated by local police, national security authorities, and immigration officials.

For these reasons, researchers should be very careful about the kinds of personal information they collect in the first place. In addition to following data security procedures, researchers can further minimize the risk of exposure to their subjects by collecting only personal information that is directly relevant to their research and actively avoiding all other personal details. For example, researchers can tell participants that they are specifically not interested in information that could potentially be embarrassing or incriminating.

BALANCING RISK AND BENEFIT

As part of the review process, most ethics boards weigh the potential benefits of a proposed research project against the risks it may involve. If the potential benefit to the public is high, the ethics board is more likely to approve some level of risk.

Suppose that Jonas Salk, on the verge of developing the first successful vaccine for polio, has submitted his research proposal to the IRB at his institution. An ethics review board looking at Salk's work might decide that the potential benefit to society of his polio vaccine might outweigh the risks of vaccine research. The point here is that you aren't Jonas Salk. In the humanities and social sciences, a research project's benefits to society are typically less clear-cut and predictable. This means that the risk of harm to subjects is still very real while the potential benefits of our research can be vague. A review board is not likely to approve a research design that contains any significant risk to human subjects if its benefit to society is too hard to quantify.

If you are a graduate student working on a thesis or dissertation, it is important for you to recognize that the only person who can reasonably expect to benefit from your research is you. You are the one who will get your degree, publish your research, and go on to a career in academia or elsewhere. In most cases almost no one else will benefit from your research, at least not in any measurable way. In fact, the number of people who are likely to read your thesis is relatively small. Master's theses and doctoral dissertations serve very valuable educational purposes within academic programs, but the vast majority receive very little attention outside the immediate field. Intentionally or not, researchers can end up using research subjects to further their own careers, often with no clear benefit the subjects. Clearly this outcome is not ideal and is usually unintentional, but it is often the default.

In sum, the potential benefits of research on social issues are rarely solid enough to justify taking any significant risk with human subjects, whether individuals or groups. Research designs that include vulnerable populations such as those we mentioned above will almost certainly be closely scrutinized by the ethics board at your institution.

MITIGATING THE RISK OF HARM

Beyond following the ethical guidelines we have outlined and those of your research institution, there are a number of strategies for mitigating possible risks to human research subjects. The ethics model described above assumes that human subjects are individuals that can be identified as individuals, that these individuals also have a reasonable expectation of privacy, and that the information you collect will be made public. There are a number of circumstances that void these assumptions.

Ethics rules apply to human individuals, not to agencies, organizations, and businesses. For example, a properly designed organizational study will almost always pass a review board if it focuses on an organization rather than the individual people in the organization. Researchers that may not be allowed to study child soldiers directly can study the organizations that provide shelter and social services to those same child soldiers.

Almost anything that these organizations do or publish is considered to be within the public domain and can be used in research.

Social movements, social issues, public events, and government programs and policies are also not private individuals. A study that focuses on social movements will probably gain the IRB's approval as long as it does not identify private individuals. Speeches by organization leaders, an organization's public activities, and any documents that it has published will probably be considered public domain. Moreover, if the subject of an interview is a public figure such as a politician, a business owner, an organization leader, or an entertainer, the expectation of privacy may not apply. Nearly anything a public figure says can be used in research.

In most cases you can use information collected in public places. If anyone could have been standing in a given public place and could have seen what you saw, heard what you heard, or taken the same picture you took, then the information is probably considered to be in the public domain. For example, a conversation with a passerby at a public event is usually allowed so long as no identifying information about that person is published. If you don't use the interviewee's name, appearance, ethnicity, dress, or anything else that could be used to identify them as a subject of the research, then the information gained in the exchange will normally be allowed.

If the information you seek was previously made public or is published in the public realm, then in most cases it is okay to use it in your research. In this era of social media, microblogging, and oversharing, an amazing amount of very personal information has already been made available on the Internet, a most public realm. Are you interested in who practices domestic or sexual abuse and why? Just subscribe to the appropriate blog and voilà, a wealth of very public personal data. With a little browsing and searching, you will find that almost any private information that you might expect to be revealed only in a confidential interview has already been revealed in public, sometimes by the same person you wanted to interview in confidence.

Researchers can mitigate harm and avoid violating privacy if they

- protect the privacy of research subjects
- avoid gathering any information that could be used to identify individuals
- avoid publishing any information that could be used to identify individuals

- use data sets that are already in the public realm
- use data sets that have all identifying information removed
- focus on groups, organizations, and agencies rather than identifiable individuals
- interview public officials and other public figures
- use personal data that is already freely available in the public realm (e.g., memoirs)
- use personal data that the subjects themselves have already made public (e.g., on blogs, forums)

While some of our suggestions may help you gain access to personal information, we should note that giving wider exposure to subjects who have already exposed themselves could still do harm in some situations. The rules for protecting research subjects still apply. Even when you collect information from public sources, it is a good idea to avoid collecting names, nicknames, usernames, and any other personal information that could lead others to identify individual research subjects.

TAP INTO EXPERTISE

Another way to avoid doing harm to research subjects is to make use of the ethics resources and experts that are available to you. Most research institutions have staff available to help researchers design and conduct ethical research. The point-person for ethics on any campus will probably have resources and guidelines specific to your institution. They may also be able to help you think through ethical issues, increase your chances of getting your research proposal past the IRB, and ultimately minimize the potential damage that your research could do to human subjects.

Looking beyond the host institution, most professional organizations have guidelines for professional behavior and research ethics available on their websites. In addition, there are guides that offer specific advice on ethical issues in particular areas of study. The following is a small sample:

"Ethics in Research with Children" (Farrell 2015)

"Ethical Issues in Image-Based Research" (Clark, Prosser, and Wiles 2010)

Media Ethics (Patterson and Wilkins 2013)

Professional Lives, Personal Struggles: Ethics and Advocacy in Research on Homelessness (Valado and Amster 2012)

Researching War: Feminist Methods, Ethics and Politics (Wibben 2016)

If the proposed research calls for work in a cultural setting that is unfamiliar to you, then tapping into local resources is very important. The standards for ethical research vary from culture to culture (Israel 2015). No matter what your topic and research site are, there are probably local experts who can help you with both your substantive topic and related ethical concerns. Make contact with local academics, experts, organizations, government officials, lawyers, healthcare workers, and others who have experience working in the town, city, or region in which you are conducting research. These local experts are often grappling with the same ethical issues, and they are likely to be more familiar with the issues, norms, and concerns of their particular community. Taking the time to identify and speak with local experts can help you pinpoint particular ethical concerns associated with doing research in the region.

Impact of Research on Social Groups

Beyond harming individuals, academic research can also do harm to social groups and sectors of society (Mertens and Ginsberg 2008). Academic research becomes part of the public domain when it is published. The researcher does not retain control over how their research and findings are used, so they can have unintended consequences. Published research can directly or indirectly contribute to social stereotypes that negatively impact disadvantaged groups such as women; racial, ethnic, and religious minorities; poor people; LBGT; immigrants; disabled people, and the mentally ill, among many other groups. Other types of harm to social groups that research can cause include, but are not limited to

- stigmatization
- discrimination by individuals
- persecution
- institutional and legal discrimination
- loss of public services

- criminalization
- vigilantism
- racial and ethnic violence

In many cases, individual researchers and the institutions that support their research are not aware that they are doing harm because it can be subtle, pervasive, and persistent. It may manifest in a variety of unanticipated ways, take years to manifest, and/or persist from generation to generation. As a result, it can be difficult to quantify the damage and determine exactly who its perpetrators and victims are. The issue of *studying down* highlights the important role that social power plays in research ethics.

STUDYING DOWN

The modern social sciences developed primarily as a tool for studying modern urban social problems such as poverty, crime, deviance, and mob violence. Unfortunately, this means that the history of social research is largely the history of "studying down." By studying down we mean studying the poor, less powerful, and criminalized segments of society. Given this history, it should not be a surprise that social research still tends to focus on the people and issues that mainstream society defines as "problems." Researchers still study those who are at a disadvantage in terms of race, class, and gender. We rarely study the wealthy, the powerful, or the law abiding, or "normal," dominant, or mainstream culture. Rather, it is the wealthier mainstream that sponsors research about those who are in some way considered abnormal, unusual, exotic, taboo, or otherwise outside social norms. Researchers are often drawn to social issues that involve illegal gangs and subcultures, immigrants, criminals, victims of crime, and victims of natural disasters. As a result, researchers often interview the homeless, street children, transvestites, transsexuals, prostitutes, child soldiers, the terminally ill, and refugees.

Marginalized groups are popular subjects of research almost precisely because they are outside social norms. In this sense, studying down can give research very disturbing voyeuristic and sensationalistic qualities. The researchers may study down with the best of intentions but still do great harm unintentionally. The very qualities that make marginalized groups fascinating are the same qualities that can make them vulnerable to being stigmatized, ostracized, persecuted, arrested, or deported. For these reasons, most research institutions now have rules and guidelines for doing research on vulnerable populations.

SOCIAL POWER, ACADEMIC AUTHORITY, AND THE PRODUCTION OF KNOWLEDGE

The reverse side of intersectional disadvantage is privilege. The impact of the power dynamics of privilege and intersectional disadvantage on research is an ethical concern. Any power differential between the researcher and research subjects should trigger a number of ethical considerations because differences in power, authority, and vulnerability create opportunities for subjects to be coerced or harmed, whether intentionally or not.

The social status of a researcher can influence their subjects. Differences in gender, class, race, and age can impact subjects in the same way they affect other social interactions. The greater the status differential between researcher and subject, the more likely these factors will influence the research process. Take, for example, the subject's decision to grant consent. This decision is greatly influenced by the subject's level of trust in authority, which is in turn affected by the social statuses of the researcher and subject. Differences in status can be even more important in the difficult decision to withdraw consent after the research has already started. This was one of the ethical concerns raised about the Stanford Prison Experiment (Zimbardo 2007). In this experiment student volunteers were arrested, imprisoned at a mock prison, and subject to discipline by volunteer wardens. The research got out of hand, and some subjects playing the role of prisoner were deliberately humiliated by their wardens in authority positions. Over time, it was no longer clear that the distraught prisoners still felt free to withdraw from the study. At that point, their participation could no longer be considered voluntary.

In addition to social status, most researchers hold a certain authority that comes with being a credentialed expert—the same kind of authority that, Stanley Milgram showed, can come with a white lab coat and clipboard (Milgram 2009; Blass 2009). Researchers also have the authority that comes with representing a respected academic institution. You are in this position if you are at a university that can afford to have graduate students and invest time and resources in training graduate students, teaching them to design research, use research methods, apply for research funding, and carry out and publish actual research. Being affiliated with an established research institution adds a layer of authority to your normal social status and increases your social power.

With this kind of academic expertise and institutional authority comes responsibility. Could the authority of the researcher unduly influence the subject's decision to participate in the research? Can the coercive power of authority be used to prevent subjects from withdrawing their consent? Who in the research relationship is the credentialed expert? Who has the power to publish research and produce knowledge about whom? Who stands to gain from the research? Who is more vulnerable to being harmed by the research? Does the research subject have the training necessary to understand the research, its significance, and its consequences? Does the subject have the authority, credentials, resources, and opportunity to contest the research findings? Could they publish a rebuttal? In most cases the answer is clearly no. Researchers must carefully consider the impact their academic authority may have on individual research subjects and their safety, well-being, right to privacy, and ability to give and revoke their consent.

The ethics of social power also plays an important role in conducting research about social groups. When academics "study down" on social groups, many of the same power dynamics are at work. Did the population being studied give their consent to, or even know about, the research? Do they understand the purposes of the research and the possible impacts it could have on them? Who stands to gain from research conducted about marginalized groups? Do the people being studied have the credentials, authority, and resources to produce academic knowledge about themselves? Do they have a means to challenge your conclusions about them? Can they appeal the verdict of science? The less powerful and more vulnerable the population, the greater the obligation of the researcher to carefully avoid doing harm.

GLOBAL RESEARCH ETHICS

Looking back in history, we can see that supposedly objective scientific research during the colonial and imperial periods that sought to categorize the races and cultures of the world did grievous harm to millions of people. It is not as easy to look at the present and recognize that this danger is still very real. We may use different terminology—development, inequality, human rights, humanitarian aid, and the environment—but it is important to understand that some aspects of the power dynamics between former colonizers and formerly colonized peoples endure in the present (Clitandre 2011). The knowledge that the global north produces about the global south can still have the same kinds of self-serving and damaging consequences that it had during earlier colonial periods.

Many global north researchers studying issues associated with the global south often regard these issues as "problems" that need to be solved by outsiders (Lunn 2014). This paternalistic positioning by global north researchers "studying down" on developing nations, cultures, and peoples can contribute directly or indirectly to

- discrimination against refugees, immigrants, and other displaced people
- reprisals against political rivals
- ethnic or racial violence
- civil war or regional conflict
- interruptions to tourism or foreign investment
- interruptions in humanitarian and foreign aid
- international sanctions and "failed state" status

The ethical dimensions of power take on new meaning in global contexts (InterAcademy Partnership 2016). Researchers should ask themselves: Do the populations that are the subjects of their research have a say in the research? Do they have an equal opportunity to participate in creating the knowledge that shapes national and international policies that impact their lives and futures? Do the subjects of knowledge production have equal power to produce their own kinds of knowledge? Do they have the kinds of economic, political, social, and military power required to counter the knowledge being produced about them?

ETHICAL PLURALISM

The ethical dimensions of global studies research often reach beyond the individual researcher and subject, beyond the various social groups in one society, and out into global contexts. These global contexts can include not one, but many ethical traditions. Every society has its own ethical, moral, and legal systems that developed in very specific historical, cultural, and religious traditions. The way a given society understands research ethics will necessarily reflect their unique traditions (Israel 2015). This means that researchers interested in global issues are likely to encounter cultures and ethical traditions that are very different from their own. For instance, modern legal and development practices often violate indigenous values based on collective forms of identity and ownership (Anker 2014). When faced with this kind of ethical pluralism, it is not enough to arbitrarily apply one's own ethics without regard for other people and their ways of understanding. To put this another way, the plurality of ethical perspectives in global contexts calls for a more cosmopolitan approach to the issue of ethics. A cosmopolitan approach recognizes and engages the multiplicity of ethical perspectives, without elevating one over the others. Global scholars must learn to engage global issues from more than one ethical perspective and be ever vigilant about their own ethical biases and assumptions (see Chapter 2).

We do not wish to present engaging with the ethical dimensions of research at individual, social, and global levels as quick or easy. In our view, research ethics should be more than just a mandatory paragraph in a research proposal. The fact that there are different ways of knowing, and a plurality of ethical systems, should change the way global studies scholars go about designing, conducting, and publishing their research. Similarly, engaging with the ethical and cultural plurality of global contexts is not something one does over their lunch break. It isn't even something one can say one has finished doing. Engaging with ethical pluralism in global contexts should be part of the ongoing practice of research.

MULTIPLE PERSPECTIVES AND VOICES

If global studies scholars are to engage with the plurality of cultures and ethics, we suggest that they start by decentering the production of knowledge (see Chapter 2). It is not enough for privileged scholars from elite institutions to ponder the plights of less fortunate peoples. Standpoint theory makes it clear that what and how each of us can know are shaped and constrained by our lived experiences. In any intercultural exchange, each side's knowledge about the other is constrained by their respective experiences. Intellectual engagement alone cannot give scholars the knowledge and experience required to represent other peoples and their cultures. In any intercultural endeavor, the peoples of the world must ultimately be allowed to represent themselves. Similarly, women and minorities in a given culture must be allowed to represent themselves and their lived experience.

In any intercultural research, the members of each culture should participate in the production of academic knowledge about their own cultures and about global issues that impact them. This kind of participation requires the inclusion of scholars, experts, and other representatives from the communities involved in the research process. Wherever possible, representatives of these communities should be encouraged to participate in research grants, research design, data collection, analysis, conclusions, and publications.

At first glance, the idea of embracing the plurality of cultures, ethics, and ways of knowing can be overwhelming. However, these varied ways of knowing create productive opportunities to triangulate multifaceted global issues. Bringing a plurality of perspectives to the analysis gives us a deeper understanding of what the key global issues really are and whom they impact most. This plurality of perspectives may complicate "scientific" theories and methods, but this complication is precisely what we require to overcome the limitations of Western knowledge of global issues and the limitations of Euro-American academic models (see Chapter 3). Embracing the plurality of perspectives can give global research the complexity, validity, and relevance that it requires to take on contemporary issues.

DOING BALANCED RESEARCH

The heuristic interaction of theory, method, and data drives empirical research. As with much in life, however, the trick is finding the balance-point between observation, analysis, and application. Good research should describe empirical data but take the analysis beyond pure description. Researchers should use theory where appropriate, but they should not be dogmatic in applying it or remain wedded to any one theory. Researchers should apply methods diligently, but they should recognize that each data collection method has strengths and weaknesses. Researchers should keep an eye on the practical applications of their research without letting desired outcomes corrupt the research process, and without letting the ends justify the means. The most useful kinds of research strike a balance between these different impulses.

Global issues, dimensions, theories, and methods that are relevant to a given study are limited only by its central research question. For example, if your research question draws connections between local customs and global markets, you should feel free to mix ethnographic or qualitative methods with econometric or quantitative methods. If you find that historical details are relevant to your question, you should use historical methods and data to support those aspects of your research. Wherever different analytical and methodological approaches lend themselves to the various aspects of an issue, global studies researchers should not hesitate to use those different theoretical and methodological approaches to address it. *Simply put, your research question should drive your entire research design, including which issues you will examine, which of the many theoretical frameworks you will employ, your overall methodology, and the specific data collection and analytical methods you will use, without regard for disciplinary boundaries.*

The question-driven approach may seem abstract and difficult to operationalize in a research project. Fortunately, we have found that there are several ways for researchers to implement this approach. How to develop a question-driven methodology is the subject of Chapter 5. One of the best ways we have found to implement a viable research methodology is through the global case study approach that we describe in Chapter 6.

5 Global Methods and Methodologies

Much has been written about data collection methods by the various disciplines over the decades, and it is not our intention to cover ground that has been covered at length elsewhere. In the first section of this chapter we discuss the distinction between methods and methodologies as well as between primary and second research. We then list the standard data collection methods used in conventional academic work. Hundreds of books—literally—are dedicated to each of these methods (Lewis-Beck, Bryman, and Liao 2004, see also footnote 9). We only seek to identify the basic methods one finds in much social science and humanities research. We then turn to the concept of *mixed methods*. This approach has become increasingly essential for many scholars, and we believe it is very important, though not obligatory, for global studies scholars in particular.

In the second section of the chapter we discuss methodological strategies, which are in essence combinations of data collection methods designed to serve specific research objectives. After outlining conventional methodological strategies, we turn to an exploration of critical methodological strategies. What is interesting about these critical strategies is that they open up new modes of data collection and push researchers to think about what counts as evidence in scholarly work. In the final section of the chapter, we present what we call *global methodological strategies*. These cumulative, inclusive research strategies incorporate many of the features found in critical methodologies and we have found them to be very applicable and effective in conducting global studies research.

METHODS VERSUS METHODOLOGIES

A research methodology is different from the actual methods used to collect information and evidence. Feminist scholar Sandra Harding makes a clear distinction between the concepts of *methodology* and *method*. She writes, "A research methodology is a theory and analysis of how research does or should proceed." In contrast, "A research *method* is a technique for (or way of proceeding in) gathering evidence" (Harding 1987: 2–3). Elaborating on this distinction, Linda Tuhiwai Smith notes, "Methodology is important because it frames the questions being asked, determines the sets of instruments and methods to be employed, and shapes the analyses . . . Methods become the means and procedures through which the central problems of the research are addressed" (Smith 2012: 144). Putting this another way, a methodology is the elaboration of a clear strategy for gathering evidence, including the specific data collection methods to be used, the kinds of evidence to be collected, and the approach for analyzing the evidence.

A research design in global studies has the same general outline as in other fields: theory, thesis, methods, data collection, analysis. However, the methodological challenges of global studies research are compounded by the interdisciplinary nature of the field. Since global studies spans the humanities and the social and natural sciences, scholars have a great many qualitative or quantitative methods or techniques available to them. A scholar could conceivably use any of the standard methods associated with conventional disciplines as diverse as anthropology, communication, economics, geography, law, history, linguistics, philosophy, political science, environmental science, health, psychology, and sociology, among others. Depending on the research design and the nature of the research question, the researcher selects from a wide range of established qualitative and quantitative data collection methods in order to gather the kinds of information needed to answer the central research question. When thinking about research design the most important issue is: If the research design were fully and successfully implemented, could it produce the kind of evidence needed to answer the original research question?

The challenges involved in doing global studies research make certain aspects of the research design process more crucial than they may be in some disciplines, or even in other interdisciplinary fields. Certain fields have clearly defined research goals and a relatively limited range of accepted methods, so the methodology may appear in abbreviated form. It may simply explain, for example, how the researcher will apply a specific set of methods. Global studies research, however, has a very wide range of potential methods and approaches, and these can be applied nearly anywhere in the world under an even wider array of possible conditions. Hence, it is extremely important for global studies scholars to explicitly deal with their overall research goals, the basic assumptions underlying their research design, their methodological choices, their analytical and ethical concerns, and the significance of their expected outcomes and conclusions.

PRIMARY AND SECONDARY RESEARCH

Most conventional methods textbooks make a clear distinction between primary and secondary research. Primary research happens when the researcher collects their own original data using one or more of the primary data collection methods (interviews, observations, surveys, etc.). In contrast, secondary research uses data that has already been analyzed by someone else. For example, a meta-analysis of existing academic articles would be considered a form of secondary analysis.

Designing, funding, and carrying out one's own primary research is generally understood to be the more difficult, expensive, and time-consuming mode of doing research (Bryman 2016: 11). Conducting primary research requires substantial planning, extensive knowledge of the literature, considerable training in specialized methods, a successful grant proposal to fund the research project, not to mention the rigors and duration of the data collection process. The entire research cycle from planning to funding, execution, and publication of results can take years and cost thousands of dollars. There are also some important risks associated with primary research. There is no guarantee that a primary research project can be completed as planned or that it will actually produce the kinds of data needed to address the original research question.

In comparison, secondary data analysis can be relatively quick and easy. For example, students do secondary research when they use books and articles from the campus library to write their papers. Secondary research can also be achieved by analyzing the mountains of census and political data produced every year by the United Nations (UN), national governments, and a host of other international and local organizations. Much of this secondary data has only been analyzed in the most cursory of ways. This means that huge data sets are already out there, either completely unanalyzed or ready to be analyzed in new and creative ways. Furthermore, many of these data sets are inexpensive or freely available to researchers. This means that for the average scholar, doing secondary research on existing data can be more convenient, much faster, and less expensive than trying to do one's own primary research to collect new data.

Still, a number of circumstances require researchers to conduct primary research. Naturally, if the data that is necessary to study a given topic does not already exist, the researcher must consider doing original research to develop raw data. Another reason that researchers do primary research is that data sets are not infinitely flexible. Data collected by specific researchers in specific disciplines for specific purposes cannot always be adapted for other kinds of studies. For example, the data collected by a political survey may or may not produce information that is useful for other kinds of research. Whether the data can be retasked for a new purpose depends on the original survey design, the narrowness of the survey questions, and the new purpose to which the data is being applied.

For our students, there is one other important reason to do primary research. Primary research is often required in academic programs that have a thesis or dissertation requirement as part of the MA and PhD degrees. To complete their dissertations, students must demonstrate that they can conceive, design, fund, and implement their own primary research projects, and then write up their results in a coherent summary that is relevant to their field of study. No primary research, no dissertation.

The rather simplistic distinction between primary and secondary data can be useful for instructional purposes. However, this distinction gets rather fuzzy in places. For instance, a statistical analysis of data the researcher did not collect can be considered primary research if the data was not previously analyzed. There are also circumstances where archival, discourse, text, and content methods can be considered to be either primary or secondary analysis depending on the research question and design (Salevouris and Furay 2015). Further, a mixed-methods research design can incorporate both primary and secondary research in one project. And, as we have previously noted, researchers often use information from both primary sources (interviews) and secondary sources (literature) in the early stages of design, even if these sources are not ultimately listed in the methods section. In sum, the distinction between primary and secondary research is largely academic, and in most cases it doesn't pay to apply it too strictly.

BASIC DATA COLLECTION METHODS

There are dozens of research methods used in the humanities and social science disciplines (Given 2008; Lewis-Beck, Bryman, and Liao 2004). For the purposes of clarity, we make a distinction here between the dozens of specialized research methods and a small group of basic data collection methods. The seven basic data collection methods introduced below are the building blocks that can be used in different combinations to make almost all of the other research methods and strategies. For example, a researcher deploying the community-study method might use a combination of archival, observation, interview, survey, and statistical methods.

Historical-Archival Research

Archival research is one of the most fundamental and widely used data collection methods. The classic example of archival research is a bespectacled historian poring over dusty historical records (Storey 2009). Anytime a researcher analyzes material that has been collected and archived, however, they are doing archival research. For example, students do archival research when they use their school libraries. There are many different kinds of archives and a very wide range of materials that can be archived, including books, magazines, newspapers, historical documents, blogs, art, music, film, personal letters, maps, government reports, church records, court records, and many others. And because academic literature is also archived in libraries, we think it is safe to say that most academics routinely use archival research at several different points in the processes of designing, implementing, and publishing their research.

Global scholars should use evidence in historical and cultural archives carefully and critically. Historical records and cultural artifacts can be forms of evidence that do represent some aspect of a particular time and place, but exactly what they represent and how they represent it should not be taken for granted (Salevouris and Furay 2015: 169). Some records and artifacts are produced by persons or institutions with specific motivations or purposes in mind (Howell and Prevenier 2001: 18). Other sources can be unreliable or incorrectly translated, artifacts incorrectly described or dated, and records intentionally falsified or altered (Howell and Prevenier 2001: 58).

Historians explicitly recognize different qualities of sources when they make the distinction between *primary* and *secondary* sources of evidence (Brundage 2013: 20). A primary source is a record created during the period under investigation, for example war records created during a war. Reliable primary sources are likely to be closer to the events, to what actually happened at that time, to the experience of historical reality (McCullagh 1984: 4). A secondary source is an account created afterward, and typically includes analysis and interpretation of one or more primary sources. As narrative interpretations of evidence about the past, secondary sources introduce a number of complex debates about representation, the meaning of history, and historiography more generally (Carr 1967; Hobsbawm 1997; Laslitt et al. 1997). Primary and secondary sources differ in the degrees of immediacy, interpretation, and potential distortion. But as previously noted, several different kinds of sources can be considered either primary or secondary depending on how the source is used. Researchers should recognize that the reliability and quality of sources can differ greatly and are impacted by many factors including the when, where, why, how, and who of their creation, as well as how the researcher is using the source.

Archival research is particularly important for students that are developing their own global studies research topics. Students with very limited time and money can make great progress in defining and developing their research projects using the archives available to them at their home institutions and online. The first archival resource to turn to should probably be the academic literature on the student's substantive topic. In addition, organizations such as the UN, World Bank, International Monetary Fund (IMF), World Trade Organization (WTO), European Union (EU), and North Atlantic Treaty Organization (NATO), among many others, provide huge amounts of information on a variety of global issues in the form of detailed government reports, summary reports, bibliographies, pictures, graphs, tables, charts, and more that are all freely available online. Students of all skill levels can use these resources to quickly develop supporting evidence for their theses, proposals, and public presentations.

Beyond their chosen substantive topics, students should use the available archives to systematically build their own analytical, methodological, and regional expertise. Archival sources can help students learn about the history and culture of the region they are interested in, ongoing current events, regional demographics, industry and business news, and a great deal of other background information that may be relevant to their research topics. Knowledge about the social, political, and economic contexts for a given research topic can go a long way in strengthening theses, dissertations, and grant proposals.

You can also use archives and online resources strategically to track down concrete specifics for research and grant proposals. In most cases it is possible to identify specialized archives in the area of study, local academics and academic institutions, experts working in a region or on a particular substantive topic, and/or organizations doing work in related areas. It may also be possible to find internship opportunities with governmental agencies, nongovernmental organizations, and/or businesses working in the region. A sprinkling of these details can go a long way toward strengthening a research proposal. Further, developing ties to institutions and organizations that are already working in the region can help you identify and access other local resources. Local organizations can give you a place land and a reason to be there. Using archival resources to develop prior knowledge and contacts is usually a much better strategy than showing up in a place without a plan.

Archival research can also take you beyond the limits of the Internet (shocking news). Wherever our research takes us, we encounter university archives, local public libraries, historical and rare manuscript archives, monuments, church records, museums, art galleries, and other local sites with loads of valuable information that is not necessarily available online. Accessing these archives can be easy and very productive. It often only requires a little advanced planning—a phone call or a letter on department letterhead—to access amazing materials and even some of the world's great historical treasures. As a bonus, meeting the local experts that curate these specialized archives can be a most informative and memorable experience.

Observation and Participant Observation

Observation is another fundamental empirical method. It involves "the systematic description of events, behaviors, and artifacts in the social setting chosen for study" (Marshall and Rossman 1989: 79). The researcher carefully observes the subject of the study using their five senses and notes their observations. For example, a chemist might observe and take notes on a chemical reaction in the laboratory. Similarly, an anthropologist might observe and take notes on a wedding ceremony in another culture. As part of their observation, researchers may take photographs or otherwise record the events they observe. In the natural sciences it is assumed that the researcher's presence does not change the events being observed. Observing a chemical reaction is not meant to change the reaction itself. In the social sciences, however, the presence of an observer can and often does change events. We are almost always participants, whether we intend to be or not.

Participant observation is "the process of learning through exposure to or involvement in the day-to-day or routine activities of participants in the researcher setting" (Schensul, Schensul, and LeCompte 1999: 91). Participant observation has long been one of the main methods of ethnographic fieldwork (DeWalt and DeWalt 2011). It builds on basic observation methods by recognizing that in social situations the observer very often impacts the events being observed in some way. The researcher who performs the observation is not separated from the social action, but is involved or actively plays a role in the events they observe. This distinction is important because active participation provides the researcher with a subjective dimension that can profoundly change the way they understand the social action they observe. Generations of anthropologists have found that this kind of first-person participation is particularly important when trying to understand events that take place in the context of another culture.

Interviews

Interviewing is another basic data collection method that is very widely used (Weiss 1994; Seidman 2013). It is a qualitative method that aims to explore the thoughts, opinions, beliefs, experiences, and motivations of people around a particular subject. Interviews have the potential to be more interactive than other data collection methods, like surveys or statistical analysis. Ideally, this interactive quality can provide the interviewer with a deeper understanding of what people think than they would typically gain otherwise.

In practice, research interviews can range from brief, informal chats to long, formal sessions. An example of a very informal interview is talking with a street vendor or taxi driver during a routine business transaction. A more formal interview might be a planned meeting with a government official to discuss specific aspects of a proposed project.

Interviews also vary in their degree of structure. They can be very structured, semistructured, or almost entirely unstructured. A structured interview usually involves the interviewer asking a series of preformed questions designed to elicit specific kinds of information. For example, a very structured interview might be similar to administering a written survey, but with the interviewer asking questions verbally. The structure of this format gives the interviewer more control over the course of the conversation. In contrast, a less structured interview gives the person being interviewed more freedom to determine the topics of discussion and the direction of the conversation. This approach can be very useful when interviewing someone who knows a great deal about the topics that interest you. Unstructured interviews are particularly important for finding out information that you may not initially have thought relevant.

We suspect that the average researcher uses the interview method far more often than they may realize. Academics can often be found drinking coffee and talking to other academics about what they are reading (their archival research) and their projects, findings, and publications. Before they even begin to formally design a research project, they begin by talking to other academics in that area of specialization during meetings and conferences. Talking to knowledgeable people inside the academy and beyond has always been a crucial part of learning, doing, analyzing, and disseminating research.

Doing interviews is a skill. Some researchers have the knack for simultaneously maintaining an active presence and participating thoughtfully in a two-way conversation while at the same time minding their research purpose, recording, analyzing, and even selectively guiding the conversation. Most researchers can develop these skills with time and practice. One of the more important interview skills, however, is identifying the right kinds of people to talk to. A skilled interviewer identifies people that have a stake in, a unique perspective on, or specific knowledge about the research topic. It is a good idea to select interviewees from different points on the local-global continuum. Depending on the research, it may make sense to talk to policy makers and local regulatory agencies, leaders of multinational corporations and small business owners, international experts and local academics, community leaders, local residents, and transient workers. These actors will have their own relationships to and understanding of the issues involved. Learning to tap into these various understandings is a key skill in understanding multifaceted global issues.

Focus Groups

The focus group method brings a small group of people together so that the researcher can facilitate a semistructured group interview (Morgan 1997). For example, a focus group may be used to test audience reactions to a television commercial or political advertisement. While executing focus group research, the researcher may use one or more of the basic data collection methods, such as interviewing, observation, and surveying, to study the group's responses. What makes the focus group unique, however, is that it can be used to study social interactions within the group itself. The focus group method recognizes that people are profoundly influenced by groups and group behavior. People often react differently in groups than they do when they are studied individually. Focus groups can be used to study group reactions and the formation of collective responses to a given stimulus (Kitzinger 1994). The collective response aspect makes the focus group method very important to fields such as media studies where audience response is a key issue.

Surveys

The survey method is one of the most useful methods for collecting self-reported information from large groups of people, usually groups that are selected for specific reasons (Engel et al. 2015; Fowler 2014). Common examples are a national census or a survey of the attitudes of likely voters about an upcoming election.

Rather than surveying every member of a population, survey researchers typically use sampling logic to select a smaller sample that is representative of the larger group (see "Sampling Logic," Chapter 4). The representative sample is then given a predefined set of questions designed to obtain the kinds of information the researcher seeks. The questions can be asked on a written questionnaire, via phone, or in person. The product of the survey is typically a large set of quantitative data that can be statistically analyzed.

Unfortunately, conducting a survey that properly represents a large population can be very difficult and costly. Conducting a representative survey requires several distinct skill sets, each of which involves considerable training. First, designing and administering a survey instrument that produces the kinds of information that can be successfully analyzed is not as easy as one might think. Survey researchers must use mostly closed-end survey questions that are unambiguous and will make sense to, and garner intelligible answers from, a wide array of people from very different backgrounds. Survey researchers must also understand sampling logic and statistical analysis. Using all three of these skill sets to produce useful findings takes time and practice. Further, the costs associated with carrying out a representative survey on a large population are beyond the means of most researchers. For these kinds of surveys, most researchers will need substantial extramural support in the form of survey grants. Learning to write, submit, and win survey grants can add significant time to the survey research cycle. In general, beginning researchers should not plan to do large-scale survey research without adequate training and the ongoing mentorship of someone with experience conducting surveys.

For global scholars, the challenges of survey research in intercultural settings can further complicate matters. Designing and conducting an effective survey in a foreign culture adds some serious challenges. These challenges go well beyond simple language translation. The survey questions must unambiguously make sense in local languages and social contexts, as well as across different sectors of society. Making a survey that works in a foreign culture usually requires collaborating with a local survey expert that has experience doing successful surveys in that specific culture. We encourage these kinds of collaborations in nearly any form of intercultural research for a number of practical and ethical reasons (see "Ethical Dimensions of Global Research," Chapter 4).

Fortunately, a survey does not need to be huge, scientifically quantitative, randomly selected, or expensive to provide useful information. While doing a full probability survey of large-scale populations may be out of reach for many researchers, there are ways to use smaller-scale and less formal questionnaires to effectively collect information that is less statistically representative but still empirical information. For example, if you were studying the history of a particular community you could ask the head of each household how and when the family came to live in the community, as well as the ages and occupations of the people living at that address. The skill sets and resources required for a less formal questionnaire like this one are well within reach of most researchers. The information that this kind of questionnaire would produce may not be complete, random, or scientifically representative of the entire community, but you would have learned a great deal about the community, met many families, let people know why you were there, developed many opportunities for further interviews, and probably even found new avenues for further research.

You can also use less formal questionnaires to survey organizations. You could survey all social clubs on campus, businesses in a particular consortium, or industry groups in a particular sector. Or you could survey NGOs working on a particular social issue or in a particular region. In cases like these, the less formal questionnaire can help you identify and gain access to particular sets of organizations, develop qualitative and quantitative information about them, and introduce yourself and your research project to key contacts within them. Deployed properly, the questionnaire can be a very effective empirical tool for collecting many different types of quantitative and qualitative data.

OTHER RESEARCH METHODS AND STRATEGIES

The basic data collection methods we introduced above are just a few of the commonly used methods. Most of the dozens of research methods available to global scholars combine one or more of these basic methods to create a coherent methodology that is suited to a specific kind of research. Table 1 provides a small sampling of these other methods and examples to examine.

Many of these methods are far more sophisticated and specialized than the basic data collection methods. But all of them, even the most sophisticated and powerful, have strengths and weaknesses. It seems that the more specialized and powerful an individual research method is in one way, the weaker it is in another way. This is one reason why global scholars should consider triangulating their findings with more than one kind of research method wherever possible (see "Triangulation" in Chapter 4 and "Mixed Methods" in this chapter below).

GENERAL METHODS OF ANALYSIS

As noted above, global scholars can make use of a very wide range of theoretical and methodological approaches. Since different research methods produce different kinds of evidence, global scholars must employ the analytical approaches that are appropriate to the kinds of evidence produced

Table 1   Research Methods

Method	Resources
Action and Participatory Action Research	McIntyre 2008; Chevalier and Buckles 2013; Reason and Bradbury-Huang 2008; Stringer 2014; Herr and Anderson 2015
Case Study	Stake 1995; Willig 2008; Yin 2014 see also Chapter 6
Community Study	Hacker 2013; Stoecker 2013; Halseth et al. 2016
Development Studies	Haynes 2008; Sumner and Tribe 2008; Desai and Potter 2014
Ethnography	Marcus 1995; Burawoy et al. 2000; Gille and Ó Riain 2002; O'Reilly 2012; Falzon 2009
Feminist Methods	Reinharz 1992; Hartsock 1999; Harding 2004; Hesse-Biber 2014; McCann and Kim 2013; Tong 2014
Field Research	Bailey 2006; Rossman and Rallis 2017
Life History	Rosenzweig and Thelen 1998; Caughey 2006
Organization Studies	Powell and DiMaggio 1991; Czarniawska 1998; Clegg et al. 2006; Knights and Willmott 2011
Program Evaluation	Fitzpatrick, Sanders, and Worthen 2011; Bamberger, Rugh, and Mabry 2011; Royse, Thyer, and Padgett 2016
Visual Research	Margolis and Pauwels 2011; Rose 2016

by their chosen methodology. Unfortunately, talking about the research process in terms of theory-method-data can make it seem that the choice of analytical techniques is an afterthought determined by the types of data gathered. In many cases, the reverse is more accurate.

In empirical research there is a necessary relationship between the conceptual framework, research question, methodology, types of evidence produced, and methods for analyzing the evidence. The relationship between these elements of research design, however, is not unidirectional. Some research approaches start with data and work toward theory (Glaser and Strauss [1967] 1999). But it is the analysis that must ultimately answer the research question, so in many cases the type of analysis to be used determines the rest of the research design. A researcher may employ a particular methodology because it provides the evidence they need for the analysis.

In very general terms, research questions that deal with quantitative issues—for example, the impact of education on income or the impact of foreign direct investment on economic output—call for more quantitative or econometric types of analyses (Treiman 2009; Martin and Bridgmon 2012). Research questions that deal with qualitative issues—for example, why people discriminate or how viewers understand a foreign film—call for more qualitative types of analyses (Wertz et al. 2011; Miles, Huberman, and Saldaña 2014). A question about a work of art might call for visual methods of analysis (Van Leeuwen and Jewitt 2001; Helmers 2005). On the other hand, a question about an autobiography could call for a *qualitative* narrative analysis (Kim 2016; De Fina and Georgakopoulou 2015) or a *quantitative* narrative analysis (Franzosi 2010). A mixed-method research design could call for any two or more types of analysis, depending on the nature of the research question and the researcher's aims. For many graduate students, this is the crux of the matter. They can't design their research project because they don't have a specific-enough research question, one that can be answered with a specific type of analysis.

Some types of evidence or data can be used in more than one analysis—for example, basic demographic statistics such as race, gender, class, age, and education level. These statistics explain so much variation in social outcomes that they are used by researchers in many different fields. As one starts to deal with more specialized information, however, it gets progressively harder to make data that was collected for one purpose apply to other purposes. As we noted above, most evidence necessarily reflects the original purpose for which it was collected. Accordingly, it enables certain kinds of analysis and disables others. Much of the evidence that researchers collect is used for a specific analysis and might never be used again.

People who have not done primary research and have not tried to analyze evidence they have collected themselves do not know how hard it can be to collect data that can be analyzed systematically. It may sound like a simple thing to do, but if a researcher does not have prior experience analyzing evidence, it may not be easy for them to collect analyzable evidence. Every year some unfortunate student returns from their field research with "tons of data," only to find that what they have collected is a heap of disorganized information that cannot be analyzed in any meaningful way.

If a researcher is not familiar with the analytical techniques they propose to use, if they have never tried to analyze their own data before, they are much less likely to be successful at collecting the kinds of data they need. To design a methodology that is capable of producing analyzable evidence, the researcher must first come to terms with the constraints of different types of evidence and analytical approaches.

Two broad categories of analysis are *content analysis* and *statistical analysis*. These approaches are used across the humanities and the social and physical sciences, and they encompass a wide range of research designs and methods.

Content Analysis

We use the term *content analysis* to refer to a variety of methods that can be used to study culture by analyzing cultural products—words, art, images, songs, and so on. The broad category of content analysis should not be confused with the specific method of textual analysis that is also called content analysis (Krippendorff and Bock 2009), nor should it be confused with the interdisciplinary field of cultural studies (Barker and Jane 2016). Researchers doing content analysis analyze cultural artifacts, the products of culture. These include visual art, performance, crafts, literary works, film, broadcast and print media, and architecture, but can also encompass clothes, household products, coins, toys, and many other forms of material culture. There are a number of analytical approaches for different types of cultural artifacts—literature (Parker 2015; Zimmermann 2015), media (Jensen 2012; Ott and Mack 2014), music (Collins 2013), performance (Madison and Hamera 2006; Schechner 2013), visual art (Van Leeuwen and Jewitt 2001; Helmers 2005), and so on.

Content analysis methods tend to be qualitative in the sense that they rely on the researcher's ability to observe, analyze, and interpret the artifacts in relation to specific cultural contexts. There are also, however, several quantitative methods of content analysis. For example, there are both quantitative and qualitative methods for textual analysis (Jockers 2014; Kuckartz 2014) and discourse analysis (Schiffrin, Tannen, and Hamilton 2001; Gee 2014).

Content analysis can be used very effectively to analyze culture. For example, in recent years content analyses of mass media have provided timely investigations into the ways that media reflect gender and racial biases in society. This method can reveal a great deal about society, but it does not typically reveal much about processes of cultural production (e.g., a creator's intent in creating an artifact). Nor can it reveal much about audience reception of an artifact. For this reason it can be difficult to show any correlation between the production of cultural artifacts (e.g., violence in film) and specific social behaviors (e.g., violence in society) through content analysis alone. Exploring the processes of cultural production and reception require the use of additional methods such as interviews and focus groups to give wider social context.

Statistical Analysis

Statistical analysis is another broad category of analytical approaches. Statistical analyses are quantitative techniques used to summarize, analyze, and interpret variable numerical data (Vogt and Johnson 2016). Statistical methods are widely used in many different fields, such as economics, geography, political science, psychology, and sociology. Statistical procedures can be used to study relationships and associations between variables in very large data sets. Typically the statistical analyst does not collect their own data; they work on data sets that were collected by someone else. A researcher interested in the impact of college education on individual income, for example, could use census data to analyze the relationships and associations it contains between education and income variables.

Generally speaking, statistical procedures break down into several areas. There are descriptive statistics, which can be used to describe the basic features of a data set (mean, median, range, percentile, etc.) (Holcomb 1998). There are procedures for exploring data with visualization techniques such as box plots, histograms, scatter plots, and multidimensional scaling (Kirk 2016). Linear and logistic regression models can be used to estimate relationships among variables (Schroeder, Sjoquist, and Stephan 1986). The analysis of variance (ANNOVA) can be used to study the differences among group means (Iversen and Norpoth 1987). There are regression diagnostics (Fox 1991), the goodness of fit (R-squared), statistical significance (F-test), and tests of individual parameters (T-tests). There are also distinct procedures for time series analysis and multivariate analysis, among many others.

Statistical analyses are widely used because they have several important advantages. A statistical analysis is an efficient way of dealing with large amounts of quantitative data. As a quantitative method along with experiments and surveys, it is consider by some to be more empirical, scientific, and unbiased than qualitative methods. There are mountains of virtually unanalyzed data on nearly any global topic online, freely available in spreadsheet format. Many governments and international organizations such as the UN, World Bank, IMF, WTO, EU, and NATO make their data sets available to researchers via their websites. Unlike with the survey method, the time-consuming and costly task of assembling large data sets is already taken care of by these organizations. Researchers with the required statistical skills can download relevant data and start the analysis portion of their research straight away.

There are also some serious limitations to statistical analysis. To begin with, not everyone has the skills required to do this kind of analysis, and acquiring them can take considerable time and effort. There are also limitations built into the various statistical models (see Burawoy 1998: 12; Stiglitz, Sen, and Fitoussi 2010; Darian-Smith 2016). For example, the regression model is built on an assumption of linear causality—that the independent variables in a data set cause the variation observed in the dependent variables. This kind of linear causal logic does not always fit social phenomena. Another limitation to statistical analysis is in the range of questions a researcher can ask of quantitative data. There is a tendency for researchers to restrict their questions to ones that can be answered with the kinds of data at hand.

OTHER METHODS OF ANALYSIS

Table 2 provides a list of analytical methods and source examples for further reference.

Table 2 Analytical Methods

Method	Resources
Comparative-Historical Analysis	Mahoney and Rueschemeyer 2003; Lange 2012; Mahoney and Thelen 2015
Content, Textual, and Hermeneutic Analysis	Krippendorff and Bock 2009; Jockers 2014; Kuckartz 2014; Zimmermann 2015
Demographic Analysis	Hinde 1998; Wachter 2014; Yusuf, Martins, and Swanson 2014; Rowland 2003
Discourse Analysis (Foucauldian and socio-linguistic)	Stubbs 1983; Schiffrin, Tannen, and Hamilton 2001; Johnstone 2008; Dunn and Neumann 2016; Gee 2014
Econometrics	Simon and Blume 1994; Hayashi 2000; Chiang and Wainwright 2005
Geographic Information System (GIS)	Bodenhamer, Corrigan, and Harris 2010; O'Sullivan and Unwin 2010; Steinberg and Steinberg 2015
Grounded Theory	Glaser and Strauss (1967) 1999; Charmaz 2014; Birks and Mills 2015
Meta-Analysis	Borenstein et al. 2009; Cooper 2016; Wolf 2013
Network Analysis	Wasserman and Faust 1994; Jackson 2010; Newman 2010; Borgatti, Everett, and Johnson 2013
Policy Analysis	Weimer and Vining 2016; Bardach and Patashnik 2015; Patton, Sawicki, and Clark 2012

ANSWERING A GLOBAL RESEARCH QUESTION

It is easy to get bogged down in the details of an analytical technique and lose sight of the big picture. No matter which analytical techniques you ultimately employ, it is important to bring your analysis back to your original research question—the global research question (see Chapter 4). Depending on the analysis, you may find it necessary to explicitly address

- the overarching research question
- specific research questions
- the aspects of the research question(s) that can be addressed by empirical analysis

- key analytical concepts used
- the logic behind the research design and methodology
- the types of evidence used in the analysis
- the analytical techniques used
- how the evidence and analytical techniques address the research question

When doing global research, it is a good idea to remember that the audience reading your work may not know anything about global research. For this reason, we recommend making an effort to address the questions: Why did you use a global approach? What specifically makes your analysis global? Be explicit about the kinds of global issues, characteristics, perspectives, and dimensions that inform your research and analysis (see Chapters 2 and 3). Elaborate which global-scale issues your research addresses and how they intersect. Explain how and where the analysis is holistic, integrative, critical, interdisciplinary, and decentered. Discuss the impact of relevant local-global, spatial, historical, political, economic, sociocultural, intersectional, and ethical dimensions on the analysis. Not all researchers need to cover every one of these characteristics and dimensions. We recommend, however, that you explicitly engage those that are relevant and add to your analysis. For a more detailed discussion of how global issues and their dimensions might be used in the analysis of a global case study, see "Deploying Global Perspectives and Analyzing Global Dimensions" in Chapter 6.

MIXED METHODS

In some fields, the majority of research uses monomethod research designs. There is nothing wrong with these research designs as long the one method they employ is capable of producing the evidence required to answer the research question. Nonetheless, there are some very good reasons why global scholars might want to consider using a mixed-method research design (Plano Clark and Ivankova 2016). The first reason is one we have already mentioned: every method has its strengths and weaknesses. As we mentioned in Chapter 4, global scholars can greatly enhance the reliability and/or validity of their research by triangulating with multiple research methods.

Note that the term *mixed methods* is sometimes used to refer exclusively to research designs that integrate both qualitative and quantitative research methods (Creswell 2015). By this definition, mixing one qualitative method with another qualitative method, or mixing two or more quantitative methods, would not qualify as a true mixed-method design. Research designs with multiple methods that are only either qualitative or quantitative are sometimes called "multimethod" research designs to distinguish them from mixed-method research designs that do combine qualitative and quantitative approaches.

We are not sure that defining "mixed methods" around the qualitative/quantitative distinction is really helpful for triangulation. This narrow definition comes from the possibility that two methods might share the same kinds of limitations and weaknesses if they are too similar to each other, and therefore may not triangulate sufficiently. By this logic, mixed methods should be far enough apart to yield different kinds of evidence. For some, using a qualitative method with a quantitative one guarantees this distance. Others will take the argument even further and argue that a maximally effective triangulation must use methods from the humanities and from the social sciences. Still others might argue that a truly robust research design will include different methods from the humanities and the social, natural, and behavioral sciences. Rather than trying to define a successful triangulation by the types of methods it uses, we argue that the research design should determine the methods. The correct mix of methods need only produce types of evidence that are sufficiently different to achieve the desired degree of triangulation.

Other definitions of mixed methods go so far as to exclude research designs that simply import external data into the analysis stage of the research. To be a mixed-methods design, then, both qualitative and quantitative methods would have to be integrated into it from the start. We disagree: adding data analyses from organizations such as the World Bank or World Health Organization in the analysis section can in certain cases be sufficient for triangulating findings from other types of methods.

The second reason to consider a mixed-method research design is that this type of design is often more appropriate for multiperspectival global analyses. Global-scale issues can encompass both micro and macro dimensions in ways that require a researcher to, for instance, pair interviews with town officials with quantitative data for the region. However, this is just a glimpse of the possibilities for creatively mixing one's methods. Qualitative methods are often associated with micro analyses and quantitative methods with more macro analyses, but global scholars need not be bound by this. In practice, we find that qualitative interviews can be used very effectively to address macro global issues. An interview with the right expert, public official, or industry leader can cut right to the heart of global issues and make them more accessible than they would otherwise be. Similarly, quantitative data can be used very effectively to address micro issues. For example, calculating the ratio of boys to girls in schools in a particular place can sometimes cut to the heart of gender issues more quickly than any number of interviews with local officials.

Third, employing different kinds of methods can provide researchers with creative ways to follow complex global issues across geographic and temporal boundaries. You can use regional statistics to link what is going on in one community to larger, regional patterns. Or you can conduct interviews with refugees to gain indirect access across borders that you cannot cross or to conflict zones that you should not enter. Or you can mine historical archives to link current issues to their deeper histories. Using mixed methods can enable you not only to span the local-global continuum but to cross geographic, political, and historical boundaries as well.

Fourth, employing more than one method is usually much easier than it sounds. You can significantly increase the reliability and/or validity of your research with little additional effort. It is so easy to mix multiple methods that many scholars do it without realizing it. For example, it is often observations about what is going on in the world that lead researchers to their research question in the first place. When we access the substantive literature on a topic, we are already carrying out archival research. When we talk to experts on a topic or region, we are using the interview method. People that identify themselves as qualitative researchers often use quantitative graphs and charts to enhance their arguments. Survey researchers often do a handful of qualitative interviews with survey respondents to get feedback on their survey questions, possibly leading to improvements in the survey itself. Mixing methods in these ways can lead to better research and stronger arguments that reach wider audiences. Depending on the additional methods chosen, employing more than one method can be easy, inexpensive, and very rewarding.

In sum, global scholars should base their choice of a mono-, multi-, or mixed-method research design on the kinds of questions they are asking and the types of data they need to answer their questions. Some research questions can be answered with evidence that just one method will yield. Other research questions can only be answered with different kinds of evidence that require more than one method to produce. Whether you ultimately choose a mono-, multi-, or mixed-method research design, you should be ready to justify that choice in your dissertation proposal, grant proposals, and publications. Researchers need to be able to explain why they chose a particular research design, how the design addresses their research questions, and how they will use the evidence produced by each method to address their research questions.

CRITICAL METHODOLOGICAL STRATEGIES

Complex global issues do not have just one side, or even two. It is important to recognize that people around the world have their own cultures, religions, values, and ways of knowing and interpreting, and that diverse ways of understanding the world are grounded in historical traditions and validated by lived experiences. There is never just one community, history, or truth since each cultural tradition's epistemologies, understandings, and systems of meaning are dynamic and change over time. Thinking critically means being willing to think openly—to challenge one's own assumptions; to reflect on how knowledge is produced, by whom, and with what possible impact; and more generally, to question the implicit bias involved in various forms of communication. As we discussed in Chapter 2, one of the most significant reasons why global studies is important is that it fosters critical thinking. This includes the ability to think about an issue from multiple perspectives that may not represent one's own, and in the process reflect upon the limitations of one's worldview and its culturally embedded assumptions. The process of reflection, or what is often referred to as *reflexivity*, makes standpoint and intersectional theories and concepts such as *cosmopolitanism, intercultural communication, pluralism,* and *multiperspectivism* key to global studies (Smith 1977; Collins 1990; Appiah 2006; Beck and Sznaider 2006; Darieva et al. 2012; Gunn 2013).

In pursuing particular methodological strategies, many scholars in global studies endeavor to recover voices and perspectives that are typically disregarded in mainstream discourse about globalization. This mainstream discourse tends to view global trade and finance as the drivers of globalization, and as a result focuses on macroeconomic processes, global markets, international and regional trade, and development agendas. Macroeconomic analyses, however, often fail to see the finer details of social reality, and they may displace localized processes and further marginalize voices from the periphery of the global economy. Similarly, focusing on the macropolitical relations between countries—a typical approach in the fields of international relations and international political economy—too often skims over the complexity of all that is happening within and between countries and the influential interventions of a wide range of nonstate actors in local, regional, national, and transnational sectors of society (see Cohen 2014).

Global studies as an emerging field seeks to counterbalance these top-down, macro perspectives by encompassing the entire local-global continuum, which necessarily includes the voices of women, racial and ethnic minorities, indigenous peoples, postcolonial subjects, unemployed people, the precariat, people living in poverty, immigrants, and refugees and displaced persons, among others. By definition, then, global studies scholars seek to incorporate multiple intersectional dimensions of discrimination—gender, race, ethnicity, class, sexuality, religion, health, and citizenship—and underscore the unfairness in a global system that includes extreme poverty, human rights abuses, exploitation of human and natural resources, environmental degradation, governmental corruption, and regional violence and genocide.

Discussions of critical methodological strategy have become very important across a range of disciplines and fields of inquiry. Many of these discussions are concerned with ensuring that the social sciences and humanities remain relevant and applicable in our complex globalizing world and seek to transcend the so-called science wars that position the "hard" physical sciences against the "soft" social sciences and even "softer" humanities. As Bent Flyvbjerg argues, it is inappropriate and misleading to compare the physical sciences with the social sciences since the latter are not designed to be explanatory, predictive, or find universal theories that posit the "truth about the nature of things" (Flyvbjerg 2001: 166). Rather, he declares, the social sciences should focus on people and how they make meaning of their world:

> We must take up problems that matter to the local, national, and global communities in which we live, and we must do it in ways that matter; we must focus on issues of values and power like great social scientists have advocated from Aristotle and Machiavelli to Max Weber and Pierre Bourdieu ... If we do this, we may successfully transform social science from what is fast becoming a sterile academic activity, which is undertaken mostly for its own sake and in increasing isolation from a society on which it has little effect and from which it gets little appreciation. We may transform social science to an activity done in public for the public, sometimes to clarify, sometimes to intervene, sometimes to generate new perspectives, and always to serve as eyes and ears in our ongoing efforts at understanding the present and deliberating about the future. We may, in short, arrive at a social science that matters. (Flyvbjerg 2001: 166)

For Flyvbjerg, making social science matter carries methodological implications. He argues that researchers need to focus on how people create values, place power at the center of their analyses, nurture multiple perspectives and interpretations, and ensure that specific contexts and grounded case studies provide the mechanism from which to generalize on the important, "big" questions. As he notes, this decentering methodological approach draws on Clifford Geertz's notion of "thick description." Taking as its point of departure local micropractices, it means always "searching for the Great within the Small and vice versa ... doing work that is at the same time as detailed and as general as possible" (Flyvbjerg 2001: 133–34; Darian-Smith 2002).

Below we list some of the more widely used critical methodological strategies that are helping to ensure that social science and humanistic research continues to matter as we move into the middle decades of the twenty-first century. The list is not comprehensive, but we hope it gives a sense of the range of innovative methodological approaches and why they may be important for global studies scholarship. Each of these critical methodologies is deployed by scholars in a variety of ways, and there is much debate and nuance among those who use them. Much depends on the researcher's ontological, epistemological, political, cultural, and ethical profile, which in turn informs a scholar's research questions and research design choices. Moreover, each of these methodological approaches may use a full range of methods or techniques for accessing, collecting, and analyzing data. Critical methodologies can be micro and macro in orientation and can use qualitative, quantitative, and mixed methods. These approaches are as scientific and empirical as the more standard methodological approaches used in conventional disciplinary research.

What the many types of critical methodologies have in common is that they bring into question the taken-for-granted assumptions and concepts of Euro-American scholarship and the distortions of social reality that this scholarship produces (Morrow and Brown 1994). As feminist scholars have argued, movements for social liberation "make it possible for people to see the world in an enlarged perspective because they remove the covers and blinders that obscure knowledge and observation" (Millman and Kanter 1987: 30). For this reason, critical methodological strategies are sometimes controversial and often vulnerable to being characterized by conservative scholars as biased, subjective, marginal, unscientific, and nonauthoritative. Fortunately, critical global studies scholars tend to be innovative thinkers who are open to methodological approaches that seek to make the familiar unfamiliar and that open up intellectual space for exploring complex global issues.

Transcending Methodological Nationalism

GENERAL DESCRIPTION

Following on from our discussion of decentering the nation-state in Chapter 3, one of the most widely used critical methodological approaches is that of moving beyond nation-states as the assumed "container" of societies and social relations (Beck and Willms 2004: 13).

Joseph Stiglitz and Amartya Sen (former Nobel laureates in economics) caution against simple correlations between nations, particularly when that comparison involves data sets collected by the countries themselves. In a report titled *Mismeasuring Our Lives: Why GDP Doesn't Add Up*, Stiglitz and his two co-authors reflect upon the use of measurements in people's everyday lives and underscore the limitations of economics that is constrained by a nation-state framework (Stiglitz et al. 2010). They argue that "the theories we construct, the hypotheses we test and the beliefs we have are all shaped by our system of metrics. Social scientists often blithely use easily accessible numbers, like GDP, as a basis of their empirical models, without enquiring sufficiently into the limitations and biases in their metrics. Flawed or biased statistics can lead us to make incorrect inferences" (Stiglitz et al. 2010: xix). Overall, the report's findings were that conventional GDP indicators are inadequate and a more holistic approach needs to be developed that includes "multiple metrics." This is particularly the case with respect to global issues such as the environment. According to the Commission, "When problems of globalization and environmental and resource sustainability are combined, GDP metrics may be essentially misleading" (Stiglitz et al. 2010: xxii; see Darian-Smith 2016; Hodgson 2001; Shionoya 2001).

Important contributions to scholarship that decenters the nation-state come from global historians who have been particularly important in problematizing the nation-state and forging new modes of inquiry that contextualize nations within intercontinental flows of ideas, cultures, resources, and movements of people (Hughes-Warrington 2005; Bentley 2013; Conrad 2016; Pernau and Sachsenmaier 2016). Together these scholars call for the removal of the "analytical shackles of 'methodological nationalism'" (Zürn 2013: 416). As practitioners in a relatively new subfield of inquiry, global historians reflect upon historiographical conventions and point to the limitations of national histories that have dominated the past two hundred years in the Euro-American academy. They are keen to explore how modes of cultural exchange and conceptual translation that flowed across state boundaries and plural cultures shaped events, including the very construction of nations and nationalist identities. So instead of taking the nation-state as a given and then making comparisons between them, global historians explore how nations developed over time as a product of transnational events, complex social relations, and geopolitical forces (e.g. Frühstück 2014; Goebel 2015).

METHODOLOGICAL IMPLICATIONS

Migration scholars Andreas Wimmer and Nina Glick Schiller wrote about the need to develop new concepts and approaches to better examine transnational and global processes:

> In order to escape the magnetism of established methodologies, ways of defining the object of analysis and algorithms for generating questions, we may have to develop (or rediscover?) analytical tools and concepts not colored by the self-evidence of a world ordering into nation-states. This is what we perceive, together with many other current observers of the social sciences, as the major task lying ahead of us. (Wimmer and Glick Schiller 2002: 324–5)

This task is taken up in the edited volume *Beyond Methodological Nationalism: Research Methodologies for Cross-Border Studies* (Amelina et al. 2012). Here a range of scholars from across the disciplines seek to move beyond a critique of the nation-state framework and explicitly engage with methodological issues in doing transnational research (Nowicka and Cieslik 2014). They ask a range of new questions such as: How does one design a research agenda and strategy that adequately enables empirical analysis of global processes? What is the appropriate context and spatial container of social, economic and political relations? How can one keep in sight the importance of inter/national relations without prioritizing these and excluding the vast assortment and assemblages of nonstate actors, institutions, relations and social and cultural translations operating across different historical times and different geopolitical spaces?

Developing new analytical tools and concepts is not an easy task, as all the contributors in *Beyond Methodological Nationalism* acknowledge. What unites their various approaches and concerns—be they exploring global cities, labor markets, indigenous movements, or migrant communities—is focusing research on the exploration of a specific site, group, or process. This is not to privilege or essentialize the "local" but to examine the specified "container" as a site through which multiple intersecting transnational processes are occurring concurrently and in fact shaping the container over time and the ways we recognize it as such. Particular care is given to see relations as fluid and integrated and not necessarily correlating to national territories or predetermined geopolitical social and political entities. Hence Nina Glick Schiller in her work on migrations to cities is keen to explore the city as a lens or portal through which immigrants embed transnationality in the places of people's everyday experiences. Her focus on the transnationality of cities sees local migrants as building new forms of alliance that may resist and shape urban restructuring, link migrant labor with local labor, and possibly contribute to global struggles for social justice. Writes Glick Schiller, "These struggles will be both site-specific and able to critique a world of global disparities in wealth and power. Solidarities and alliances can be built that are simultaneously spatial and global" (Glick Schiller 2012: 36).

CONTRIBUTIONS TO GLOBAL STUDIES

Transcending the conceptual and analytical limitations of methodological nationalism has important implications for global research design. In global studies, it is not sufficient to simply compare one set of national data with another set of national data, as if all that is going on is a simple correlation between two monolithic entities. One can compare two countries in one's research project. However, the concept of the nation-state should not be taken as a given or used in such a way that it excludes nonstate actors. A global methodological strategy should open up analytical space for transnational processes as well as translocal voices that participate in global processes and in shaping and making meaningful the nation-state framework in the first place. An excellent example of this type of nation-state comparison is Paul Amar's *The Security Archipelago*, which we summarize in Chapter 7.

Transcending methodological nationalism also implies that global scholars should pay attention to the experiences of people that are displaced by political and economic forces or are marginalized within the nation-state framework. The flows of migrants, refugees, and circulating diasporic communities complicate notions of modern identity and make static and territorialized forms of citizenship increasingly problematic (Cheah and Robbins 1998; Fangen, Johansson, and Hammarén 2012). Global scholars should be sensitive to the limitations of methodological nationalism and work to overcome its conceptual, theoretical, analytical, and methodological constraints. However, this is not an easy task given the dominant state-centered thinking that still prevails in the Euro-American academy.

Feminist Methodologies

GENERAL DESCRIPTION

Many books have been written about the rise of women's studies in the 1960s and 1970s as a new field of interdisciplinary scholarship (e.g., Smith 2013). Around the world, in Canada, the United Kingdom, India, the United States, and elsewhere, individual scholars started exploring women's history, economics, literature, and psychology and the ways in which women were affected by different forms of discrimination. As we discussed in Chapter 1, in the US women's studies developed alongside ethnic studies programs in black studies, Chicano/a studies, and Asian American studies, as well as area studies programs in African studies, Latin American studies, Asian studies, East Asian studies, European studies, and Pacific studies.

There is a large body of literature exploring the theoretical and methodological frameworks used in feminist scholarship (e.g., Harding 1987; Ramazanoğlu and Holland 2002; Naples 2003; Tong 2014). We are not about to reproduce these discussions here, but do note that the changes associated with first-, second-, and third-wave feminism together highlight differences and debates in feminist scholarship around the world. These waves of feminist thought and activism also underscore the field's dynamic and evolving agendas and theories. These dynamics are to some degree reflected in the transition from women's studies programs to feminist and gender and sexuality studies programs in many institutions in recent years. Across varieties of feminist scholarship, critical feminist methodologies highlight the asymmetrical power relations between genders and the systemic patriarchy that is in play in much of the world, including in the United States and other so-called democratic societies.

METHODOLOGICAL IMPLICATIONS

Feminist methodologies present an explicit challenge to conventional ways of analyzing social relations. They expose power dynamics and enduring mechanisms of oppression and discrimination, particularly as these pertain to women's lives and experiences. In her introduction to the groundbreaking book *Feminism and Methodology* (1987), Sandra Harding, an eminent philosopher of feminist and postcolonial theory, identified a number of distinctive methodological features of feminist research at the time. These included the role of women's experiences in research and knowledge production; designing research agendas expressly for women, rather than by men operating on behalf of women; and locating the researcher on the same critical plane as the subject to avoid the supposed objectivism of those who claim to be scientists. With respect to the first of these features, Harding argued that women's experiences offered a new theoretical and empirical resource for rethinking who gets to speak for whom and what power dynamics are in play in this process of representation. Harding was keen to emphasize that there is no singular woman's experience, arguing that "Masculine and feminine are always categories within every class, race and culture in the sense that women's and men's experiences, desires, and interests differ within every class, race and culture" (Harding 1987: 7).

Harding's focus on women's experiences drew on second-wave feminist Dorothy Smith's earlier concept of *standpoint theory*, which Smith outlined in *Feminism and Marxism* (1977). Standpoint theory argues that knowledge is based in experience. And since women have very different experiences from men, they also have different knowledge, and sometimes very different truths. For example, men rarely register experiences of male privilege. As a result male-based forms of knowledge and authority typically do not recognize male privilege as an issue. For most men the problem does not seem urgent or pressing. But for women the experience of male privilege can be a pervasive daily reality. They may experience male privilege in their homes, workplace, with shocking frequency in the media, and nearly every social interaction involving men. Standpoint theory makes it clear that men and women are not capable of fully understanding each other's experiences, and as a result they cannot fully represent each other, be it in the operation of government, implementation of policy, adjudication of law, education, or the production of knowledge. From this perspective, functional representation can only be achieved with the full participation of women in the democratic process, in positions of power and decision making.

Feminism's call for participatory representation resonates with other groups organized around experiences of disempowerment. Standpoint theory has since contributed to the development of race, class, queer, disability, and postcolonial theories in several very important ways. Racialized others, marginalized others, indigenous peoples, LGBTI communities, the disabled, children, the elderly, and so on, have their own unique standpoints, and must also have a seat at the table in order to achieve full participation in political, economic, and social life.

The resonance of feminist standpoint theory with other marginalized groups led legal scholar Kimberlé Crenshaw and sociologist Patricia Hill Collins to develop what is known as *intersectional theory*. Drawing on the concerns for diversity within third-wave feminism, Crenshaw and Collins combined feminist standpoint theory with critical race theory to elaborate the notion of *intersectionality*. Collins argued that the structures of domination and discrimination that put women, racial and ethnic minorities, and poor people at a disadvantage are not mutually exclusive, but rather overlapping and in many ways cumulative (Collins 1990; Crenshaw 1991; Butler 1990). This approach saw a poor black woman as being cumulatively disadvantaged by her class, race, and gender. The position of a black woman in society, intersectional theory contends, is *overdetermined* by multiple structures of domination—what Collins calls a "matrix of domination."

Patricia Hill Collins's theorization of intersectionality centered on women in developed Western countries (Collins 1990; Collins and Bilge 2016; Hancock 2016). It and other early elaborations of intersectionality did not take into account global and postcolonial contexts and the disadvantaged statuses of the global south citizen, indigenous person, religious minority, immigrant, refugee, or asylum seeker. As Bonnie Smith argues, "One thing that [economic interconnections and rapid communication of knowledge] revealed was the vast array of differences among women depending on where they lived in the world. The experiences of women were shaped by global differences and shared commonalities as never before. These connections—often unequal, at other times shared—have become central issues in Women's Studies" (Smith 2013: 60). Feminism has come a long way from first-wave to global women's movements.

CONTRIBUTIONS TO GLOBAL STUDIES

The overlapping agendas of feminist studies and global studies are considerable (McCann and Kim 2013). For instance, the impact of multinational corporations and global capitalism on women in the labor force has emerged as a huge issue in contemporary feminist scholarship. A related concern revolves around women's participation in mass migrations and global diasporic networks in search of opportunity—work, freedom, security. A third, also related concern is that of human rights as a global discourse mobilized in defense of women against violence (Merry 2006). And of course global poverty and political disenfranchisement disproportionately affect women and children in many part of the world. Women's poverty has become a prominent rationale for the World Bank and other agencies and NGOs to impose development policies and promote intervention in the global south on behalf of so-called victimized women. The important role that women play in issues such as literacy, education, health, human rights, conflict, social and economic development and our need to understand how the women involved understand these same issues underscore the significance of feminist methodologies for global studies scholarship.

Over the past decade, scholars have begun to use the concept of intersectionality that black feminists in the United States first developed in a wide range of global contexts (Bose 2012; Chow et al. 2011; Purkayastha 2012; Sen and Durano 2014). In her recent publication Patricia Hill Collins acknowledges that intersectionality has been adopted and adapted by activists around the world (Collins and Bilge 2016). As the concept moves into global analysis and informs a methodology by which to engage with larger processes of structural inequality and discrimination, it takes on new analytical force and significance. Moving beyond the horizons of the individual to encompass groups, movements, and transnational networks, intersectionality can be flexibly adapted across space and time. A more global intersectional theory implies that the disadvantages of millions of women are overdetermined not only by their gender, race, and class statuses, but also by their postcolonial, native, immigrant, and refugee statuses (Wing 2000). Compounded, intersectional modes of oppression are intertwined with deep global histories and institutions of colonialism, imperialism, racism, and contested power relations (Grewal and Kaplan 1994; Brah and Phoenix 2004). A theory that takes into account these temporal and spatial dimensions of women's subjectivities and disadvantages is an important conceptual and methodological tool for global studies. A global understanding of intersectionality spotlights the complex connections between such phenomena as gender, labor, and the environment and women's movements, ethnic movements, and indigenous movements. It opens up a whole new field that links the literatures, research topics, and mutually constitutive perspectives surrounding them.

Standpoint theory is as important to global studies as a global understanding of intersectionality (Harding 2004; Hartsock 1999). It underscores that there are many different perspectives and subject positions in whatever topic a researcher is examining, and that these standpoints represent variations in people's ways of knowing and experiencing the world. This has important ethical implications (see "Ethical Dimensions of Global Research," Chapter 4). Think of a woman in a refugee camp. She is probably as intersectionally disadvantaged as anyone else in the world. This does not mean her perspective is of lesser value or can be dismissed, as much Euro-American scholarship is apt to do. Global studies as a field of inquiry seeks not to essentialize or reify the subjectivity of this woman refugee, or of any other woman. Rather, global studies aims to valorize the woman's perspective as constitutively important in any analysis of refugee law, refugee aid, and refugee experiences and practices. The field provides an inclusive and receptive platform for women's voices and experiences to be heard the way they themselves want them to be heard. Global studies legitimates women's perspectives, recognizing their due weight and authority in constructing new knowledge about the world's pressing challenges.

Critical Race Methodologies
GENERAL DESCRIPTION

Theories of race and racism have been a central plank in the canon of modern social theory. Building on the work of influential thinkers such as W. E. B. Du Bois, C. L. R. James, Eric Williams, Frantz Fanon, Edward Said, and Stuart Hall (see Chapter 3), contemporary critical scholars have had a growing concern with the racialized structures and institutions that have defined and shaped differentiations between First and Third Worlds and global south and global north. Scholars such as Cedric Robinson, Paul Gilroy, and Howard Winant have highlighted global structural formations of racism and their deep legacies in slavery and former periods (Robinson (1983) 2000; Gilroy 1993; Winant 2004).

Critical race methodologies are often associated with specific groups of scholars from across the social sciences and humanities, in fields such as black studies, postcolonial studies, and critical race theory. In its original formulation, critical race theory emerged within American law schools to focus on the intersections of law, power, and racial discrimination and bias that informed structural inequalities in society (Matsuda 1987; Crenshaw 1988; Williams 1992; Delgado and Stefancic 1993, 1998, 2001; Harris 1993; Crenshaw et al. 1995). One of its earliest proponents was Derrick Bell, a professor at Harvard Law School, who wrote:

> Critical race theory writing and lecturing is characterized by frequent use of the first person, storytelling, narrative, allegory, interdisciplinary treatment of law, and the unapologetic use of creativity. The work is often disruptive because its commitment to anti-racism goes well beyond civil rights, integration, affirmative action, and other liberal measures. This is not to say that critical theory adherents automatically or uniformly "trash" liberal ideology or method (as many adherents of critical legal studies do). Rather, they are highly suspicious of the liberal agenda, distrust method, and want to retain what they see as a valuable strain of egalitarianism which may exist despite, and not because, of liberalism. (Bell 1995: 899)

Bell was well known for championing the use of stories to draw attention to alternative views and the experiences of ordinary people. He argued that storytelling by people who were often marginalized and silenced in conventional scholarship was essential for opening up the academy to new interpretations and "expressing views that cannot be communicated effectively through existing techniques" (1995: 902). As he went on to explain, "I prefer using stories as a means of communicating views to those who hold very different views on the emotionally charged subject of race. People enjoy stories and will often suspend their beliefs, listen to the story, and then compare their views, not with mine, but with those expressed in the story" (1995: 902; see also Williams 1992).

As with gender issues, experience plays a key role in how issues of race are understood. For example, whites very rarely register the experience of white privilege. Over the centuries the abolition and anti-apartheid movements have shown that white forms of knowledge and power actively deny that racism and white privilege are an issue. In the United States, despite the long and bloody history of slavery, civil war, segregation, and ongoing racial discrimination, many whites today still deny that white privilege exists. Nonetheless, for people of color the fact of white privilege is a daily experience. They see it in government, the economy, healthcare, in their neighborhoods and schools, and all too frequently in the news. It is part of their everyday reality. The experience could hardly be more real.

METHODOLOGICAL IMPLICATIONS

Critical race methodologies typically take a bottom-up, grounded approach, often presenting stories and narratives that give voice to marginalized peoples, particularly people of color. Storytelling is often associated with first-person novels, interviews, and other creative formats such as autobiographies. But it also includes retelling third-person stories and narratives, as well as narratives that draw on various forms of "data" "to create composite characters and place them in social, historical, and political situations to discuss racism, sexism, classism, and other forms of subordination" (Solórzano and Yosso 2002: 33). For critical race scholars, all scholarship is composed of stories in the sense that no analysis is entirely objective. Mainstream scholarship legitimates master narratives that present politically neutral analyses removed from cultural contexts, structural oppression, and historical memory. Hence the main objective of critical race scholars is to promote counter-storytelling as a form of resistance and empowerment.

The expanding authority and applicability of critical race scholarship, and its intersections with class, gender, sexuality, ethnicity, religion, and so on, is evident in its expansion well beyond law schools setting and its significant impact across the humanities and social sciences in North America (Essed and Goldberg 2001; Parker and Lynn 2002; Omi and Winant 2015). It has helped nurture a range of submovements, such as critical race feminism (Wing 2000), Latino critical race studies (LatCrit) (Bernal 2002; Delgado and Stefancic 1998), Asian American critical race studies (AsianCrit) (Chang 1993), South Asian American critical race studies

(DesiCrit) (Harpalani 2013), and American Indian critical race studies (TribalCrit) (Brayboy 2005). Critical race methodologies use "the transdisciplinary knowledge and methodological base of ethnic studies, women's studies, sociology, history, law, and other fields to guide research that better understands the effects of racism, sexism and classism on people of color" (Solórzano and Yosso 2002: 27). As critical race scholars note, "This is important to the research process because it offers the critical-race researcher an array of research methodologies to consider, especially those methodologies that have developed in an attempt to capture and understand the experiences of marginalized communities better than more traditional research methods" (Malagon, Pérez Huber, and Vélez 2009: 254).

CONTRIBUTIONS TO GLOBAL STUDIES

The overlay between global studies and critical race scholarship—as with global studies and feminist studies scholarship—is considerable (Wing 2000). The broad structural implications of theories of racism and racialization is slowly expanding beyond the borders of the North American academy, and its unique theoretical and methodological contributions are contributing to a worldwide scholarly appreciation of the deeply embedded racial dimensions of social organization. Critical race methodologies offer global studies a range of approaches to complex contemporary problems such as the worldwide phenomenon of Islamophobia and the accompanying rise of right-wing politics, terrorism, and religious conflict in many regions of the world. Deep histories of colonialism and imperialism over hundreds of years have created new lines of cultural differentiation in what some scholars, referencing the earlier work of Du Bois, call a "global color line" (Winant 2004; Silva 2007; Lake and Reynolds 2008). Where it includes the standpoints and perspectives of minorities, global studies provides an inclusive and receptive platform for the voices of racialized peoples and for understanding the racialized structures of the current world order.

Postcolonial Methodologies

GENERAL DESCRIPTION

Critical postcolonial methodologies highlight individual and collective experiences in contexts of historical and enduring colonialism and

contemporary imperialism (Lezra 2014). The origins of European colonialism can be traced back before Columbus to the year 1095 when Pope
Urban II issued a papal decree titled *terra nullius*, a phrase meaning
"nobody's land." In the process of providing a legal framework for the First
Crusade (1095–1099), the pope declared all non-Christian lands to be
effectively uninhabited under Roman law. This authorized Christian
European states to occupy and own lands inhabited by non-Christians. In
that moment the non-Christian populations of the world were effectively
dehumanized, and their rights to life, property, and self-determination
were summarily suspended.

Not coincidentally, it is from that moment on that the European powers began to expand and take colonies. Over the course of the crusades
Europeans captured the "Holy Land" and parts of the Mediterranean.
After the Fall of Constantinople in 1453, the Portuguese began seeking
new trade routes to the east and so began the "Age of Discovery." Europeans
began colonizing parts of North Africa and islands in the Atlantic. In
1493, shortly after Columbus discovered the Americas on behalf of Spain,
Pope Alexander VI assigned all lands in the east to Portugal and all the
newly discovered lands in the west to Spain. For the next four hundred
years the Portuguese, Spanish, Dutch, English, and other European powers would go on to colonize the rest of the world.

For more than five hundred years the European colonial powers used
ideologies of cultural and racial superiority to justify the conquest, annihi-
lation, subjugation, enslavement, and exploitation of colonial peoples.
Colonial subjects, who would eventually come to include the majority of
the world's population, were in almost all cases treated as inferior and
denied the basic rights of citizenship.

Following a period of rapid decolonization in the mid-twentieth century, many former colonies gained political independence. However,
former colonies were quickly lumped together as the "Third World" and
marginalized in world affairs by leading Western nations. Today, many of
the former colonies continue to experience new forms of structural domination, neoimperialism, and racial tension wrought by modernization,
industrialization, and development. Organizations such as the World
Bank and WTO have furthered the impacts of economic globalization
and exploitation through practices such as structural adjustment, and

through international policies associated with the War on Drugs and the War on Terror. In the twenty-first century, the postcolonial majority still struggle to be recognized, to be treated as equals. Their labor and natural resources are siphoned off to support the "First World," but more than fifty years after decolonization they have yet to participate as equals in that world.

Postcolonial studies is largely associated with rethinking the dominant European historiography that places the West at the center of the world. It posits a plurality of cultural perspectives that challenge the idea that Europeans are a superior culture because of their Christian values and scientific rationality. Associated with South Asian scholarship, subaltern studies, and literary studies, as well as with analyses of resistance, postcolonial studies emerged from the global south in the 1980s and thereafter gained an increasing presence in Anglo-European universities (Prakash 1990, 1992; Chakrabarty 1992; O'Hanlon and Washbrook 1992). There has been much debate over the meaning and scope of postcolonial studies' terminology and political agenda with the proliferation of postcolonial research (Williams and Chrisman 1994; Schwarz and Ray 2000). Despite these ongoing deliberations, it is helpful to turn to the most significant implications of a postcolonial perspective—those that mark it as distinct from yet complementary to other critical methodologies, including feminist, critical race, and indigenous approaches.

Postcolonial theory emphasizes the ongoing significance of colonized peoples in shaping the epistemologies, philosophies, practices, and shifting identities of dominant and taken-for-granted Western subjects and subjectivities (Santos 2007). Postcolonial scholars foreground the cultural and psychological relations between the formerly colonized and former colonizers, who, they argue, cannot be understood except in conjunction with each other (Gandhi 1998). Postcolonial scholars acknowledge that colonialism was experienced differently under different regimes. Nonetheless, while paying attention to specific contexts, it is important to remain aware of the enduring presence of macro discourses that posit "civilized," "progressive," and "lawful" Europeans against "barbaric," "static," and "lawless" native populations. So even though the experiences of former colonial subjects are unique, they share a common experience of colonial and ongoing neoimperial domination.

Today, postcolonial scholarship is more widely recognized than ever before (Darian-Smith 1996, 2013b; Comaroff and Comaroff 2006; Mongia 1996; Dann and Hanschmann 2012). The terms of the conversation, however, have shifted to apply to current geopolitical realities. Early postcolonial scholars focused on the relationships between colonizing nations and colonized peoples, framing these in the binary language of Western/non-Western. In contrast, contemporary scholars have shifted from examining specific national colonial enterprises to a more global, post-Westphalian worldview that takes into account transnational, regional, state, and local historical, economic, and cultural processes (Loomba et al. 2005).

This shift in postcolonial scholars' lens is important in that it opens up the conversation to include the oppression of all communities that historically have been treated as racially and ethnically inferior to the dominant members of a colonizing society, whether or not these communities self-identify as having been colonized. This shift also acknowledges new forms of colonialism, such as the colonizing of East Timor by Indonesia and Eritrea by Ethiopia, and the occupation of Palestinian territories by Israel (see Weldemichael 2012). And it takes into account neocolonial activities by Western nations that continue to exert economic and political power or "soft imperialism" over their former colonies (Nkrumah 1966). Importantly, today's neocolonial activities also include the soft imperialism of non-Europeans, such as China's pursuit of natural resources in Africa, and "new wars" in regions such as the Congo that allow for an economy of extraction and exploitation by foreign capitalists over local communities, often in collusion with local elites (Kaldor 2006; Ferguson 2006).

METHODOLOGICAL IMPLICATIONS

Postcolonial methodologies challenge mainstream social science and humanistic scholarship in the Euro-American academy by focusing on issues of power, race, and oppression. Postcolonial scholars are keen to interrogate the power relations between people and demonstrate how these concepts have been used historically to marginalize and disempower certain individuals and communities. They specifically set out to critique Western discourses of modernity and the imposition of concepts such as time, progress, and development that privilege specific forms of knowledge and agendas yet are deemed universally applicable (Escobar 1995; Ogle 2015).

In implementing these objectives, postcolonial methodologies "utilize social, cultural, and political analysis to engage with the colonial discourse" and include "voices, stories, histories, and images from people traditionally excluded from European/Western descriptions of the world" (Bauchspies 2007: 2981). In exploring transnational historical and political processes and then connecting these processes to people on the ground, postcolonial scholars work within frameworks that are not necessarily contained by nation-states and that transcend a conventional international relations paradigm (Amelina et al. 2012, Chapters 8 and 10).

CONTRIBUTIONS TO GLOBAL STUDIES

The methodological implications of postcolonial studies for global studies are considerable. Similar to critical feminist, race, and indigenous methodologies, postcolonial methodologies stress the standpoint and perspectives of people typically ignored in Western scholarship. In short, there is a great deal of overlap between these critical approaches. However, postcolonial studies adds a deep historical dimension and a focus on the structural power relations between the global south and global north that continue to play out in today's global political economy and culture wars. These asymmetrical power relations between countries and cultures inform contemporary global issues such as mass migration, terrorism and security, and the disproportionate impacts of climate change on vulnerable populations.

Indigenous Methodologies

GENERAL DESCRIPTION

Indigenous peoples around the world constitute approximately 350 million people who represent a vast array of cultural and linguistic traditions. The cultures and histories of the indigenous peoples of the world are long, complex, and unique. At the same time many indigenous peoples share experiences of colonialism, imperialism, exclusion, systemic marginalization, and genocide.

While indigenous peoples are often lumped into the category of "minorities," many indigenous peoples argue against this classification on the basis that their societies existed in places around the world well before colonialism and imperialism. The modern European colonial powers introduced the concept of the modern liberal state, which in turn created the categories of national citizens, colonials, majorities, and minorities. While "minorities" are considered part of modern society, many indigenous peoples were pushed to the margins, relocated or otherwise excluded from modern society altogether.

For many indigenous peoples the conquest and colonization of the world was experienced as genocide or assimilation. They were infected with new diseases, forced to convert to Christianity, and those that survived were often enslaved or relocated to reservations on marginal lands. Those that tried to remain free—fighting to resist slavery and protect families, lands, cultures, beliefs, and languages—were ultimately annihilated by colonial powers. Millions of men, women, and children were slaughtered and entire regions were depopulated and unique cultures wiped out. In many cases there is barely a historical record to mark their passing. Thus depopulated, indigenous lands could then be repopulated with settlers, as well as slaves and colonial laborers that were often taken from other regions of the world.

For many indigenous people the genocide that began with conquest and colonialism continues to this day in that many remain politically, economically, and socially invisible (Moore 2003). Some have no citizenship or are classified as second-class citizens, without constitutional protections or legal recourse. National policies of "assimilation," "re-education," and "retraining" are often explicitly designed to bring about the end of indigenous cultures, languages, and ways of life. Many still do not have access to health care, education, or employment. In addition, many indigenous peoples are now beset by a range of globally oriented issues related to increasing economic inequality, deforestation, mining and resource grabbing, and the cumulative impacts of climate change. In short, many are still struggling to be rehumanized, and to regain fundamental human rights to life, property, and self-determination that were taken from them. They still struggle to be respected, to be recognized as citizens of the world, to retain their cultural identities and beliefs, without being converted to someone else's religion and without being forced to assimilate into the modernist, nationalist, capitalist, and consumerist ideologies that people living in the global north often take for granted.

METHODOLOGICAL IMPLICATIONS

Indigenous scholarly communities are developing a broad spectrum of projects and methods around what can generally be labeled an *indigenous research agenda* (Chilisa 2011; Lambert 2014). This research agenda has emerged from a wider global indigenous peoples' movement that seeks change through decolonization and demands a role in the production of new forms of knowledge (Mutua and Swadener 2011). The agenda expressly recognizes concepts, causal logics, and nonlinear time frames that may be unfamiliar to Western scholars. It may also draw on unconventional forms of texts and aesthetics, such as songs, aural traditions, symbols, and rituals that often play an important role in indigenous communities (Allen 2012).

Very simply, an indigenous research agenda is research conducted by and for indigenous peoples "using techniques and methods drawn from the tradition and knowledge of those people" (Evans et al. 2009: 897). Writing from her perspective as a Maori woman living in New Zealand, Linda Tuhiwai Smith characterizes an indigenous research agenda in terms of the ebb and flow of tides. She draws this tidal metaphor from Pacific peoples, who rely so heavily on the ocean (fig. 10):

> Although there are many directions that can be named, the chart takes the Maori equivalent of the four directions: the northern, the eastern, the southern and the western. The tides represent movement, change, process, life, inward and outward flow of ideas, reflections and actions. The four directions named here—decolonization, healing, transformation and mobilization—represent processes. They are not goals or ends in themselves. They are processes which connect, inform and clarify the tensions between the local, the regional and the global. They are processes which can be incorporated into practices and methodologies. (Smith 2012: 120)

Differences between scholarship produced by indigenous researchers and scholarship produced by nonindigenous researchers is particularly pronounced in the British settler colonial societies of Canada, Australia, New Zealand, South Africa, and India and in the United States (Cavanagh and Veracini 2013). Indigenous scholarship is also produced by native scholars in postcolonial settings within the African continent, the Middle East region, and the wider Asian geopolitical region.

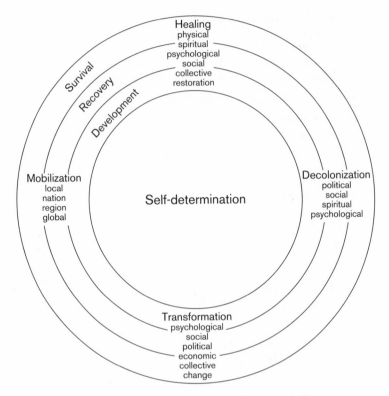

Figure 10. The Indigenous Research Agenda in Linda Tuhiwai Smith's
Decolonizing Methodologies: Research and Indigenous Peoples (2012).

Decolonizing methodologies find a ready audience among indigenous
scholars, and increasingly nonindigenous scholars are taking them seriously as well. As Norman K. Denzin and Yvonna S. Lincoln note in the
preface to *Handbook of Critical and Indigenous Methodologies*:

> We believe that over the past quarter century, a significant number of indig-
> enous and nonindigenous scholars have moved into the spaces we attempt
> to chart in this handbook. These scholars are from a host of different nations
> and disciplines, from health care to business, organization studies, advertis-
> ing and consumer research, education, communications, social work, sociol-
> ogy, anthropology, psychology, performance studies, and drama. They are
> committed to using qualitative research methods for social justice purposes.
> (Denzin and Lincoln 2008: xii–xiii)

As an increasing, albeit small, number of indigenous scholars are securing jobs in universities, and demanding "a seat at the table" through their teaching and research, their decolonizing perspectives have gained traction among mainstream scholars who find it more and more difficult to entirely ignore or avoid them (Clifford 2013). The embracing of indigenous methodologies can be understood as an ethical response by nonindigenous scholars that recognizes the equal dignity and authority of non-Western knowledge and practices. But more and more it is also a pragmatic response to dealing with social issues that may not easily correlate to nonindigenous experiences. For instance, the Center for Population Health Research at the University of South Australia is conducting an extensive study of the role of environmental factors in cardiometabolic health in remote Australian Aboriginal communities.[1] The center focuses on the wider contexts in which people live and that ultimately impact their consciousness and capacities to practice better health behaviors. Understanding how indigenous peoples engage with and experience their environment—as either one of enduring colonial oppression or one of self-determined spaces of community investment—translates into better lifestyle options and practices.

CONTRIBUTIONS TO GLOBAL STUDIES

Indigenous methodologies are making significant interventions in the Euro-American academy. Indigenous analyses are sensitive to the global dimensions of indigenous people's historical oppression, rightly viewing colonialism as a global phenomenon of land grabbing and resource extraction that is not limited to the specific context or framing of any one nation-state. There is a growing movement within indigenous studies to "read the

1. Environments and Remote Indigenous Cardiometabolic Health (EnRICH) Project, 2012 http://www.unisa.edu.au/Research/Sansom-Institute-for-Health-Research/Research /CPHR/Spatial-Epidemiology-and-Evaluation/EnRICH/ (accessed January 31, 2016). This kind of study learns from indigenous methodologies and seeks to incorporate some of those insights into its own methodology. Its approach includes stakeholder engagement and community mapping throughout the life of the project, which in turn build regular feedback and flexible data collection methods into the project's implementation. In this way, the center's research objectives are in part shaped and determined by the subjects of the study itself. It is hoped that this methodological approach will produce more effective public health and policy initiatives that will ultimately better serve indigenous communities (see also West, Stewart, Foster, and Usher 2012; Hole 2015).

global *through* the local" and in the process challenge dominant political
theories and resist "a geography that flows from dreams of imperial domination" (Magnusson and Shaw 2003: viii). Moreover, indigenous methodologies are opening up the Euro-American academy to non-Western
knowledge and indigenous peoples' experiences. Global studies scholars
should be particularly sensitive to indigenous perspectives given longstanding histories of oppression and violence that underscore centuries-
long waves of global imperialism and capitalist colonial expansion. We
hope that indigenous methodologies will become more widely embraced
within global studies in the coming decades.

GLOBAL METHODOLOGICAL STRATEGIES

At the core of the emerging field of global studies is an explicit attempt to
engage a wide range of cultural, racial, political, economic, and social
issues that inform our world and everyone's place in it (see Chapter 2).
Critical methodologies based in the experiences of marginalized peoples
can provide global scholars with new ways of understanding people and
the issues they face. By engaging with women's social movements, issues,
and standpoints; by recognizing the racialized structures of the geopolitical order; by being sensitive to long histories and legacies of colonialism
and enduring forms of imperialism; and by embracing indigenous viewpoints and alternative ways of understanding, global scholars have the
potential to engage with processes of marginalization and postcoloniality
that are still going on—albeit under new guises. This deeply intersectional
approach offers global scholars the opportunity to advance a more profound and critical understanding of globalization and global issues that
are often couched in value-free economic determinism, superficial analyses of political power, and parochial interpretations of global social
organization.

Global studies owes an enormous debt to all critical methodologies; it
is hard to imagine its emergence without them. Critical methodologies
such as the feminist, race, postcolonial, and indigenous methodologies we
discussed in this chapter highlight the need to accommodate bottom-up
perspectives, pay attention to multiple relational histories, valorize situ-

ated identities, conceptually transcend the nation-state paradigm, and think in terms of power and who is acting on behalf of and upon whom. Perhaps most important of all, critical methodologies underscore the necessity to acknowledge, appreciate, and learn from the plural ways in which individuals and communities know, conceptualize, understand, and narrate their experiences and subjectivities. As indigenous studies scholar Margaret Kovach, a member of Pasqua First Nation located in southern Saskatchewan, reminds us, "We know what we know from where we stand. We need to be honest about that" (Kovach 2009: 7).

We argue that one of the most profound contributions of a global studies methodology is that it fosters a *global standpoint theory* that is *deeply intersectional*. Global studies recognizes that everyone has a different standpoint, so it advances cross-cultural interpretations, hybrid subjectivities, cosmopolitanism, and plural ways of knowing and being in the world that should not be ignored or discounted. Global studies recognizes that institutions and organizations such as the UN and the World Bank present certain perspectives that must be taken into account, as should those of social movements such as the antinuclear movement or labor movements. In short, what makes a methodological strategy global is working across, within, and among plural epistemologies and standpoints to understand a problem or issue from multiple perspectives. The standpoint of a dark-skinned Muslim woman in a refugee camp highlights the limitations of the standpoints of privileged scholars from the global north trying to understand her situation. Appreciating that limitation goes to the heart of what makes global studies unique and important. It does not mean that the researcher has to address all perspectives on every issue—that would be impossible. But it does mean that the researcher has to recognize that other standpoints exist, that they are important and of value, and that their very existence highlights the inadequacies and limitations of analyses that present only the researcher's point of view. It is that simple.

Global studies scholars have a great deal to learn from those who use critical methodological approaches (see Sandoval 2000). Listening and learning from communities of scholars and sectors of society that are typically not well represented within the academy opens up opportunities to create new research methodologies, new data collection methods, and new ways to theoretically and conceptually frame intellectual inquiries that deal with the complexities of our current world. Critical methodological approaches underscore three essential points that global studies scholars should take very seriously:

1. Methodology, just like the many theories that inform it, represents a dynamic process. Methodologies are not static strategies of inquiry but rather are constantly evolving to address new research questions and new agendas.

2. Critical methodologies seek to reframe our conceptual and analytical scaffoldings so as to incorporate new perspectives, epistemologies, issues, conversations, voices, collaborations, and contexts. The flexible and largely problem-driven approaches of most critical methodological strategies expressly engage with issues of social justice and as a result are highly relevant to a great deal of global scholarship.

3. All methodological strategies are political, whether this is openly acknowledged or not by individual scholars or academic disciplines, and they tend to be deeply interwoven with ethical choices and moral positions. For instance, a scholar who deliberately adopts a critical race methodology is, through that choice, consciously attempting to open up scholarly engagement beyond conventional understandings that may have—often inadvertently—marginalized analyses of racism. In a similar way, claiming that one's research methodology is apolitical or objective fails to take into account long histories of European imperial dominance that have positioned the global north as the authoritative center of the world's knowledge production, a position that in turn sustains claims of European thought's universal applicability.

Of course, critical methodologies, like critical social theories, are not essential to all forms of global studies research. As we stated at the beginning of this chapter, in global studies all methods are available, as are all methodological strategies. Whether you choose to use qualitative, quantitative, or mixed methods, or whether you choose to adopt a conventional or a more critical methodological strategy, is entirely up to you. The methods you choose will depend on the nature of the project, the type of data needed to answer the research question, the context of the study, and the availability of resources.

That being said, as a field of inquiry global studies provides a platform for multiple critical methodologies to be used concurrently. And critical methodologies can provide us with important building blocks upon which to build more inclusive global studies scholarship. In embracing the insights of critical methodologies to better understand real-world social justice issues from multiple perspectives and subject positions, the hope is that global scholars will be able to speak across academic disciplines as well as to Western and non-Western scholars in the global south and global north. Embracing critical methodologies also suggests that global scholars will be better equipped to speak beyond the academy and communicate with audiences that may include health organizations, law and policy makers, civil society associations, community groups, teachers, doctors, psychologists, urban planners, union organizers, capitalists, politicians, and a wide range of state and nonstate agencies across a broad swath of local, regional, national, transnational, and global sectors.

In the next chapter, we bring together discussions about research design (Chapter 4) and research methods and methodologies (Chapter 5) to explore the advantages of adopting a multidimensional case study approach (Chapter 6). This approach offers an expedient way to cumulatively incorporate all of our discussions so far about the components of a viable global studies research project. The multidimensional case study approach has been proven to be successful with our junior students as well as with our senior colleagues. Articulating what exactly a multidimensional case study is offers a practical way forward and answers the central question with which we began this book: As an individual researcher, how do you begin the formidable task of doing global research?

6 A Global Case Study Method

In this chapter we outline a case study research method for global studies. The case study method is not new, but the synthesis we offer here adapts the approach to the study of complex global contexts and the degree of theoretical and methodological flexibility that, we have argued, they require. Our experience has shown that the synthesis outlined here is accessible and flexible in a way that makes it useful for new students and experienced researchers. We are not arguing that this is the only way to do global research. There are clearly many different methodologies that can be used to study global issues (see Chapter 5). Our point is simply that the approach detailed here has proven to be effective for researchers at very different skill levels, and with limited time and resources, to carry out global studies research.

As earlier chapters in this book have noted, global studies presents a series of daunting methodological challenges. In Chapters 1 and 2 we argued that global-scale issues are complex and interconnected and have many intersecting dimensions that play out across geopolitical boundaries, as well as up and down a local-global spatial continuum. In Chapter 3 we argued that the interdisciplinary theoretical and analytical frameworks that can be used to analyze global-scale issues must be equally varied and complex, drawing from across the social sciences and humanities and from scholars in the global south and global north. In Chapter 4 we discussed the value of developing a global studies research question and implementing an appropriate research design. In Chapter 5 we argued that global-scale issues often call for multimethodological strategies that are capable of addressing multifaceted issues from numerous perspectives at different points on the local-global continuum. At first glance, these collective demands make the methodological challenges of global studies research appear daunting indeed.

Fortunately, we have found that conducting global research does not have to be that complicated. There are contained and feasible approaches to global issues. The global case study is one possible methodological synthesis that can simplify the process. Before we discuss the global case study, however, it may help to briefly review the conventional case study method.

THE CASE STUDY METHOD

The case study research method should not be confused with the case method that is often used in teaching (see Lynn 1998; Andersen and Schiano 2014). The case study method we discuss here is a research method along with surveys, statistical modeling, and experimental and historical comparative research.

The modern case study approach developed out of the physical and medical sciences in the 1800s. One of the more famous examples is Jean Itard's study of the "Wild Boy of Aveyron," who was found living in the woods of France in 1798 (Itard 1802). Another example is Dr. John M. Harlow's medical study of Phineas Gage, a man whose behavior changed dramatically after an accident in which a large iron rod passed right through his skull (Harlow 1848). By the 1830s the method was being adapted for the social sciences, as evidenced by Frédéric Le Play's *Les Ouvriers Européens*, a series of thirty-six monographs featuring typical household budgets of working families across Europe (Le Play [1855] 1878). By the 1900s the case study was in wide use as a distinct research method (Mills, Eurepos, and Wiebe 2010: xxxi).

Both Sigmund Freud and Jean Piaget used and helped further define the case study method. Freud used case research to explore the histories and symptoms of his patients. Drawing upon material from these cases, he elaborated his now famous theories about the structure and function of intangible human psyche. Many aspects of Freud's theories have been criticized, but the case study method that he used allowed him to develop basic vocabulary and analytical concepts that are still influential in the field of psychology and wider society. Piaget, initially influenced by Freud, also drew on case studies in his work on the cognitive processes of children. Piaget was extremely important in forging the field of developmental psychology particularly as it relates to child education. Moreover, as we discussed in Chapter 3, Piaget was important for introducing the concept of *transdisciplinarity* and exploring the construction of knowledge within a holistic framework. Together, Freud and Piaget helped to underscore the value of the case study method, which has since been adapted for use in many disciplines in the natural, behavioral, and social sciences (Mills et al. 2010: xxx).

In simple terms, the case study method is an intensive analysis of a contemporary real-world phenomenon in relation to a wider field of comparable cases and their social and historical contexts. As Carla Willig asserts, case studies "are not characterized by the methods used to collect and analyze data, but rather [by their] focus on a particular unit of analysis: a case" (Willig 2008: 74). The *subject* of the case study (e.g., a person, a community, an institution, an event) provides evidence that is used to analyze the *object* of the study (e.g., inequality, policy impacts, mental disorders). Case study research typically begins with a detailed description based on close empirical observation of a single subject carried out over a significant period of time (Creswell 2013). The case study approach tends to be holistic in that it relies on multiple sources of evidence and multiple research methods that can be qualitative, quantitative, or both (Yin 2014: 62).

Case study research can focus on just one case, usually in reference to a wider field of cases, or it can compare two or more cases directly to each other. The selection of cases to be studied can be done in a number of ways and for a number of different purposes, depending on the *analytical frame* (the theoretical or conceptual approach) that the researcher employs. Most cases are selected because they are *typical*, *key*, or *excep-*

tional. Typical cases represent a common occurrence or norm and can be helpful when doing exploratory work, establishing a basic vocabulary, or developing a general typology. Key cases are not necessarily representative of a group but are selected because they highlight a specific aspect or characteristic for the analysis (e.g., rule violation, contradiction, lacunae). Exceptional or outlier cases are generally used to illustrate the extremes of variation in a field of cases.

There are many examples of outstanding case studies that transcend disciplinary frameworks and have had an impact on the way the case study method is used in different fields. Here are some key examples:

- *Argonauts of the Western Pacific* by Bronislaw Malinowski ([1922] 1984)
- *Middletown: A Study in American Culture* by Robert Lynd and Helen Merrell Lynd ([1929] 1956)
- *Street Corner Society: The Social Structure of an Italian Slum* by William Foote Whyte ([1943] 1955)
- *The Affluent Worker in the Class Structure* by John H. Goldthorpe, David Lockwood, Frank Bechhofer, and Jennifer Platt (1969)
- *Awakenings* by Oliver Sacks (1973)
- *Slim's Table: Race, Respectability, and Masculinity* by Mitchell Duneier (1992)
- *The Challenger Launch Decision: Risky Technology, Culture, and Deviance at NASA* by Diane Vaughan (1996)

Even though various academic fields employ the case study method differently, there are several features of the method that remain relatively constant across the disciplines. In general terms, case study research

- relies on direct observation and is empirical
- focuses on a single tangible case with real-world implications
- recognizes the complexity of cases
- explores multiple facets of an issue: multiple possible causes and potential outcomes; multiple actors, including individuals, groups, organizations, governments; conflicting expectations, rules, laws, and cultural norms
- recognizes that the different facets of the case may interact in complex ways

- looks at each case in depth
- adopts a holistic approach, understanding the case from multiple perspectives
- recognizes case studies can be interdisciplinary
- recognizes case studies can be analyzed through mixed methods (Yin 2014: 103)
- recognizes that cases tend to have a historical dimension that explains some aspects of the case
- situates the case in a field of comparable cases
- compares two or more cases
- deploys one or more concepts or theories to explain real-world outcomes
- appreciates that analysis relies on the interpretive skill and insight of the analyst

The characteristics listed above mean that the case study research method lends itself to

- numerous analytical frameworks
- multiple data collection methods
- mixed quantitative and qualitative approaches
- combined exploratory and explanatory approaches
- combined empirical and interpretive approaches

In summary, the case study method is particularly useful for studying complex social interactions that are often difficult to capture with conventional, monomethod research designs. Moreover, the historical and holistic dimensions of the case study method make it very useful for studying social interactions that have a historical dimension or play out over time. The case study method excels when the researcher wants to go beyond the questions of "What?" and "How many?" to ask, "How?," "Why?," and "What does it mean?" in social context (Yin 2014: 5–6). *What ultimately makes the case study approach useful in so many different fields, and especially in global studies, is that it can yield multiperspectival analyses of multifaceted issues.*

A GLOBAL CASE STUDY METHOD

The challenge of dealing with global processes calls for a new approach that can engage with the kinds of complex, global-scale issues that we have discussed in previous chapters. We are proposing an adaptation of the conventional case study approach that can deal with multifaceted and multidimensional issues from a number of analytical perspectives. The approach outlined here explicitly situates the case study in a global context that includes, but is not limited to, the following dimensions:

- local-global continuum
- spatial and geographic dimensions
- temporal and historical dimensions
- intersecting political, economic, social, and cultural dimensions
- intersectional dimensions (e.g., race, class, gender, ethnicity, religion)
- global ethical dimensions (e.g., structural inequality, asymmetrical power relations)

The methodological synthesis we propose rests on several important insights. First, because the local and global are mutually constitutive, most global issues can be studied from a local perspective. As discussed in Chapter 1, even the largest and most abstract global issues manifest somewhere in the real world in the lives of ordinary people, and hence can be studied at the local level. Once researchers recognize that the local-global continuum is a mutually constitutive process—that the global is in the local and vice versa—it becomes possible to study global issues almost anywhere at any time. Researchers can study the global in any retail shop, in any one person's life history, or in the supply chains enabling food and water for the evening meal. In short, making a local case study global only requires seeing the connections and interplay between the various global dimensions in the issue that is being explored.

Second, by definition, every substantive global-scale issue has multiple dimensions to it. Researchers looking into the local manifestations of global issues tend to find as many intersecting dimensions as they care to look for. Does the issue have political, economic, sociocultural, religious, historical, and spatial dimensions? The answer is almost by definition going to be, "Yes, there are multiple global dimensions in my study." Are intersections of race, ethnicity, gender, and class relevant to the study? Again, the answer will almost certainly be "Yes." When students look they find that many, if not all, of these dimensions are not only present but also relevant to their analyses.

Third, any given global-scale issue is likely to be interconnected with other global-scale issues. Researchers investigating what looks like a local environmental issue are likely to find that their issue is impacted by global climate change, global market forces, international immigration, regional conflict, or any number of other global issues. Once researchers are alert to these interactions, they are likely to find that any or all of the dimensions listed above may be relevant to their study. The methodological problem is not that there are too few intersecting dimensions; it is almost always the case that there are more intersecting dimensions than we imagined or know what to do with.

Fourth, as we argue throughout this book, what makes an issue or process global is the questions one asks that reveal its global dimensions, even if on the surface it appears small-scale and localized (Darian-Smith 2013c). Thus to make a research project global, the researcher may not need to change what they are doing or even how they are doing it. The researcher can employ nearly any analytical framework or methodology to conduct global research. They need only ask the kinds of questions that engage the multiple global dimensions that are almost always present in, and relevant to, pressing real-world issues. As we discussed in Chapter 4, developing a global research question often involves critical, reflexive, and ethical elements. Beyond these characteristics that are common to good research questions in many disciplines, global studies favors questions that are inherently global in their recognition of global contexts and the local-global continuum. Acknowledging the interconnectedness of various political, economic, and sociocultural processes is not the end point of a good global studies research question, but rather the starting point. Global studies research questions examine the historical continuity of these intersections and go on to interrogate the *who*, the *why*, and the specific ways these interconnections register across a local-global continuum.

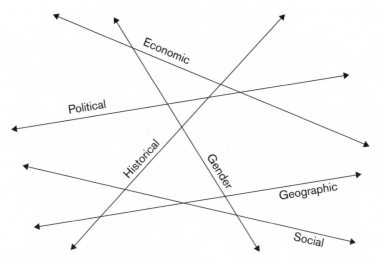

Figure 11. Divergent Dimensions.

Finding a Focal Point

If the first trick to doing global studies research is developing a good research question, then the second trick is to find a *focal point* related to the subject of your case study. For the purposes of global studies, the focal point can be nearly anything: a place; a person or group of people; a festival; a local business or transnational organization; a social, economic, or political process; or, as we will see, even an object such as a T-shirt or a single fish. The most important feature of the focal point is that it is situated at the intersection of the kinds of global issues and dimensions that you, the researcher, want to investigate.

As we have mentioned, when researchers learn to see global dimensions they tend to find more and more of them cutting through their topics. At first they may think of the various global dimensions passing through their area of interest as separate issues. When crosscutting issues come into view, it is often as a tangled jumble of seemingly unrelated dimensions (fig. 11).

Identifying a focal point, however, will bring order to the chaos. The focal point is the place where all the dimensions you want to study intersect (fig. 12).

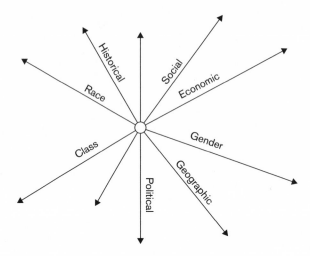

Figure 12. Dimensions Intersecting at a Focal Point.

For students, it can be a difficult exercise to find a focal point in the real world where the issues that interest them all intersect. We want to be clear, however, that finding a focal point is a worthwhile exercise. There is a knack to it; it can be learned, and it does get easier.

Take supply chain studies as an example of a focal point. Several of the earliest and most well-known studies of global processes followed one product such as a T-shirt or pair of shoes through the entire global supply chain (Bateman and Oliff 2003; Iskander 2009). Commodity chain studies can be used to examine the production of a single product from the initial gathering of raw materials, through the international production chain, through distribution and retail markets, on to consumption, into the waste dumps, and finally back into the environment (Rivoli 2005; Hohn 2012). Focusing on the lifecycle of a single product through the global supply chain in this way allows researchers to highlight the increasing complexity of global commodity chains. It can also illuminate a surprising range of social, political, and economic issues, including the consumption of natural resources, the exploitation of human labor, human rights, economic development, international trade, and the cultural and environmental impacts of mass production and consumption. By picking a focal point and asking the right kinds of questions, a researcher of global processes can use a single object to show how these apparently disparate issues are in fact interconnected.

Another example of a focal point is the lifecycle of a single fish. Imagine tagging a single salmon and following it from birth in the headwaters of a river, through its migration downriver and into coastal waters and the ocean, and ultimately its return upriver to spawn in the headwaters again. The migration of that one fish would touch on a host of environmental matters, such as water pollution and biodiversity, and regulatory practices around issues such as water quality, recreational boating, tourism, fishing, and species protection. The river might pass through tribal land at some point. This could introduce topics relating to indigenous cultures, religions, traditions, and sovereignty. There might be concerns related to dams, water supply, irrigation of farmland, and hydroelectric energy production. Food regulations and interstate transport and commerce would almost certainly be involved. If our one little salmon was lucky, she might survive the river, pass through the estuary, swim through highly regulated coastal waters, and make it into international seas. Here the little fish could play a small but important part in ocean fisheries, related laws and international treaties, and perhaps even be the object of conflict between countries and commercial fishing operators. The point is that even a single salmon can act as a focal point for intersecting global processes.

The Fair Trade Exercise

Finding a focal point becomes a good deal easier once the researcher learns to explicitly engage with the kinds of issues that span the local-global continuum. To demonstrate this for our students, we often use the subject of fair trade. We ask: How may a researcher go about studying the impact of Fair Trade marketing on coffee production? What, if anything, does buying coffee labeled "Fair Trade" at your local coffee shop do for the coffee plantation workers in developing countries? For this exercise, we assume that the supply chain for Fair Trade coffee reaches from plantations in the global south, through global markets, through regional wholesale distribution, and finally ends at retail consumption. A topic like Fair Trade could conceivably be studied at any point along this supply chain, from producer to consumer. How does one go about identifying a focal point with so many options? It turns out not to be as difficult as it may sound.

For the purposes of this exercise, we pick as our focal point a specific Fair Trade coffee cooperative. This particular cooperative is made up of coffee growers from a specific region of Costa Rica, but we could have picked a cooperative from nearly anywhere around the world. Focusing the investigation of Fair Trade on this kind of cooperative has a number of advantages. To begin with, the cooperative's own website makes it clear that it is designed to serve as a pivot point between local growers and world markets, intentionally and explicitly connecting the local to the global and vice versa. By simply picking this regional cooperative, we have already situated our study at a midpoint that gives us easy access to the entire local-global continuum.

In this case, the cooperative's website also conveniently lists the specific benefits that membership in the Fair Trade cooperative brings to local coffee growers. The benefits it lists, and even the order they are listed in, are very interesting:

- solidarity
- increased land tenure
- better pay and job security
- health benefits
- education for families

Each of these claimed benefits can be converted into a research question with the potential to lead a student to the evidence they will need to address the original question about fair trade's impact on local growers. In the exercise, we ask students to develop a set of research questions based upon the cooperative's claims. The result is an amazing variety of questions. What is "solidarity" in this context and why is it listed first? Does belonging to a fair trade cooperative significantly increase land tenure for coffee growers? Some of the claims made by the cooperative can even be converted directly into testable hypotheses. Do plantation workers in the cooperative have more job security than workers outside the cooperative? Do they get more benefits such as education and health care?

In this example the local coffee growers, including members and non-members of the fair trade cooperative, provide a ready-made field of comparable cases. There are also a number of other actors involved, including transnational fair trade networks, government officials, cooperative operators, plantation owners, and plantation workers and their families. Each group of actors would almost certainly have a different perspective on the issue. It is not hard for most students to see how they could build any number of viable research projects using the cooperative as a focal point.

Further, as part of the exercise we ask students to consider the distributors' perspective by examining the claims that retail coffee outlets make on their corporate websites. These claims are frequently stated in terms that are very different from those used by producers. Major coffee outlets use terms such as accountability, corporate social responsibility or CSR, equity, ethics, fairness, sustainability, and transparency. To round out the exercise we ask students to survey their fellow students on campus about what they think fair trade coffee does, or does not do, for coffee producers in other countries. The responses of the students provide a quick and easy way to access consumer expectations about the purpose and impact of fair trade. Most of the students voice expectations in terms that are again very different from both the producers and distributors. Students tend to use terms such as fairness and social justice.

The fair trade example illustrates how different micro and macro analyses, as well as qualitative and quantitative methods, can be brought to bear on the cooperative as a focal point and the different global dimensions that pass through it. A focal point enables global studies scholars to use various theoretical and methodological approaches in creative ways to explore different aspects of the issue at hand. Developing a research strategy that explores different perspectives on fair trade provides a very accessible way for our students to learn about focal points and how to operationalize a viable study of global processes.

Be it a supply chain, salmon fish, or coffee cooperative, the focal point in these examples acts both as the conceptual focus and as a refractor for exploring the multifaceted global issues that happen to intersect at that point. This approach allows the researcher to concentrate on one case, but it also gives them a way to connect the case to wider global concerns. We have found that using the global case study approach allows students to use one example of human trafficking, for instance, to explore trafficking in global contexts. No matter which case of trafficking is chosen, this approach allows students to speak to their specific case and reflect on the global problem of trafficking and its many dimensions *without making them attend to all forms of human trafficking everywhere in the world.* Further, they can discuss the various gender, race, and class dimensions of their specific case of trafficking without making themselves responsible for entire bodies of literature dealing with gender, race, and class.

Freedom, Coherence, and Containment

A focal point allows the researcher to corral complexities into one tangible place, thing, or process. A focal point can localize, concretize, humanize, and personalize global research in analytically productive ways that make studying complex global-scale processes much more feasible for most researchers. A focal point provides conceptual clarity, analytical freedom, and practical containment of the project, making it possible to produce a coherent project with the limited time and resources that are typically available to a researcher.

Suppose that a student decides that they want to study the intersection of very abstract issues such as gender, the environment, and inequality. Each of these is an enormous topic and the bodies of literature that could be relevant are very large. With a focal point the researcher becomes responsible for explaining just one real-world case. They can choose to talk about how race and inequality impact the specific case, but they are not required to summarize all the attendant literature on these large topics. The researcher's responsibility is simply to discuss how the topics factor into the specific case. In short, with the case study approach researchers do bit need to summarize the works of Marx, Durkheim, Weber, and Du Bois, and everyone that came after. They need only incorporate the specific aspects of the literature that touch directly on their particular case.

We recognize that there are practical limitations to how much time one can spend searching for the right focal point. At the same time, we do not want students to settle for a focal point that does not allow them to address all of the issues they may want to address. Our experience as researchers and teachers indicates that if students keep looking, delve further into their topics, read more, learn more, and meet more people working in their area of interest, they will almost certainly find a point where the issues that interest them come together in one tangible example. Once found, the focal point can be used as the starting point for designing a global research project that is viable and relatively contained. The initial effort spent in finding a good focal point repays the researcher many times over in the clarity and containment of the project.

A focal point also provides coherence to the researcher. Finding a tangible focal point changes how they talk about what are often very abstract ideas. As teachers we can often hear the transition when students go from referring to intangible and incoherent interests to describing a specific and tangible example of their interests. In short, having a focal point saves time, money, and the researcher's sanity! For these reasons, spending the time to find a focal point is almost always worth the effort.

A Multidimensional Methodology

Once the researcher has elaborated a central research question and identified a focal point for the study, the next step is to design a viable research project around that focal point. This is where the multidimensional case study comes in. A case study may focus on one subject or case, but that subject is not the end goal or objective of the study. It is a starting point for an exploration of how global issues play out along the local-global continuum.

The anatomy of the multidimensional case study is basically the same as that of the conventional case study. Remember that in a conventional case study there is a real-world subject or case that serves as its focal point. The subject can be nearly any discrete, real-world unit (e.g., person, group, institution, event) where the global issues that interest the researcher intersect. The subject is studied empirically, in depth, over time, and in reference to a field of comparable cases. The empirical study of the subject should yield evidence that is in some way relevant to the object of the study.

In global studies, the *object* of a study can be nearly any political, economic, or sociocultural issue. Global cases can be analyzed using one or more analytical frames. The frames should explicitly tie the *subject* to one or more global-scale issues (e.g., inequality, religious conflict, immigration, climate change, emerging economies, commodity chains, global markets). The analytical frames should also explicitly situate the *subject* and *object* of the study on the local-global continuum (e.g., local, state, national, regional, transnational, and/or global). Further, the frames can incorporate other global dimensions (geographic, historical, intersectional, ethical, etc.) where needed for the analysis.

Like the conventional case study method, a multidimensional case study should begin with close empirical observation and detailed description of a specific case. As should be clear from Chapter 5, there is no limitation on the kinds of empirical methods that can be used to gather evidence about the case. In global studies research it is possible to use nearly any academic method that has been shown to produce reliable evidence. Similarly, there is no need to put disciplinary limitations on the analytical frameworks, theories, concepts, and methods that the researcher employs in the analysis. As long as the overarching analytical framework is essentially and explicitly global, researchers should feel free to draw on the theoretical and conceptual developments of any field in the humanities and social and behavioral sciences. *In global studies the entire research design, including the theory, methods, and analysis, should be driven by the central research question and the kinds of evidence needed to address it, regardless of disciplinary boundaries or conventions.*

Due to its holistic and in-depth approach and its analytical and methodological flexibility, the multidimensional case study method provides researchers with the opportunity to transcend the much-debated distinctions between qualitative, quantitative, empirical, and interpretive research. The multidimensional case study method outlined here is flexible enough to be as qualitative, quantitative, empirically rigorous, and subjectively interpretive as one might feel necessary.

Moreover, as with conventional case studies, the multidimensional case study tends to defy the distinctions between exploratory, explanatory, and descriptive research (see Chapter 4). Most case studies can be said to be descriptive because they begin with a close empirical description of the case and case history. And because the cases themselves and the issues being studied are complex and multifaceted, case studies tend to include elements that can be approached from either the exploratory or the explanatory perspective, or both. A well-chosen case can illuminate existing theory and then go beyond to challenge, refine, or build on established knowledge. It could be argued that case studies are at their best when they combine the exploratory, explanatory, and descriptive elements of empirical research.

Finally, given that most researchers face severe limitations on resources, the multidimensional case study provides a feasible and cost-effective research design without sacrificing the reliability and validity of one's findings. As we argue in Chapter 4, the simplest and most cost-effective way to ensure reliability and validity is to triangulate by using mixed research methods. The multidimensional case study lends itself very nicely to this kind of mixed-method triangulation. There is no reason why the researcher's own empirical data and direct observations cannot be easily and efficiently augmented with interviews, historical records, government reports, and statistical data analyses.

DEPLOYING GLOBAL PERSPECTIVES AND ANALYZING GLOBAL DIMENSIONS

While the specific analytical frameworks to be employed may vary, we argue that in order for a research project to be considered "global" it should, as a minimum (1) have an overarching research question that is informed by global perspectives, (2) explicitly address a global-scale issue or issues, and (3) include one or more global dimensions in the analysis.

In Chapter 2 we elaborated a number of characteristics of global studies research (that it be holistic, transgressive, integrative, critical, interdisciplinary, decentered, open to hybridity and fluidity, etc.) and there may well be others that we have not named. Taken together, these characteristics, including those we have not yet named, create new perspectives and a way of thinking that we sometimes call "thinking globally" (Juergensmeyer 2014a). *Thinking globally* is shorthand for the habit of putting objects of study into larger conceptually and spatially global contexts and approaching issues from global perspectives. Scholars may use this kind of shorthand when talking among ourselves, but in practice we should endeavor to be clear about which global perspectives we are employing, which global dimensions we are analyzing, and what these elements add to the research.

Global perspectives help scholars break out of old ways of thinking. They help scholars think past the nation-state, the limitations of the international relations framework, and possibly even the limitations of the modern disciplines. Global studies research should call attention to those moments when and where global perspectives do this kind of work.

Local-Global Dimensions

The first dimension that should almost certainly be discussed in any global analysis, and the one that is probably the most basic to the field of global studies, is the local-global continuum (see Chapter 2). Because the interconnection of the local and the global is a defining feature of global studies and one of the field's central concerns, nearly all global research projects should explicitly address the local-global continuum in some way. In most cases this can be as simple as connecting abstract concepts such as globalization to concrete examples at the local level. This is most often accomplished by designing a project that includes interviewing local people or observing local events and organizations, and explicitly connecting these concrete examples to more abstract global issues or processes in the analysis.

There may be special cases where the local-global connection can be left implicit. In general, though, we find this can cause confusion—if not for students and researchers, then certainly for their readers. It is better to start out making these connections more or less explicit throughout. We recommend that the local-global connection be explicitly addressed throughout the entire project, including its theoretical, methodology, analysis, and discussion sections.

In our experience, researchers tend to spend most of their time in the places and at the levels where they are most comfortable. For some that can be the local, for others the global; it can be the concrete or abstract, the micro or macro, or the qualitative or quantitative. When writing up the case study it is important to go back and deliberately bridge local and global, micro and macro, to explicitly link the *subject* and *object* of the study. Do explore the specificity of individual cases, but also recognize that it is equally important to zoom back out to the macro level and reconnect the specifics back to larger trends and relevant global issues. Or even if you find you are more comfortable in the abstract realm, we think it is important to make the effort to bring your analyses back down to earth with some local and concrete examples.

Historical and Temporal Dimensions

Another dimension of a given topic that is almost always productive for global scholars is the historical dimension (see Chapter 2). While many people tend to think of globalization as a new phenomenon, any specific case study has historical roots that may link to former eras of globalization. Huge historical processes such as colonization and decolonization are part of earlier phases of globalization and in many ways underscore deep continuities between past and present. At the same time, contemporary forms of economic and technological globalization often make sharp contrasts with traditional cultures and values. Historical dimensions can thus highlight ongoing processes of change, resistance, adaptation, appropriation, and assimilation. In our experience, appreciating the historical dimensions in one's case study can add depth to nearly any analysis and a kind of particularity and validity that a purely synchronic analysis cannot provide. Fortunately, global studies researchers can access historical dimensions in any number of ways, including historical archives, life histories, regional literature, statistical trends, and records of demographic change. Moreover, since global studies scholars are sensitive to there being competing historical narratives of the past, the standpoint of the person telling or recording any history is considered very important and taken into account in the analysis.

Geographic and Spatial Dimensions

The academic discipline of geography has influenced the field of global studies in many ways (Golledge and Stimson 1996; Cresswell 2013; Tally 2012). At a basic level, physical and cultural geography remind us that global issues have spatial and demographic dimensions, and that these dimensions can impact our analyses. Basic spatial dimensions such as distance, surface area, and elevation can be relevant. Physical features such as mountains, rivers, transportation corridors, land use, and borders can matter. Moreover, demographic elements relevant to any society or population (total population, relative size of racial, ethnic and religious groups, mobility and migration) almost always matter in some way. Whether or not a researcher ultimately chooses to include such geographic dimensions in their analysis, it is important at the start to recognize that they are present and could be relevant to the case study.

Economic, Political, and Sociocultural Dimensions

As discussed above, designing a research project that explores the economic, political, and sociocultural dimensions of an issue and the ways in which they interact is another productive area of analysis for global scholars (see Chapter 4). Most global-scale issues involve all three dimensions. In the past most academic disciplines treated these dimensions as discrete areas of study. Global studies scholars, however, see them as mutually constitutive and consider any separation of the economic from the political, for instance, to be problematic. Even a cursory engagement with global-scale issues such as religious conflict and mass migration reveals the dangers involved in trying to separate out these dimensions.

In addition to seeing economics, politics, society, and culture as interactive and interconnected, it is also important to recognize that all three are essentially Western analytical constructs that arose relatively recently, within the nineteenth-century Euro-American academy. As a result, these dimensions may not necessarily translate easily into non-Western contexts. Societies and cultures around the world may hold very different ideas about what these dimensions are and where the boundaries between them lie. To avoid these pitfalls, global studies scholars deploy these ideas critically, and deliberately emphasize the intersection of the three dimensions and their fluid boundaries. Most global studies scholars find this approach less problematic and ultimately more productive.

Intersectional Dimensions

As we mentioned in "Critical Methodological Strategies" in Chapter 5, intersectional theory suggests that forms of inequality intersect and can overdetermine a person's place in society. As you begin analyzing your data, it may help to revisit the issue of intersectionality and consider what role race, class, gender, religion, and nationality, among many other potential markers of difference, might play in your study. Are the individuals and groups that take part in your research disadvantaged by race, class, and/or gender? Where do individuals fit in the hierarchy of their communities? Where does a specific community fit in the hierarchy of society? Where does that society fit in the hierarchy of the global order? Which members of the community have more social, economic, and political power and which members have less?

When analyzing intersectional dimensions, note that they tend to operate at multiple levels up and down the local-global continuum. For example, class issues can operate simultaneously at the local, national, regional, transnational, and global levels. Furthermore, issues at different levels can interact. Class issues operating at the national level can interact with different but related class issues at the community and individual levels. Intersectional dimensions can also interact with other dimensions at any place on the local-global continuum. For example, it isn't hard to imagine a situation where laws about race at the national level could impact issues of class at the community level and gender at the domestic level, and organizations representing communities and individuals could in turn mobilize social media and influence social movements at a global level (fig. 2). A global intersectional theory might suggest that in any given situation multiple intersectional dimensions are interacting at several points on the local-global continuum. The challenge for the researcher is to tease out the specific interactions that are relevant to the analysis and their overarching research question.

Ethical Dimensions

We introduced ethics as a research design issue in Chapter 4. Once you begin the analysis stage of your research, it is important to return to the issue of ethics and consider the ethical implications in your work. Ask yourself: What role does social power play in your research design, analysis, and findings? What role do intersectional inequalities such as race, class, gender, and nationality play in your research? How might individual, structural, and systemic discrimination impact your analysis and findings? Who will benefit or potentially be harmed from your findings and conclusions? Are there cultures and ethical systems other than your own involved?

As is the case with research design and implementation, the best strategy for researchers working in unfamiliar cultural contexts is to actively seek out one or more knowledgeable representatives of that culture and involve them in your analysis, your conclusions, and the publication of research. Local scholars, experts, and community leaders should be encouraged to actively participate in every stage of the production of knowledge about their own cultures. And foreign researchers should be grateful for such local expertise and be willing to collaborate, cooperate, and copublish if at all possible. Not only will the end result be a much richer and deeper understanding of the issues analyzed, but it is a profoundly ethical stance to adopt, particularly when studying people and problems in the global south. In practice, collaboration and coproduction of new knowledge goes a long way to build trust and respect and to offset the enormous power differentials involved when scholars of the global north analyze subjects of the global south.

A GLOBAL FIELD OF CASES

As with the conventional case study method, cases selected for a multidimensional case study can be *typical* of particular categories or characteristics, *key* in that they feature a particular aspect of a global issue, or *exceptional* in that they show extremes of variation. By definition, however, cases selected for a multidimensional case study come from a wider field of comparable cases than is usually the case with a conventional case study. In global studies the field of comparable cases can be very large, even global in range and scope.

Conventional case studies within a field of comparable cases tend to be relatively similar and connected in fairly clear ways. Going back to the example of Freud, most of his cases involved people living in the same society or from culturally very similar societies in Europe. They typically shared a nationality, language, and set of cultural values, and they were often of the same ethnicity, gender, and even class. In contrast, in the multidimensional global case study the field of comparable cases can be global in scope. Individual cases from different regions and cultures can vary a great deal more than is typical in single-society case studies. For example, if the case being studied is a woman in a refugee camp, then the field of comparable examples could include women from very different cultures in very different circumstances in different kinds of camps around the world. Similarly, a multidimensional case study examining the impact of immigrants on a single community could be compared to the thousands of communities around the world that are also experiencing an influx of immigrants.

Embracing a global field of cases in some ways increases the difficulties inherent in designing global studies research. The potential for extreme variation in a global field introduces a host of analytical, methodological, intercultural, and ethical concerns, not to mention some serious practical and linguistic limitations. In the following sections we address these concerns and limitations. Still, we think that coming to terms with the extreme variation at the global level, while difficult, is a necessary step in understanding the kinds of global-scale issues the world faces today. An in-depth analysis of micro-level variation reveals the human side of the larger global forces playing out in each specific case. It is precisely these extremes in local variation that open new avenues of investigation and offer new possibilities for revising and rejuvenating Western, modern, and disciplinary ways of knowing and thinking about the world we live in.

Selection and Representation

As with all research design, any researcher contemplating a multidimensional case study must deal with issues of selection and representation. These issues become more difficult by orders of magnitude when carried into global contexts. For example, in some areas of the developing world finding a reliable sampling frame to replace the phone book and voter registration rolls can be very challenging. In active conflict zones it may be impossible to know even the most basic information about impacted populations. This kind of work can be very pressing, but researchers must thoroughly qualify any claims to representation. In such cases, they should be exceedingly careful in defining the population and clear about the limitations involved in representing it with a given subsample.

When issues of selection and representation are carried into global contexts, they take on new and very important geopolitical, historical, and intercultural implications. Throughout the modern period Western scholars have consistently represented and misrepresented other peoples to suit their own purposes, whether the "others" are women, indigenous peoples, colonized subjects, minorities, poor people, or other groups. In the context of this history, scientific observations we consider to be empirical and objective often turn out not to be as value neutral as we would like. In practice, the knowledge that Western scholars produce about non-Western "others" is almost invariably politically, culturally, and ethically loaded. It can, and very often does, have negative material impacts on research subjects who are substantially less able to influence public discourse than those who research them (see Chapter 4, "Ethical Dimensions of Global Research").

In the contemporary moment, extremes of inequality also trigger a number of very important ethical questions about selecting and representing subjects for a multidimensional case study (see "Ethical Dimensions" in this chapter). Who, for example, has the academic credentials, financial resources, and political clout to represent whom? Why are the representations in question being made, who will they have an impact on and how, and who will benefit and in what ways? The key point here is that researchers working across race, ethnicity, class, gender, and national and cultural boundaries should be mindful of the power dynamics inherent in the processes of selection and representation. Researchers should deal with these issues head-on by explicitly addressing how and why they are selecting and representing specific peoples, issues, or processes for their multidimensional case study.

Comparing Multidimensional Cases

As we have noted, the case study research method has at its core a comparative element. Case study comparisons can be either case-to-field or case-to-case.

CASE-TO-FIELD COMPARISON

In a case-to-field comparison the comparative element of the study can sometimes be more implicit than explicit. For example, a medical or psychiatric doctor may study an individual with certain symptoms in relation to particular health or behavioral norms. The reference group, in this case a healthy or symptomless population, provides a baseline for comparison. However, the study may never explicitly mention this comparison group.

In the social sciences and humanities there is often no clearly defined norm to compare cases to. In the social world the very idea of "normal" is a contested concept that often has important political implications. To treat one group as normal necessarily implies that the comparison group is in some way abnormal. Where we can define distinct social groups, it is usually better to assume a more neutral stance and simply examine their similarities and differences without making value judgments and taking care not to fall back on or reinforce existing stereotypes. Value judgments are often implied in broad terms such as positive and negative. These kinds of judgments, whether explicit or implicit, can be avoided by defining the specific dimensions along which the comparison cases vary or coincide. Groups can be relatively similar or different without being better or worse. It is possible, for example, to discuss variations in income, employment, education, and specific beliefs and attitudes without assigning values to the variations. In this way researchers can avoid triggering loaded comparative dichotomies such as normal/abnormal, assimilated/unassimilated, legal/illegal, developed/underdeveloped, positive/negative, or functional/dysfunctional.

The process of defining a comparison group can be very problematic in global studies, and can include an unusually large and diverse set of cases that span many different communities and societies around the globe. For this reason it is never a good idea to leave the comparison group undefined in global research. When the comparison group is left undefined, the researcher risks imposing their own values and norms—their own standpoint—as the basis for comparison. It is almost always better to be explicit about the reference group and the comparisons being made.

One way to deal with the difficulty of defining a baseline comparison is to make comparisons only within a specific culture. As sociocultural anthropologists point out, however, no culture is static, and it is misleading to present any one culture as a fixed or monolithic category. Moreover, making comparisons within the same culture does not necessarily get you around the issue of having to define relevant norms in a culture other than

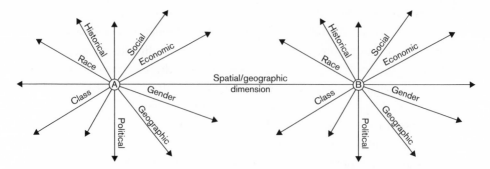

Figure 13. Multidimensional Case-to-Case Comparison.

your own. Again, anthropologists have taught us that understanding another culture's social norms well enough to make an authoritative case comparison is exceedingly difficult and should only be attempted with caution and consultation with culturally fluent members of that particular society.

CASE-TO-CASE COMPARISON

Another way to deal with the difficulties of cross-cultural comparisons is to do direct, case-to-case comparisons. While this approach might avoid some complexities of intercultural comparison, it is still necessary to deal with intercultural contexts and to define the specific dimensions of variation between the cases being compared. Figure 13 represents a hypothetical comparison of two multidimensional cases separated by one dimension, the geographic dimension. If the two case studies were carried out in the same way, at the same time, and by two different researchers, the only variation in the comparison could theoretically be the distance between the geographic sites of the two case studies.

Consider for a moment this simplified diagram and the important implications that the difference of one dimension, in this example the spatial or geographic dimension, could represent. If the two cases were separated by a few miles, that small distance alone may or may not be significant. If the distance between them, however, separated urban and rural, lowland and highland, coastal and inland, or gated community and slum, even a relatively short distance could be a very significant part of the study.

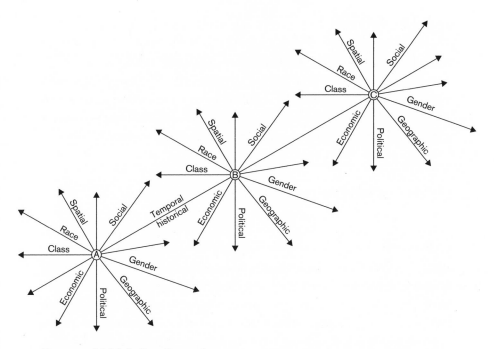

Figure 14. Multiple Case Comparisons.

If the distance were greater or included significant political, linguistic, or cultural boundaries, then the separation would almost certainly be a crucial part of understanding the differences between the cases.

The same could be said for the other major dimensions cutting through all multidimensional case studies. Take, for example, the historical or temporal dimension in a comparison of three cases, each with its own focal point (fig. 14). If the three studies were conducted only a few days apart, we might not expect that amount of time to be particularly significant. We might expect the difference between case studies separated by several decades to be more significant. However, in some instances even a short time period between cases can be very important. If one were doing research in Eastern Europe one day before the fall of the Berlin Wall and one day after, that short period of time would almost certainly impact the study in a variety of ways. Major events like the fall of the Berlin Wall, the Arab Spring, and the Brexit vote tend to create before-and-after effects that would almost certainly impact any research being done in the affected areas. Even significant local events like an outbreak of violence, a natural disaster, or a contested election can add this before-and-after element to any case study. The point is that any two global case studies separated by time or distance, by political, economic, or sociocultural boundaries, or by more than one of these factors are likely to vary in innumerable ways. A diagram of all the possible dimensions of variation could be very complex and tangled, and may look more like a large bowl of spaghetti.

SELECTIVE ANALYSIS

This is not to say that this kind of comparative work cannot be done. Rather, we are emphasizing the need to recognize that cases can vary along many dimensions and the need to deal with these variations selectively and explicitly as part of the research design process. Save yourself a lot of trouble by limiting the scope of your study to the specific dimensions that interest you. Engage with certain kinds of variation and not others. Then own it. If you design your research project to examine the intersection of x and y, give yourself permission to say the rest of the alphabet is important but for the purposes of your study will not be examined in any depth, if at all.

For example, one of our students designed a project to compare the influx of refugees from the ongoing Syrian civil war into Europe to the influx of Jewish refugees into the same countries during World War II. At first glance the differences between these two refugee crises were so huge, and the time periods so different, that any comparison seemed futile. Despite the obvious differences, however, it was clear that any similarities between these two refugee crises could be very important. By focusing on the news media's coverage of anti-immigrant hysteria in the countries receiving them then and now, the student was able to design an investigation that could be done in a relatively contained fashion. Deliberately focusing almost exclusively on one aspect of the two cases allowed that student to manage what would otherwise have been a very complex comparison across space and time.

In sum, even though global studies issues are multifaceted and interconnected, there is almost always a manageable way to compare two or more multidimensional case studies. Selecting specific dimensions through which to focus your comparison can be difficult. As we have emphasized with regard to other elements of your research, however, your central research question should drive the process of selecting dimensions of comparison. In the next chapter, we turn to four exemplary multidimensional case studies to illustrate the usefulness of this methodological strategy for exploring complex global issues.

7 Examples of Global Studies Research

In this penultimate chapter, we examine four studies by leading global scholars that we consider to be exemplary case studies. The four projects are all by scholars on our own campus, but clearly any number of other studies could have been used. The authors themselves do not use the term "multidimensional case studies," but we interpret their work as fitting within this research strategy. Clearly, in this chapter we cannot do justice to these studies, which are all theoretically rich, empirically robust, and methodologically innovative—perhaps even groundbreaking. That being said, we have chosen these four studies for the following reasons:

- Each author is a critical interdisciplinary, if not transdisciplinary, scholar who self-identifies with the emerging field of global studies.
- Together, these case studies represent scholarly training in disciplines and fields from across the social sciences and humanities: law, anthropology, history, English, political science, feminist studies, sociology, and religious studies.
- Each case study highlights many of the characteristics of global studies scholarship: taking a holistic approach, being transgressive and integrative in transcending Eurocentric modes of thinking, seeking to break down binaries and conceptual assumptions,

examining decentered and deterritorialized processes across time and space, connecting the case study to global social structures, and appreciating that people's sense of identity is hybrid and fluid (see Chapter 2).

- Each case study deploys a range of theories, analytical frameworks, research designs, and mixed-method approaches that are not unique to any one academic discipline (see Chapters 4 and 5).

- Each case study demonstrates many of the points we have made throughout this book with respect to using one's research questions to drive a project's overall research design and methods and specifically engaging with the local-global continuum and various global dimensions (see Chapter 6).

- Each case study presents a lens through which to engage with enormously complex global issues, offers significant and timely analysis, and makes innovative theoretical contributions along the way.

- The authors of the case studies represent different stages of an academic career. Two of the case studies are based on doctoral theses and were written by people who were junior scholars at the time, one was written by a midcareer scholar, and the most recent case study was written by a senior scholar in collaboration with a graduate coauthor and a large, multiyear grant. This spectrum of experience underscores that everyone can do excellent global studies research irrespective of their position along the academic career trajectory or their financial resources.

- Finally, the case studies together have been influential in both disciplinary and interdisciplinary fields and have been widely acknowledged for opening up scholarly approaches to new ways of thinking globally. Each has received numerous reviews and acknowledgments, and two have received very prestigious book awards.

BRIDGING DIVIDES: THE CHANNEL TUNNEL AND ENGLISH LEGAL IDENTITY IN THE NEW EUROPE

Eve Darian-Smith's *Bridging Divides* was published in 1999. The author practiced corporate law for some years before completing a doctoral degree in sociocultural anthropology, and this book was based on her dissertation fieldwork. The book received widespread acclaim and a major book prize, and has been described as one of the first ethnographies of globalization. Significantly, many of the issues the book raises—nationalism, identity, racism, immigration, xenophobia, and what it means to be a citizen of the supranational European Union—remain extremely relevant today. Some would argue that these issues have become even more problematic in recent years, as evidenced by the United Kingdom's Brexit vote to leave the EU in June 2016. *Bridging Divides* highlights the enduring significance of deep cultural histories underpinning today's tense relations between European countries and the EU's twenty-seven remaining member states.

What Is the Study About?

The focal point of the study is the Channel Tunnel, which runs through the sea between England and France and connects London to Paris and Brussels by fast rail. UK prime minister Margaret Thatcher and French president Francois Mitterand signed the Tunnel Treaty in 1986, and the extraordinary engineering feat was completed in 1994. The tunnel and fast rail link were part of a network of trains being built at the time in an effort to connect major cities and enable better communication between member states within the EU. The Channel Tunnel was very much an EU project. For many people in England, it represented a new era in which British nationalism and identity were being challenged by emerging political, legal, economic, and social relations between London and Brussels, capital of the EU.

In Darian-Smith's words:

> In the context of the New Europe, the Tunnel operates in a very tangible way as a catalyst for renewing and rearticulating similarities and differences between peoples and across towns, regions, nations, states, and global divides. As a symbol of the breaking down of European state borders, the Tunnel precariously affirms the ideal of a united Europe. At the same time, however, the increasing threat portrayed in the British popular media of postcolonial peoples from places such as Africa and India boarding the train in Paris and illegally entering London highlights a continuing need to demarcate differences between "east" and "west," first and third worlds, colonizers and colonized, and, in a rather circular move, again between the

English and French legal systems and national and regional social values. In a world of increasing talk about unity and transnationalism, what the Tunnel helps articulate is that there are also simultaneously emerging expressions of neo-nationalism and parochial exclusivity.

I want to make clear from the outset that the purpose of this book is not to treat the Channel Tunnel simply as a concrete entity and so to analyze how people living in England are responding to it, positively or negatively. I do not take the Tunnel as a given thing with an attached set of fixed meanings. Rather my purpose is to ask why it is that the Tunnel has come to have the object status that it has, and what the conceptual, discursive and practical effects of power are that have helped crystallize this supposedly technical apparatus of "connection" into an icon of political, moral, and ideological focus. (Darian-Smith 1999: xiii–xiv)

In What Ways Is It a Global Studies Project?

While the field of global studies did not exist at the time *Bridging Divides* was written, the case study explicitly explores the wider national and transnational implications of the localized and often rural community responses to the tunnel. Darian-Smith, in short, uses the tunnel as a focal point and lens to analyze a range of attitudes, ideologies, memories, anxieties, hopes, and reflections expressed by numerous actors, including small village residents, cosmopolitan urban business workers, mayors, public figures, politicians, and the media in general. In this way *Bridging Divides* engages the local-global continuum, looking at power and institutions as they play out across geopolitical scales at local, regional, national, transnational, and intercontinental levels, but it also moves across the continuum to examine the ways ideologies are formed and identity constructions framed (villager, county resident, English citizen, British citizen, member of the Commonwealth, European citizen, and so on).

Importantly, *Bridging Divides* is not a study of nationalism, though it engages with nationalist values, identities, and institutions. This means that the study does not take the nation-state for granted as the geopolitical unit of analysis, comparing respective British and French views on the tunnel project. Instead it takes a critical stance, problematizing the idea of the nation-state within the wider context of the EU by asking questions that reveal why some members of society understood the tunnel as challenging nationalist ideals and related national social, political, and economic relations. Through this line of interrogation, *Bridging Divides* examines the tunnel's ideological and symbolic significance to communities anxious to maintain the idea of a sovereign "island nation," on the one hand, and for communities keen to think beyond a nationalist paradigm and take advantage of all that European citizenry supposedly offers, on the other.

With respect to the characteristics of global studies scholarship that we outlined in Chapter 2, *Bridging Divides* presents a big-picture or holistic account through a bottom-up approach. This approach privileges the views of people and communities reflecting on their membership in the EU, using these as a lens through which to better understand the local impact of the EU's supranational structures and institutions. *Bridging Divides* is, at its core, an exploration of the hybrid and fluid identities people claim for themselves in contexts that challenge nationalist frameworks, histories, ideologies, and affiliations. It is a study of postnationalism, and as such presents a critical interpretation that challenges taken-for-granted modern assumptions about how the world works and how people function and give meaning to their lives.

Methodology and Research Design

Bridging Divides is very much an interdisciplinary case study, and uses a range of social and legal theory as well as mixed methods from across the disciplines. While ostensibly an ethnographic account and thus grounded in participant observation, interviews, and fieldwork, the book also draws on a wide spectrum of materials and evidence such as press reports, political cartoons, television and radio programs, official government statements, legal and historical archives, maps, tourist publicity materials, local community meetings, photographs, stamps, and etchings.

With respect to research design, *Bridging Divides* is a good example of the multidimensional case study approach. Each chapter in the book engages with a particular dimension and explores multiple perspectives on it. One chapter looks at the temporal or historical dimensions of the tunnel and delves into how Napoleon's attempts to attack England over two hundred years ago still reverberate in contemporary media and populist sensibilities. Another chapter on nationalism and racism examines widespread fears that the tunnel would allow rabid foxes to contaminate the "purity" of the island community. As Darian-Smith explains, this unfounded fear of rabies was a metaphor for racist fears of darker-skinned Africans actively seeking to enter England from the French coast and take advantage of the better socioeconomic conditions available. Interviews with locals living in rural Kent, the county at the English mouth of the tunnel, are contrasted with the views of national politicians and Londoners, who scoff at the idea of an imminent rabies infestation. Throughout the case study, Darian-Smith closely tracks intersections of its political, economic, social, and cultural dimensions, presenting a holistic understanding of the significance of the study's focal point—the Channel Tunnel—in the English imaginary.

GLOBAL ICONS: APERTURES TO THE POPULAR

Bishnupriya Ghosh's *Global Icons* was published in 2011. The author is a professor of English and affiliated faculty in film and media studies, comparative literature, and feminist studies. Her research is wide ranging, and she has contributed considerably to postcolonial theory and global media studies. *Global Icons* has received widespread attention for its rich theoretical and empirical exploration of the global dimensions of iconic figures and the role their populist symbolism plays in the eruption of social movements that transcend nation-states and link people across conventional geopolitical boundaries.

What Is the Study About?

The focal point of *Global Icons* are three contemporary icons, all associated with India and South Asia more generally, who have played a powerful role in the popular imaginary and "habitually surface in political crises where we witness eruptions of collective aspiration" (Ghosh 2011: 5). The three icons are Phoolan Devi, a renowned outlaw known as the Bandit Queen who served as a spokesperson for the Dalit and denouncer of India's discriminatory caste system and later as a member of parliament, and who was eventually gunned down outside her house; Mother Teresa, a Catholic nun who lived in Calcutta between 1946 and her death in 1997, and who was awarded the Nobel Peace Prize in 1979; and Arundhati Roy, an acclaimed Indian novelist, a Booker Prize winner for *The God of Small Things*, and an environmental and antistate activist.

Ghosh argues that the three icons are more than mere celebrities and public figures since their symbolism has the power, at certain moments, to "galvanize popular sentiment and, at times, catalyze collective action" (Prestholdt 2012: 596). According to her, the women's status as icons incorporates their personal biographies and material histories. As "bio-icons" they operate as "apertures" or spaces to connect people's aspirations in collective movements that transcend local, national, and even regional frames, even though their meanings are interpreted differently across different social and political contexts and so never fixed. As Ghosh explains, the icons represent a "paradigm of highly visible public figures whose symbolically dense images and lives circulate at high speeds in transnational (television, cinematic, print, oral, and digital) media networks" (Ghosh 2011: 4). Their mediation affords them capacities to rally human agency and build social networks across geopolitical and culturally constructed borders. These global icons are "cultural phenomena we see every day but mostly dismiss as some among so many commodities fleetingly present in our lives. Until wars break out over images. Until they move us to imagine a there we want to live in. Until iconomania erupts around us" (Ghosh 2011: 4).

Global Icons is divided into three sections that together present a theoretical tour de force to understanding the production and consumption of global mass media. Part 1 presents a materialist theory of the icon in new media technologies, focusing on the commodification and movement of symbolic images across time and space, and the bodily affects icons play with respect to their "re-territorializion" in local behaviors and social interactions. Part 2 examines the material biographies of icons in action as dynamic sites of social and political friction, corporatization, publicity, consumption, desirability, imagination, and volatility. Part 3 examines the politics of contestation over icons that become unmoored from their stable epistemological framing and are launched into wider contexts of contestation and social and political volatility.

In What Ways Is It a Global Studies Project?

Global Icons is very much a global studies project in its grappling with new forms of global media; the global consumption of symbolic, iconic imagery; and the locally embodied and situated impacts that icons have in stimulating and revitalizing dreams, desires, and claims for ways of being in the world. The book takes us on a new journey in how to read the global through the historical tracing of consumed symbolic imagery, a type of reading that up to this point has largely been overlooked in explorations of globalization and global processes. As Ghosh explains, "If our phase of globalization is marked by an increased reflexivity about 'being global'—the perception of our connection to multiple 'elsewheres' beamed at us every day—then mass-mediated signs that enter and exit local platforms can play a key role in calibrating such perceptions" (Ghosh 2011: 11). In this way, Ghosh's book is very much engaged with the local-global continuum, examining the production and consumption of global icons by different actors and institutions at different points along a spatial and conceptual scale.

Global Icons shows us that corporations pushing global icons, such as the Coca-Cola bottle, onto a global stage hope to evoke sensations, create desire, and ultimately sell products. In its moment of origination, the icon is intended to be read as global by offering a supposedly universal message that is applicable to and consumable by a global constituency. This very presumption of universality, however, is why some contemporary objects become highly contested in the process of being interpreted by local communities whom the objects confront with the communities' own immediate needs, lack of resources, or political disenfranchisement. For example, the Plachimada struggle against the Coca-Cola Company's bottling plant in southern India, which caused toxic chemicals to leak into the groundwater and poison surrounding agricultural lands, resulted in a happy global icon losing its "universal claim to speak for all" (Ghosh 2011: 14). As Ghosh argues, "As key signifiers of collective aspiration, icons that erupt into social phenomena provide further evidence of embattled responses to global modernity amid intensifying global interconnections" (Ghosh 2011: 5–6).

With respect to the characteristics of global studies scholarship we outlined in Chapter 2, *Global Icons* takes a holistic approach to exploring epistemological contestations around global symbolic imagery. The book is transgressive and integrative, explicitly giving voice and recognition to local communities dealing with the negative impacts of neoliberal economic policies. In the process, it elaborates multiple connections as well as ambiguities between the production and consumption of global icons.

Importantly, Ghosh makes a compelling argument about the materiality of global icons. Typically such images are not given much political and social significance by scholars or business entrepreneurs, relegated to the realm of corporate branding and economic calculations to expand markets and market share. But Ghosh shows us how global icons inform sectors of public consciousness and experience, and are in some cases aggressively modified and adapted for a wide range of progressive and conservative activities. She writes that

> "globality"—that place where we now live—is increasingly experientially corporeal. Our bodies become heavy with missed flights in overcrowded airports; the young lift telephones during long night shifts that rewire their bodies to different time zones; the jihadist turns from lost oil wells of wealth to fight the new world order by imploding his body. Hence, the icon, which activates intense sensations, becomes fundamental to grasping the phenomenology of the global. (Ghosh 2011: 99)

In her focus on the corporeality of global icons, Ghosh show us interconnections between what are often thought of as discrete processes of globalization that occupy mutually exclusive economic, media, or political spheres. On the contrary, Ghosh argues, these spheres of globality are deeply integrated, mutually constitutive, and never absent of political potential and possibility.

Methodology and Research Design

Global Icons presents a comparative multidimensional case study of three global icons. It is a critical interdisciplinary project that draws on cultural theory, postcolonial media studies, feminist and queer theory. Ghosh uses mixed methods ranging from archival and historical methods, content analysis, visual interpretation, and participant observation and general ethnographic methods to deep cultural studies analyses of television, film, literature, and other media, as well as propaganda and publicity.

Ghosh explores each global icon from a number of dimensions in the way we outline in Chapter 6. She situates each icon along the local-global continuum, linking local engagements with symbolic imagery to global social structures and macroeconomic processes and paying careful attention to historical materialities and local contexts. Moreover, she contextualizes each icon within intersecting political, economic, social, and cultural dimensions that break down conceptual binaries between economics and politics, consumption and consciousness, public and private, us and them, national and regional, and global south and global north.

Global Icons is designed to analyze both bottom-up and top-down global processes. It gives weight to local interpretations of global icons as expressed in political and social activism (as opposed to purely economic consumption), as well as to the top-down corporate aspirations that enable the transmission of universalized global icons in the first place (before they may take on a life of their own through circuits of social media and digital communication). In dealing with contrary modes of consumption and the unforeseen conflicts that result when real people interact with global corporate strategies, Ghosh presents a deeply ethical account that raises questions about asymmetrical power relations and exploitative neoliberal market logics.

THE SECURITY ARCHIPELAGO: HUMAN-SECURITY STATES, SEXUALITY POLITICS, AND THE END OF NEOLIBERALISM

Paul Amar's *The Security Archipelago* was published in 2013. The author worked as a journalist in Cairo, a civil rights activist in Rio de Janeiro, and a conflict-resolution specialist at the United Nations before completing his doctorate in political science. *The Security Archipelago* is a much-revised version of his doctoral thesis. The book received a very prestigious book prize for its theoretical and methodological contributions: it reframes conventional neoliberal analyses and poses new ways to understand emerging governance regimes in the global south that are shaping a new global order. Amar's work contributes in particular to the emerging field of critical security studies (Amar 2013: 19–21).

What Is the Study About?

Given Amar's experiences in Cairo and Rio, it is perhaps not surprising that *The Security Archipelago* is a comparative and multisited analysis of security regimes in the Middle East and Latin America, with a specific focus on Egypt and Brazil. The book is complex and wide ranging and does not lend itself to a summary description. That being said, the focal points of the study are the popular uprisings against authoritarian President Hosni Mubarak that took place in Egypt in early 2011 and a coinciding "revolution" in Brazil at approximately the same time under the leadership of progressive President Dilma Rousseff. Both instances involved, at least initially, elements of the military working together with progressive social and political movements. In Egypt, the military assumed control of the government "to look to the safety of the nation and its citizens" (Amar 2013: 1). In Brazil, President Rousseff encouraged the armed forces to help implement new pacification programs and humanitarian interventions intended to clean up urban slums, overhaul the corrupt police system, and combat warlords and drug traffickers.

Brazil and Egypt, of course, have very different cultural, economic, and political histories. They encompass different colonial pasts, regional pressures, and internal state politics and logics, not to mention different mixes of cultures, races, and religions. The two countries, however, also have much in common as oil and gas producers and global tourist destinations. Both have operated for decades in the geopolitical belt known as the "semi-periphery" in world-systems theory, were sexualized and racialized through tropicalist (Rio) and orientalist (Cairo) discourses under colonialism, and in the 1970s "served as pioneering test sites for neoliberalism, deployed in each site by a military junta" (Amar 2013: 28). They have both hosted landmark UN events that fostered NGOs as transnational actors in a humanitarian civil society marketplace—the Rio summit in 1992 and the Cairo summit in 1994. These common relationships they have with the global north make comparing the two countries extremely productive, as do their collaborative efforts in decolonization and development efforts within the global south throughout the 1950s and 1960s.

For Amar, then, the revolutionary moments of political organization that Brazil and Egypt experienced in 2011 only solidify the strength of their grounds for comparison. As Amar argues, these parallel moments were profoundly different from conventional understandings of state organization under the neoliberal market logics that most scholars in the global north espouse. One of the major differences was that emerging forms of political assertion in Egypt and Brazil involved new modes of "sexualized and moralized governance" and, often, surprising alliances between police and social justice movements. The focus on sexual and moral values shored up new "security state logics" that foregrounded the protection of humanity and the role of the state and military in humanitarian intervention. Neoliberalism's seductive market-driven ideology was in a sense dislodged in the ensuing reconfigurations of power, profit, class, race, gender, labor, religion, morality, and sexuality (Amar 2013: 3, 14). Writes Amar: "In the last three decades, neoliberal market legitimations and consumerist ideologies have gradually lost their power to prop up militarized forms of governance in rapidly changing regions of the Global South. Forms of humanized security discourse that generate particular sexual, class, and moral subjects have come to define political sovereignty and to articulate grammars of dialectically unfolding and internally contradictory forms of power" (Amar 2013: 6).

The Security Archipelago explores how new human-security regimes "govern through moral politics not market policies" (Amar 2013: 16). But as Amar explains, this does not necessarily translate into more just societies, since security logics can be both repressive and emancipatory. The book looks at specific moments in which human-security logics are articulated and implemented, such as the "rescue" of heritage culture, families, and prostitutes and the concurrent penalization of sex traffickers and street "thugs," and their positive and negative impacts on civilian populations and targeted sectors of society.

In What Ways Is It a Global Studies Project?

Taking a "bottom-up, Global South–centered approach," the book presents alternative perspectives to that of the global north, the orientation that most Euro-American research takes (Amar 2013: 30). Through these different standpoints, the narrative dislodges the conventional analytical frameworks that presume a modern liberal state system of political structure and organization. *The Security Archipelago* shows, in contrast, how state formations are constituted through dynamic transregional exchanges across the global south that involve various communities and movements of resistance in transnational and global-scale processes of capitalism, labor, development, and humanitarianism.

With respect to the characteristics of global studies scholarship that we outlined in Chapter 2, *The Security Archipelago* presents a deeply historical yet holistic account that challenges Eurocentric assumptions about nation-state formation and state governance. It explicitly seeks to break down binaries between the global south and global north, showing that political and ideological flows and transnational economic processes do not always originate in the West then seep outwards to Europe's peripheries. The local-global continuum is evident in the book's exploration of emergent spatial and political formations in the Middle East and South America that are both a response to and a reconfiguration of the market policies and politics of a Western-driven neoliberalism.

Methodology and Research Design

Amar explicitly draws on a wide range of literature from across the disciplines to inform *The Security Archipelago*, which he locates within the interdisciplinary field of critical security studies (Amar 2013: 19). The book deploys a mixed-methods approach, using archival, historical, and ethnographic strategies and diverse materials, including urban planning documents, public memorials, visual and musical elements, dance and public performance, community workshops, sit-ins, and interviews with people who had been involved in conflict and violence in public squares and street demonstrations.

With respect to research design, *The Security Archipelago* is a very good example of the multidimensional case study approach. It ostensibly contrasts Egypt and Brazil, but in a much more sophisticated way than a simple state-to-state comparison. The book frames these two countries and their respective megacities of Cairo and Rio within dynamic regional and global south contexts; it never presents them as static geopolitical units, as is typical in international relations scholarship. Moreover, the book's comparative analysis employs a multidimensional strategy that reveals cultural and political elements across time and space—how Egypt and Brazil were constituted through former colonial regimes, how they figured in the 1970s UN-led development paradigm, and more recently, how the two countries together and separately helped forge new subjects within a new "soft-and-smart power" humanitarian paradigm (Amar 2013: 22).

One of the most exciting contributions the book makes is its "archipelago methodology," which sets up a unique strategy for gathering and analyzing data. Throughout the book, Amar explores moments of crisis and struggles against state and parastate power, showing that it is in these "intersection zones" that the "practices, norms, and institutional products" of the new human security state are created (Amar 2013: 21, 16). These practices, norms, and products then travel "across an archipelago, a metaphorical island chain, of what the private security industry calls 'hotspots'— enclaves of panic and laboratories of control—the most hypervisible of which have emerged in Global South megacities like Cairo and Rio" (Amar 2013: 16–17). This archipelago methodology is a creative and provocative way to move beyond standard ways of researching global processes. Instead of tracing social movement mobilizations or comparing regime types, which are typical approaches in sociology and political science, the archipelago methodology allows the researcher to identify new forms of politics, actors, orderings, practices of social control, and spatial infrastructures (Amar 2013: 236). In the process, it transcends the statist methodology that still overwhelmingly dominates the Euro-American academy. A refreshing and important methodological contribution to global studies scholarship, *The Security Archipelago* reveals new conceptual horizons, imaginations, visions, voices, perspectives, and narratives.

GOD IN THE TUMULT OF THE GLOBAL SQUARE: RELIGION IN GLOBAL CIVIL SOCIETY

Mark Juergensmeyer, Dinah Griego, and John Soboslai published *God in the Tumult of the Global Square* in 2015. Juergensmeyer, the first author, was originally trained as a political scientist but became a professor of sociology and global studies. He is also one of the founders of the Global Studies Department and former director of the Orfalea Center for Global and International Studies at the University of California, Santa Barbara. Unlike the other three studies we have discussed in this chapter, *God in the Tumult of the Global Square* was grand in conception, design, and resources, and it reflects the experience and expertise of a very senior scholar in global studies. The book is the culmination of four years of collaboration and conversation among over one hundred scholars, policy makers, and religious leaders who participated in numerous workshops in Santa Barbara, California, as well as five workshops held around the world in Buenos Aires, Delhi, Cairo, Shanghai, and Moscow. The Luce Foundation provided major funding for the four-year project as part of its initiative on religion in international affairs, and the researchers received smaller amounts of funds from numerous universities and granting agencies.

What Is the Study About?

God in the Tumult of the Global Square is, as the authors describe it, a "project exploring the role of religion in global civil society"—of the social changes occurring around the world in the early twenty-first century and the role religion plays in these changes (Juergensmeyer, Griego, and Soboslai 2015: 3). The authors are particularly interested in the ways traditional religions are adapting to shifting geopolitical circumstances, the processes by which new religions are emerging in response to these changing circumstances, and how religions are in turn shaping new geopolitical dynamics. Their major research questions explore why religiosity in its various forms and institutions is re-emerging as a central platform for structuring cultural and political life. As the authors argue, this phenomenon is occurring around the world, often in different and contradictory ways. Why is secular nationalism—which involved the rolling back of religion in the public domain and characterizes the Enlightenment and the past three hundred years of national and international governance—now being severely challenged? How does one explain why religious fundamentalism has risen with such force in both Western and non-Western contexts in recent decades?

The focal point of the study is the public square as a site and space of community religious engagement. Public squares in city contexts provide arenas for demonstration and resistance by locals against state and military powers, and for hundreds of years they have functioned as battlefields for civil and political disobedience. Juergensmeyer, Griego, and Soboslai refer to events that have occurred in public squares such as Taksim Square, Istanbul; Tahrir Square, Cairo; Independence Square, Kiev; Tiananmen Square, Beijing; and Zuccotti Park, New York, throughout the book. But the book also engages with the idea of a metaphoric and symbolic global public square. The authors explore the possibility of the emergence of a new global religion that represents global civil society and a morally infused global space. This "global square" is not an actual physical place but is articulated through new forms of media and communication that transcend national cultural and geopolitical boundaries. The authors ask whether it is possible to envision this global space as a moral and spiritual base for a global community to grapple with global issues such as climate change, human rights, and world peace.

In What Ways Is It a Global Studies Project?

God in the Tumult of the Global Square is an exemplary global studies project in many ways. It is a critical interdisciplinary exploration of religious activism as enacted in new kinds of spaces that are not necessarily framed by the nation-state or institutionalized within state systems. So from the outset it does not take the national for granted as the analytical container in which old and new forms of religious expression emerge or are displayed. Instead, the authors explore religious activism in the conventional urban space of the public square as well as new forms of religiosity on the streets, in community gatherings, among displaced communities, and in the ephemeral, nowhere space of digital communications (see Sassen 2011).

Similarly, the book does not take for granted the rather narrow concept of religion as it is conventionally understood by Western scholars steeped in the tradition of the Enlightenment. That tradition posits secularism as the absence of religion—one defines the other. But as Juergensmeyer, Griego, and Soboslai argue, religion is a much more nuanced concept that takes meaning from its social, cultural, and political contexts. People can be both secular and religious simultaneously, and rarely is religiosity a discrete phenomenon that can easily be cordoned off from politics, as scholars in the Euro-American academy are inclined to think (Juergensmeyer, Griego, and Soboslai 2015: 4–5).

With respect to the characteristics of global studies scholarship that we outlined in Chapter 2, *God in the Tumult of the Global Square* illustrates a much-needed holistic account of how religiosity is unfolding against a background of turbulent global processes. At the same time, the book is attentive to the cultural, social, political, and economic strains such processes are imposing on ordinary people and their everyday lives. It takes a multicentric approach, highlighting that religious responses and activities are decentralized in that they do not only emanate from the nation-state. And it takes a distributed approach, recognizing the significance of deep historical contexts in understanding contemporary forms of religiosity that crisscross geopolitical borders and are often communicated through digital social media. The book emphasizes the lack of a center or periphery in global religion and spirituality. In so doing, it overcomes conventional binaries between secular and religious, public and private, and global south and global north and transcends the typical characterization of religions as monolithic yet discrete systems of belief and behavior. *God in the Tumult of the Global Square* above all underscores the interconnections between various forms of political power and religious engagement and the pitfalls of Western scholars' tendency to underestimate the power of religion in understanding global affairs.

Methodology and Research Design

God in the Tumult of the Global Square employs a critical methodological strategy very pertinent to global studies research. It involves mixed methods and sources: archival research, ethnographic research, interviews, reports, statistics, news and social media, and primary and secondary literatures. And it is informed by a wide-ranging transdisciplinary theoretical framework: the study's participants encompassed a broad spectrum of people representing different perspectives from across the world, each with a particular story to tell about religion and its shifting role in social and political life. These people also represented different institutions, communities, classes, ethnicities, and relative power positions within their given societies.

This kind of project involves a lot of travel by many people, requiring substantial funding, administrative resources, and university support over several years. The researchers involved have to write grants, submit reports, and publish material to secure continuing financial support for a project of this scale. This kind of research agenda is clearly not available to everyone, nor is this the kind of research project that anyone can manage and sustain for four years. That being said, the basic research design and critical methodology of *God in the Tumult of the Global Square* are ones that a single researcher with considerably less resources could emulate, albeit at a much more modest scale.

While it is not made explicit in *God in the Tumult of the Global Square*, the book adopts the kind of intersectional global standpoint theory that we have outlined in Chapter 5. It gives voice to numerous individuals and groups and explores their various viewpoints, be these at local, community, regional, national, transnational, or global levels. Its methodology is explicitly designed to advance cross-cultural interpretations by acknowledging the presence and power of hybrid subjectivities, cosmopolitanism, and plural ways of knowing and being in the world specifically as they relate to religious beliefs and spiritual practices. And as a multidimensional case study of comparative religious experiences and responses, it engages with global ethical issues such as structural inequalities, asymmetrical power relations, governmental legitimacy, religious authority, and the question of who gets to speak and act on behalf of whom.

The four multidimensional case studies we have discussed in this chapter are exemplars of global research projects. They represent critical interdisciplinary theoretical frameworks, draw on a wide range of mixed methods, and reflect global designs and methodologies. Although not necessarily explicit in the books, each study grapples with how local sites, places, events, and communities are embedded within a range of global processes and structural and institutional relationships that transcend conventional geopolitical borders and boundaries. In other words, they are all engaged with the local-global continuum and see the range of local, regional, national, transnational, and global conceptual and analytical planes of that continuum as relational and, in many instances, operating simultaneously.

Conclusion

DECENTERING THE PRODUCTION
OF GLOBAL KNOWLEDGE

The primary goal of this book is to make the process of doing research on complex global issues more accessible to global studies scholars, scholars in other fields, and students looking to do interdisciplinary research on global issues. The approach we have outlined is a synthesis of new global perspectives, transdisciplinary theoretical approaches, and methodological and analytical implications of those elements. We hope that our effort makes it possible for researchers in nearly any field to ask distinctly global research questions, design viable research projects that empirically engage global issues, and produce research that is relevant to contemporary challenges.

In the first two chapters we outlined some of the basic concepts and approaches that we feel characterize global scholarship, whether it be scholarship in the relatively new field of global studies or emerging global scholarship in more established fields. We argued that the kinds of complex global challenges playing out across the local-global continuum call for innovative research strategies. Hence, we emphasized the importance of deploying new global perspectives and recognizing new global-scale issues in designing, conducting, and analyzing global research. The subsequent chapters began the process of developing a coherent global research agenda that provides a practical way for researchers to incorporate these perspectives and engage these pressing issues.

The third chapter outlined a **global transdisciplinary framework** that we hope encourages thinking beyond conventional modern disciplinary boundaries and their limitations. The framework recognizes both transnational and translocal forces that together are challenging the centrality of nation-states from above and below. In order to maximize the potential for both **methodological** and **conceptual triangulation**, the framework includes theories from across the humanities and social sciences. It makes it possible to study multifaceted global-scale issues in a holistic fashion, deploying various perspectives at multiple levels and across spatial and temporal dimensions.

The transdisciplinary theoretical framework forms the basis for developing global research designs that can incorporate multiple methodological and analytical approaches and that are sufficiently flexible to address the enormous array of global issues confronting the world today (see Chapters 4 and 5). In Chapter 5 we also argued that one of the most profound contributions of a global studies methodology is that it fosters a **global standpoint theory that is deeply intersectional**. By this we mean that the new field recognizes that everyone sees and experiences the world from his or her own particular place in the world. In a quote we have cited a number of times throughout this book for its pithiness and bite, "We know what we know from where we stand. We need to be honest about that" (Kovach 2009: 7). But whereas feminist and other critical methodologies often take the nation-state as the framing horizon of a person's standpoint, a global methodology explicitly widens the lens to incorporate a local-global continuum upon which one's standpoint can be positioned. Moreover, a global methodology takes into account that a person's standpoint has numerous intersecting political, economic, social, and cultural dimensions and arises from intersectional relations of class, race, ethnicity, gender, and religion that involve cumulative forms of power, oppression, and discrimination. We then moved on in Chapter 6 to elaborate a multidimensional case study approach that serves as an example of the kinds of methodologies that allow researchers to maintain conceptual focus while at the same time providing the freedom to be as qualitative or quantitative, as empirical or interpretive, or as abstract or grounded as needed to answer the original research question.

The global transdisciplinary framework specifically calls for the inclusion of marginalized perspectives and epistemologies in the production of new global knowledge. Rereading national histories as more inclusive global histories requires us to recognize the brutal impacts of colonialism and imperialism. Dealing with these histories involves recognizing the role of modern forms of rationality and science in epistemological imperialism and the repeated incidents of epistemic violence and wholesale "epistemicide" that make up those histories (Santos 2014; Moore 2003). Scholars can only begin to bridge the divides between First and Third Worlds, developed and developing worlds, East and West, and global north and south if they acknowledge these histories and understand that forms of epistemological imperialism persist in development, free market, humanitarian, and human rights discourses. A truly decentralized production of global knowledge must do more than replicate these earlier forms of imperialism.

In the current moment, processes of globalization are bringing every locale into increasing contact with the radical diversity of the world's cultures. This diversity has always been there, but the increasing frequency of intercultural encounters is forcing global scholars to engage with intercultural conflict and the world's extremes of inequality. Wrote Edward Said over twenty years ago, "We are mixed in with one another in ways that most national systems of education have not dreamed of" (Said 1993: 328). Prophetically, Said went on to say, "To match knowledge in the arts and sciences with these integrative realities is . . . the cultural challenge of the moment" (Said 1993: 331; see also Said 1983). Global perspectives remind scholars that the "minority" populations of Euro-American societies, populations that have historically been underrepresented in the Euro-American academy, are the majority of the world's population. These majorities disproportionately experience the impacts of global issues such as inequality, climate change, conflict, and migration. These same majorities will almost certainly be impacted by the knowledge being produced about global issues. Surely shared global histories and shared global futures mean that the peoples of the world have every right to be recognized as self-determining geopolitical actors and to participate fully in the production of knowledge about the issues that will inevitably impact us all.

In this book we argue that the characteristics of global research—that it be holistic, transgressive, integrative, decentered, deterritorialized, critical, pluralistic, ethical, and so on—highlight the need to rethink the basic intellectual approaches and research strategies that have dominated the Euro-American academy for well over a century. To put this differently, engaging in global research is an adaptive response to the clear limitations of conventional research approaches from the global north, which continues to be locked in a worldview that reflects outdated concepts of modernity—science, rationalism, individualism, and nationalism.

Narrow-minded thinking, or what some call parochialism, is most evident when academic disciplines continue to present a state-based approach that does not accurately reflect the complex geopolitical realities of our times and their various assemblages of power, authority, and sovereignty—assemblages that no longer correlate to a "wealth of nations" schematic (Sassen 2008). As many commentators have noted, we now live in a post-national and post-Westphalian era in which nation-states are only one set of actors in regional, transnational, and global affairs. Unfortunately, the nation-state still dominates most discipline-based research, containing thought and constraining innovation.

The problem with thinking in terms of sovereign nation-states and nationalism is that these concepts sustain an exaggerated preoccupation with the political, economic, and cultural status of one country vis-à-vis other countries. Is China rising and overtaking the United States? Is China declining, and can the United States reassert its superpower status? What other emerging economies present the next big political and financial threat? Where stands Russia in all of this? What is the impact of Brexit on the other member-states in the European Union? What role does Turkey play in Middle East politics? What about the recent economic demise of Brazil? Can the United States return to an isolationist foreign policy? While these questions are not unimportant, the way they are framed harks back to former periods of imperialism and colonialism, as well as conjuring the more recent Cold War mentality of the second half of the twentieth century. These questions evoke a sense of nostalgia for an era in which categories of comparison and competition were clear and one could map the world—or so it seemed—in terms of nation-state relations with corresponding monocultural national identities and an us-versus-them framing.

Another limitation in the Euro-American academy is that conventional theories, methods, and analyses fail to take into account today's interrelated complexities. Thinking primarily in terms of sovereign nation-states precludes the innovation and creativity that is necessary for dealing with the global challenges that everyone currently faces. Given that no one country will be able to address these challenges, the dominance of such narrow-minded thinking in countries like the United States leaves them enormously vulnerable to being left behind. Anachronistic thought closes down the mind and prevents people from imagining alternative futures in which states, regions, and continents will necessarily have to collaborate, cooperate, and compromise. As Saskia Sassen argues, "When we confront today's range of transformations—rising inequality, rising poverty, rising government debt—the usual tools to interpret them are out of date" (Sassen 2014: 7).

Global research in general, and the emerging field of global studies in particular, presents a theoretical, methodological, and analytical synthesis through which to forge powerful and flexible intellectual tools and research strategies for interpreting today's wide range of global issues and transformations. The research model we outline here offers scholars the possibility of overcoming blind spots, identifying the multifaceted complexity of global issues, and understanding whom these issues impact most and why.

The interdisciplinary field of global studies is increasingly being taught to students around the world. It is arguably revitalizing a liberal arts curriculum and forging a more balanced, holistic, inclusive, and relevant approach that speaks to the lived experiences of a generation of young people facing difficult, globally interconnected realities. Doing global research offers the possibility of increasing the applicability, validity, and relevance of scholarship to global contexts, making its contribution to the academy more significant and valuable. Perhaps most important of all, embracing the promise of global research means rethinking our positions relative to other peoples, cultures, epistemologies, ontologies, values, institutions, political organizations, and religions that together speak to how people are relating and being in the world. This calls for the decentering of the production of knowledge away from the assumed intellectual superiority of the global north and building more inclusive, accessible, and collaborative research agendas that embrace voices, perspectives, and interpretations from the global south. In methodological terms, it opens up new opportunities for **epistemological triangulation**.

Decentering the production of global knowledge is not just an ethical response to the centuries of colonialism and imperialism that have marginalized the ideas of non-Western societies in Western scholarship—though it is that. More profoundly, decentering the production of global knowledge is absolutely essential if scholars are to think through viable solutions to the world's problems, which conventional disciplines, single countries, and monolithic worldviews cannot solve. In other words, decentering, or what some scholars call *decolonizing*, the production of global knowledge means that we must all learn from one another to develop the kinds of solutions that global challenges require. It is not enough just to listen to others as a token of respect. We must all be open to learning from each other and be prepared to transform dominant concepts, ideas, and notions of self and community to better speak to our intertwined collective futures. We believe that engaging in inclusive global research presents all scholars, from any intellectual background, with the potential to produce innovative and transformative scholarship.

A GLOBAL CASE STUDY OUTLINE

RATIONALE OR PURPOSE OF THE STUDY

global issue(s) to be studied
significance of the issue(s)
overarching research question
more specific research questions

RESEARCH DESIGN

conceptual or analytical framework(s)
    definition of object of study
    definition of subject(s) of study or unit of analysis
    criteria for selection of the subject(s) of study
field of comparable cases
case methodology
    empirical strategy
    specific data collection methods
data analysis techniques
intercultural and ethical considerations

DESCRIPTION OF THE CASE(S)

relevant context(s)

case history or biography

direct observations and interviews

representation of plural and intercultural perspectives

ANALYSIS

descriptive summary of observations

discussion of patterns, conspicuous omissions, and/or contrary evidence, if applicable

discussion of context

relevant global issues

conceptual frame(s)

unit of analysis

intersecting global dimensions

larger field of cases

cross-case comparisons

FINDINGS

summary of analysis's outcome

reference to original purpose of study

reference to original research questions

discussion of study's significance

APPENDIX B LIST OF GLOBAL STUDIES JOURNALS

This list is not intended to be exhaustive as new journals appear frequently.

Asia Journal of Global Studies
http://www.aags.org/journal

Global Europe—Basel Papers on Europe in a Global Perspective
https://europa.unibas.ch/en/research/basel-papers/

Global Networks
http://www.wiley.com/WileyCDA/WileyTitle/productCd-GLO3.html

Global Societies Journal
http://www.global.ucsb.edu/globalsocieties/

Global Studies Journal
http://onglobalisation.com/journal/

Global Studies Law Review
http://openscholarship.wustl.edu/law_globalstudies/

global-e: A Global Studies Journal
http://www.21global.ucsb.edu/global-e

Globality Studies Journal (open access journal)
http://globality.cc.stonybrook.edu/

Globalizations
http://www.tandf.co.uk/journals/titles/14747731.asp

Glocalism: Journal of Culture, Politics, and Innovation
http://www.glocalismjournal.net/

Identities: Global Studies in Culture and Power
http://www.tandf.co.uk/journals/titles/1070289x.asp

Indiana Journal of Global Legal Studies
http://ijgls.indiana.edu/

Journal of Critical Globalisation Studies (open access)
http://www.criticalglobalisation.com/

Journal of Environment & Development
http://jed.sagepub.com/

Journal of Global Ethics
http://www.informaworld.com/smpp/title~db=all~content=t714578955

Journal of Global History
http://journals.cambridge.org/action/displayJournal?jid=JGH

Journal of International and Global Studies (open access)
http://www.lindenwood.edu/jigs

Journal of World-Systems Research
http://jwsr.pitt.edu/ojs/index.php/jwsr

New Global Studies
http://www.bepress.com/ngs/

Third World Quarterly
http://www.tandf.co.uk/journals/CTWQ

Transcience: A Journal of Global Studies
http://www.transcience-journal.org/

Yale Global Online
http://yaleglobal.yale.edu/

References

Allen, Chadwick. 2012. *Trans-Indigenous: Methodologies for Global Native Literary Studies*. Minneapolis: University of Minnesota Press.

Althusser, Louis. 1990. *For Marx*. Translated by Ben Brewster. London: Verso.

Amar, Paul. 2013. *The Security Archipelago: Human-Security States, Sexuality Politics, and the End of Neoliberalism*. Durham, NC: Duke University Press.

Amelina, Anna, Devrimsel D. Nergiz, Thomas Faist, and Nina Glick Schiller, eds. 2012. *Beyond Methodological Nationalism: Research Methodologies for Cross-Border Studies*. London: Routledge.

Amin, Samir. 2009. *Eurocentrism*, 2nd ed. Translated by Russell Moore and James Membrez. New York: Monthly Review.

Andersen, Espen, and Bill Schiano. 2014. *Teaching with Cases: A Practical Guide*. Cambridge, MA: Harvard Business School Publishing.

Anderson, Benedict. 1983. *Imagined Communities: Reflections on the Origin and Spread of Nationalism*. London: Verso.

Anheier, Helmut K., and Mark Juergensmeyer. 2012. *The Encyclopedia of Global Studies*. 4 vols. Thousand Oaks, CA: SAGE.

Anker, Kirsten. 2014. *Declarations of Interdependence: A Legal Pluralist Approach to Indigenous Rights*. Farnham, UK: Ashgate.

Apostel, Léo, Guy Berger, Asa Briggs, and Guy Michaud, eds. 1972. *Interdisciplinarity: Problems of Teaching and Research in Universities*. Paris: Organisation for Economic Co-operation and Development.

Appadurai, Arjun. 1996. *Modernity at Large: Cultural Dimensions of Globalization*. Minneapolis: University of Minnesota Press.

———. 2000. "Grassroots Globalization and the Research Imagination." *Public Culture* 12 (1): 1–19.

Appelbaum, Richard P., and William I. Robinson, eds. 2005. *Critical Globalization Studies*. London: Routledge.

Appiah, Kwame Anthony. 2006. *Cosmopolitanism: Ethics in a World of Strangers*. New York: Norton.

Arias, Santa, and Barney Warf, eds. 2008. *The Spatial Turn: Interdisciplinary Perspectives*. London: Routledge.

Axford, Barrie. 1995. *The Global System: Politics, Economics and Culture*. Cambridge: Polity.

Bailey, Carol A. 2006. *A Guide to Qualitative Field Research*, 2nd ed. Thousand Oaks, CA: SAGE.

Bales, Kevin. 2016. *Blood and Earth: Modern Slavery, Ecocide, and the Secret to Saving the World*. New York: Spiegel & Grau.

Balibar, Étienne. 2015. *Citizenship*. Cambridge: Polity.

Bamberger, Michael, Jim Rugh, and Linda Mabry. 2011. *RealWorld Evaluation: Working under Budget, Time, Data, and Political Constraints*, 2nd ed. Thousand Oaks, CA: SAGE.

Baran, Paul. 1964. "On Distributed Communications Networks." *IEEE Transactions of the Professional Technical Group on Communications Systems* CS-12 (1): 1–9.

Bardach, Eugene, and Eric M. Patashnik. 2015. *A Practical Guide for Policy Analysis: The Eightfold Path to More Effective Problem Solving*, 5th ed. Washington, DC: CQ.

Barker, Chris, and Emma A. Jane. 2016. *Cultural Studies: Theory and Practice*, 5th ed. Thousand Oaks, CA: SAGE.

Bateman, Lucy, and Etienne Oliff, directors. 2003. *Flip Flotsam*. Documentary video available at http://www.viewchange.org/videos/kenya-flip-flotsam. See also "Fortune on the Flip Side" *The Scottsman Newspaper*, Nov 29, 2003.

Bauchspies, Wenda. 2007. "Postcolonial Methods." *Blackwell Encyclopedia of Sociology*, vol. 6, edited by George Ritzer, 2981–86. Hoboken, NJ: Wiley-Blackwell.

Bauman, Zygmunt. 1996. "From Pilgrim to Tourist—or a Short History of Identity." *Questions of Cultural Identity*, edited by Stuart Hall and Paul du Gay, 18–36. Thousand Oaks, CA: SAGE.

———. 1998. *Globalization: The Human Consequences*. Cambridge: Polity.

Beck, Ulrich. 1992. *Risk Society: Towards a New Modernity*. Thousand Oaks, CA: SAGE.

———. 2006. *Cosmopolitan Vision*. Translated by Ciaran Cronin. Cambridge: Polity.

————. 2009. *World at Risk*. Cambridge: Polity.

Beck, Ulrich, and Natan Sznaider. 2006. "Unpacking Cosmopolitanism for the Social Sciences: A Research Agenda." *British Journal of Sociology* 57 (1): 1–23.

Beck, Ulrich and Johannes Willms. 2004. *Conversations with Ulrich Beck*. Cambridge: Polity Press.

Bell, Derrick A. 1995. "Who's Afraid of Critical Race Theory?" *University of Illinois Law Review* 1995 (4): 893–910.

Bentley, Jerry H., ed. 2013. *The Oxford Handbook of World History*. Oxford: Oxford University Press.

Berg, Bruce L., and Howard Lune. 2011. *Qualitative Research Methods for the Social Sciences*, 8th ed. New York: Pearson.

Berger, Peter L., and Thomas Luckmann. 1966. *The Social Construction of Reality: A Treatise in the Sociology of Knowledge*. New York: Doubleday.

Bernal, Dolores Delgado. 2002. "Critical Race Theory, Latino Critical Theory, and Critical Raced-Gendered Epistemologies: Recognizing Students of Color as Holders and Creators of Knowledge." *Qualitative Inquiry* 8 (1): 105–26.

Bernard, H. Russell. 2011. *Research Methods in Anthropology: Qualitative and Quantitative Approaches*, 5th ed. Lanham, MD: AltaMira.

Bertalanffy, Ludwig von. 1969. *General Systems Theory: Foundations, Development, Applications*, rev. ed. New York: George Braziller.

Bhabha, Homi K., ed. 1990. *Nation and Narration*. London: Routledge.

Birks, Melanie, and Jane Mills. 2015. *Grounded Theory: A Practical Guide*, 2nd ed. Thousand Oaks, CA: SAGE.

Blass, Thomas. 2009. *The Man Who Shocked the World: The Life and Legacy of Stanley Milgram*. New York: Basic Books.

Blassnigg, Martha, and Michael Punt. 2012. "Transdisciplinarity: Challenges, Approaches, and Opportunities at the Cusp of History." White paper, Network for Science, Engineering, Arts, and Design. https://seadnetwork .files.wordpress.com/2012/11/blassnig_final.pdf.

Bodenhamer, David J., John Corrigan, and Trevor M. Harris, eds. 2010. *The Spatial Humanities: GIS and the Future of Humanities Scholarship*. Bloomington: Indiana University Press.

Bombaro, Christine. 2012. *Finding History: Research Methods and Resources for Students and Scholars*. Lanham, MD: Scarecrow.

Borenstein, Michael, Larry V. Hedges, Julian P. T. Higgins, and Hannah R. Rothstein. 2009. *Introduction to Meta-Analysis*. Malden, MA: Wiley-Blackwell.

Borgatti, Stephen P., Martin G. Everett, and Jeffrey C. Johnson. 2013. *Analyzing Social Networks*. Thousand Oaks, CA: SAGE.

Bose, Christine E. 2012. "Intersectionality and Global Gender Inequality." *Gender and Society* 26 (1): 67–72.

Brady, Henry E., and David Collier, eds. 2010. *Rethinking Social Inquiry: Diverse Tools, Shared Standards*. Lanham, MD: Rowman & Littlefield.

Brah, Avtar, and Ann Phoenix. 2004. "Ain't I a Woman? Revisiting Intersectionality." *Journal of International Women's Studies* 5 (3): 75–86.

Brayboy, Bryan McKinley Jones. 2005. "Toward a Tribal Critical Race Theory in Education." *Urban Review* 37 (5): 425–46.

Brenner, Neil. 2001. "The Limits to Scale? Methodological Reflections on Scalar Structuration." *Progress in Human Geography* 25: 591–614.

———. 2004. *New State Spaces: Urban Governance and the Rescaling of Statehood*. Oxford: Oxford University Press.

Brettell, Caroline B., and James F. Hollifield, eds. 2014. *Migration Theory: Talking across Disciplines*. London: Routledge.

Brown, Wendy. 2014. *Walled States, Waning Sovereignty*. New York: Zone.

———. 2015. *Undoing the Demos: Neoliberalism's Stealth Revolution*. New York: Zone.

Brundage, Anthony. 2013. *Going to the Sources: A Guide to Historical Research and Writing*. Malden, MA: Wiley-Blackwell.

Bryman, Alan. 2016. *Social Research Methods*, 5th ed. Oxford: Oxford University Press.

Burawoy, Michael. 1998. "The Extended Case Method." *Sociological Theory* 16 (1): 4–33.

———. 2009. "The Global Turn: Lessons from Southern Labor Scholars and Their Labor Movements." *Work and Occupations* 36(2): 87–95.

———. 2014. Preface to Keim et al., *Global Knowledge Production in the Social Sciences*, xiii–xvii.

Burawoy, Michael, Joseph A. Blum, Sheba George, Zsuzsa Gille, Teresa Gowan, Lynne Haney, Maren Klawiter, Steven H. Lopez, Seán Ó Riain, and Millie Thayer. 2000. *Global Ethnography: Forces, Connections, and Imaginations in a Postmodern World*. Berkeley: University of California Press.

Burnett, Ron. 2008. "Is Transdisciplinarity a New Learning Paradigm for the Digital Age?" In Nicolescu, *Transdisciplinarity*, 245–52.

Butler, Judith. 1990. *Gender Trouble: Feminism and the Subversion of Identity*. London: Routledge.

Campbell, Patricia, Aran MacKinnon, and Christy Stevens. 2010. *Introduction to Global Studies*. Malden, MA: Wiley-Blackwell.

Carson, Rachel. 1962. *Silent Spring*. Boston: Houghton Mifflin.

Carr, Edward Hallet. 1967. *What Is History?* New York: Vintage.

Casid, Jill H., and Aruna D'Souza, eds. 2014. *Art History in the Wake of the Global Turn*. New Haven, CT: Clark Studies in the Visual Arts, Yale University Press.

Castells, Manuel. 1996. *The Rise of the Network Society*. Oxford: Blackwell.

Caughey, John L. 2006. *Negotiating Cultures and Identities: Life History Issues, Methods, and Readings*. Lincoln: University of Nebraska Press.

Cavanagh, Edward, and Lorenzo Veracini. 2013. "Editors' Statement." *Settler Colonial Studies* 3 (1): http://www.tandfonline.com/doi/full/10.1080/18380743.2013.768169.

Chakrabarty, Dipesh. 1992. "Postcoloniality and the Artifice of History: Who Speaks for 'Indian' Pasts?" *Representations* 37: 1–26.

———. 2000. *Provincializing Europe: Postcolonial Thought and Historical Difference*. Princeton, NJ: Princeton University Press.

Chang, Robert S. 1993. "Toward an Asian American Legal Scholarship: Critical Race Theory, Post-Structuralism, and Narrative Space." *California Law Review* 81 (5): 1241–323.

Charmaz, Kathy. 2014. *Constructing Grounded Theory*, 2nd ed. Thousand Oaks, CA: SAGE.

Cheah, Pheng, and Bruce Robbins. 1998. *Cosmopolitics: Thinking and Feeling Beyond the Nation*. Minneapolis: University of Minnesota Press.

Chevalier, Jacques M., and Daniel J. Buckles. 2013. *Participatory Action Research: Theory and Methods for Engaged Inquiry*. London: Routledge.

Chiang, Alpha C., and Kevin Wainwright. 2005. *Fundamental Methods of Mathematical Economics*. New York: McGraw-Hill Education.

Chilisa, Bagele. 2011. *Indigenous Research Methodologies*. Thousand Oaks, CA: SAGE.

Chomsky, Noam. 1999. *Profit Over People: Neoliberalism & Global Order*. New York: Seven Stories Press.

Chomsky, Noam, Ira Katznelson, R. C. Lewontin, David Montgomery, Laura Nader, Richard Ohmann, Ray Siever, Immanuel Wallerstein, and Howard Zinn. 1998. *The Cold War and the University: Toward an Intellectual History of the Postwar Years*. New York: New Press.

Chow, Esther Ngan-ling, Marcia Texler Segal, and Lin Tan, eds. 2011. *Analyzing Gender, Intersectionality, and Multiple Inequalities: Global, Transnational, and Local Contexts*. Bingley, UK: Emerald.

Chow, Rey. 2006. *The Age of the World Target: Self-Referentiality in War, Theory, and Comparative Work*. Durham, NC: Duke University Press.

Clark, Andrew, Jon Prosser, and Rose Wiles. 2010. "Ethical Issues in Image-Based Research." *Arts & Health* 2 (1): 81–93.

Clegg, Stewart R., Cynthia Hardy, Thomas B. Lawrence, and Walter R. Nord, eds. 2006. *The SAGE Handbook of Organization Studies*, 2nd ed. Thousand Oaks, CA: SAGE.

Clifford, James. 2013. *Returns: Becoming Indigenous in the Twenty-First Century*. Cambridge, MA: Harvard University Press.

Clitandre, Nadège T. 2011. "Haitian Exceptionalism in the Caribbean and the Project of Rebuilding Haiti." *Journal of Haitian Studies* 17 (2): 146–53.

Cohen, Benjamin J. 2014. *Advanced Introduction to International Political Economy*. Cheltenham, UK: Edward Elgar.

Cole, Douglas. 1985. *Captured Heritage: The Scramble for Northwest Coast Artifacts*. Seattle: University of Washington Press.

Collins, Denis, ed. 2013. *Music Theory and Its Methods: Structures, Challenges, Directions*. Frankfurt am Main: Peter Lang.

Collins, Patricia Hill. 1990. *Black Feminist Thought: Knowledge, Consciousness, and the Politics of Empowerment*. London: Routledge.

Collins, Patricia Hill, and Sirma Bilge. 2016. *Intersectionality*. Cambridge: Polity.

Comaroff, Jean, and John L. Comaroff, eds. 2006. *Law and Disorder in the Postcolony*. Chicago: University of Chicago Press.

———. 2012. *Theory from the South: or, How Euro-America Is Evolving toward Africa*. Boulder, CO: Paradigm.

Conrad, Sebastian. 2016. *What Is Global History?* Princeton, NJ: Princeton University Press.

Cooper, Harris. 2016. *Research Synthesis and Meta-Analysis: A Step-by-Step Approach*, 5th ed. Thousand Oaks, CA: SAGE.

Crenshaw, Kimberlé Williams. 1988. "Race, Reform, and Retrenchment: Transformation and Legitimation in Anti-Discrimination Law." *Harvard Law Review* 101 (7): 1331–87.

———. 1991. "Mapping the Margins: Intersectionality, Identity Politics, and Violence against Women of Color." *Stanford Law Review* 43 (6): 1241–99.

Crenshaw, Kimberlé, Neil Gotanda, Gary Peller, and Kendall Thomas, eds. 1995. *Critical Race Theory: The Key Writings that Formed the Movement*. New York: New Press.

Creswell, John W. 2007. *Qualitative Inquiry and Research Design: Choosing among Five Approaches*. Thousand Oaks, CA: SAGE.

———. 2014. *Research Design: Qualitative, Quantitative, and Mixed Methods Approaches*. Thousand Oaks, CA: SAGE.

———. 2015. *A Concise Introduction to Mixed Methods Research*. Thousand Oaks, CA: SAGE.

Cresswell, Tim. 2013. *Geographic Thought: A Critical Introduction*. Malden, MA: Wiley-Blackwell.

Czarniawska, Barbara. 1998. *A Narrative Approach to Organization Studies*. Thousand Oaks, CA: SAGE.

Dados, Nour, and Raewyn Connell. 2014. "Neoliberalism, Intellectuals, and Southern Theory." In Keim et al., *Global Knowledge Production in the Social Sciences*, 195–213.

Dann, Philipp, and Felix Hanschmann. 2012. "Post-Colonial Theories and Law." "Post-Colonial Theories and Law," edited by Philipp Dann and Felix Hanschmann, special issue, *Journal of Law and Politics in Africa, Asia and Latin America* 45 (2): 123–27.

Darian-Smith, Eve. 1996. "Postcolonialism: A Brief Introduction." "Law and Postcolonialism," edited by Eve Darian-Smith and Peter Fitzpatrick, special issue, *Social and Legal Studies* 5 (3): 291–99.

———. 1999. *Bridging Divides: The Channel Tunnel and English Legal Identity in the New Europe*. Berkeley: University of California Press.

———. 2002. "Getting Past the Science Wars," review of *Making Social Science Matter*, by Bent Flyvbjerg. *Current Anthropologist* 43 (1): 194–96.

———. 2013a. *Laws and Societies in Global Contexts: Contemporary Approaches*. Cambridge: Cambridge University Press.

———. 2013b. "Postcolonial Theories of Law." In *Law and Social Theory*, 2nd ed., edited by Reza Banakar and Max Travers, 247–264. Oxford: Hart.

———. 2013c. "Locating a Global Perspective." "Symposium: Legal Scholarship and Globalization; Engagements with William Twining," special issue, *Transnational Legal Theory* 4 (4): 524–26.

———. 2014. "Global Studies—The Handmaiden of Neoliberalism?" *Globalizations* 12 (2): 164–68.

———. 2015. "The Constitution of Identity: New Modalities of Nationality, Citizenship, Belonging, and Being." In *The Handbook of Law and Society*, edited by Austin Sarat and Patricia Ewick, 351–66. Malden, MA: Wiley-Blackwell.

———. 2016. "Mismeasuring Humanity: Examining Indicators through a Critical Global Studies Perspective." *New Global Studies* 10 (1): 73–99.

Darian-Smith, Eve, and Philip McCarty. 2016. "Beyond Interdisciplinarity: Developing a Global Transdisciplinary Framework." *Transcience* 7 (2).

Darieva, Tsypylma, Nina Glick Schiller, and Sandra Gruner-Domic, eds. 2012. *Cosmopolitan Sociability: Locating Transnational Religious and Diasporic Networks*. London: Routledge.

Davis, Mike. 2006. *Planet of Slums*. London: Verso.

Dayan, Colin. 2011. *The Law Is a White Dog: How Legal Rituals Make and Unmake Persons*. Princeton, NJ: Princeton University Press.

Dear, Peter. 2001. *Revolutionizing the Sciences: European Knowledge and Its Ambitions, 1500–1700*. Princeton, NJ: Princeton University Press.

De Fina, Anna, and Alexandra Georgakopoulou. 2015. *The Handbook of Narrative Analysis*. Malden, MA: Wiley-Blackwell.

Delgado, Richard, and Jean Stefancic. 1993. "Critical Race Theory: An Annotated Bibliography." *Virginia Law Review* 79: 461–516.

———, eds. 1998. *The Latino/a Condition: A Critical Reader*. New York: New York University Press.

———. 2001. *Critical Race Theory: An Introduction*. New York: New York University Press.

Denzin, Norman K., and Yvonna S. Lincoln. 2008. Preface to *Handbook of Critical and Indigenous Methodologies*, edited by Norman K. Denzin,

Yvonna S. Lincoln, and Linda Tuhiwai Smith, ix–xv. Thousand Oaks, CA: SAGE.

Desai, Vandana, and Robert B. Potter. 2014. *The Companion to Development Studies*, 3rd ed. London: Routledge.

Desrosières, Alain. 1998. *The Politics of Large Numbers: A History of Statistical Reasoning*. Translated by Camille Naish. Cambridge, MA: Harvard University Press.

DeWalt, Kathleen M., and Billie R. DeWalt. 2011. *Participant Observation: A Guide for Fieldworkers*. Lanham, MD: AltaMira.

Douglas, Mary. 2003 [1970]. *Natural Symbols: Explorations in Cosmology*. Reprint of 1996 ed. London: Routledge.

Du Bois, W. E. B. 1986. *Writings*, edited by Nathan Huggins. New York: Library of America.

Duménil, Gérard, and Dominique Lévy. 2004. *Capital Resurgent: Roots of the Neoliberal Revolution*. Cambridge, MA: Harvard University Press.

Duneier, Mitchell. 1992. *Slim's Table: Race, Respectability, and Masculinity*. Chicago: University of Chicago Press.

Dunn, Kevin C., and Iver B. Neumann. 2016. *Undertaking Discourse Analysis for Social Research*. Ann Arbor: University of Michigan Press.

Duve, Thomas. 2013. "European Legal History: Global Perspectives." Paper presented at "European Normativity: Global Historical Perspectives" Colloquium, Max-Planck-Institute for European Legal History, Frankfurt, Germany, September 2–4.

Emmel, Nick. 2013. *Sampling and Choosing Cases in Qualitative Research: A Realist Approach*. Thousand Oaks, CA: SAGE.

Engel, Uwe, Ben Jann, Peter Lynn, Annette Scherpenzeel, and Patrick Sturgis, eds. 2015. *Improving Survey Methods: Lessons from Recent Research*. London: Routledge.

Escobar, Arturo. 1995. *Encountering Development: The Making and Unmaking of the Third World*. Princeton, NJ: Princeton University Press.

Eslava, Luis. 2015. *Local Space, Global Life: The Everyday Operation of International Law and Development*. Cambridge: Cambridge University Press.

Essed, Philomena, and David Theo Goldberg, eds. 2001. *Race Critical Theories: Text and Context*. Malden, MA: Blackwell.

Evans, Mike, Rachelle Hole, Lawrence D. Berg, Peter Hutchinson, and Dixon Sookraj. 2009. "Common Insights, Differing Methodologies: Toward a Fusion of Indigenous Methodologies, Participatory Action Research, and White Studies in an Urban Aboriginal Research Agenda." *Qualitative Inquiry* 15 (5): 893–910.

Falk, Richard. 2002. "Revisiting Westphalia, Discovering Post-Westphalia." *Journal of Ethics* 6 (4): 311–52.

———. 2014. *(Re)Imagining Humane Global Governance*. London: Routledge.

Falzon, Mark-Anthony, ed. 2009. *Multi-Sited Ethnography: Theory, Praxis and Locality in Contemporary Research*. Farnham, UK: Ashgate.

Fam, Dena, Jane Palmer, Chris Riedy, and Cynthia Mitchell, eds. 2016. *Transdisciplinary Research and Practice for Sustainability Outcomes*. London: Routledge.

Fangen Katrine, Thomas Johansson, and Nils Hammarén, eds. 2012. *Young Migrants: Exclusion and Belonging in Europe*. Basingstoke, UK: Palgrave Macmillan.

Fanon, Frantz. 1961. *The Wretched of the Earth*. Translated by Constance Farrington. New York: Grove.

Farrell, Ann. 2015. "Ethics in Research with Children." In "Childhood Studies," edited by Heather Montgomery, *Oxford Bibliographies*. Last reviewed May 13. http://www.oxfordbibliographies.com/view/document/obo-9780199791231 /obo-9780199791231-0070.xml.

Featherstone, Mike, Scott Lash, and Roland Robertson, eds. 1995. *Global Modernities*. London: SAGE.

Featherstone, Mike, and Couze Venn. 2006. "Problematizing Global Knowledge and the New Encyclopedia Project: An Introduction." *Theory, Culture & Society* 23 (2–3): 1–20.

Ferguson, James. 2006. *Global Shadows: Africa in the Neoliberal World Order*. Durham, NC: Duke University Press.

Ferguson, Roderick. 2012. *The Reorder of Things: The University and Its Pedagogies of Minority Difference*. Minneapolis: University of Minnesota Press.

Ferguson, Yale H., and Richard W. Mansbach. 2012. *Globalization: The Return of Borders to a Borderless World?* London: Routledge.

Fitzgerald, Des, and Felicity Callard. 2014. "Social Science and Neuroscience beyond Interdisciplinarity: Experimental Entanglements." *Theory, Culture & Society* 32 (1): 3–32.

Fitzpatrick, Jody L., James R. Sanders, and Blaine R. Worthen. 2011. *Program Evaluation: Alternative Approaches and Practical Guidelines*, 4th ed. New York: Pearson Education.

Flynn, Leisa R., and Ronald E. Goldsmith. 2013. *Case Studies for Ethics in Academic Research in the Social Sciences*. Thousand Oaks, CA: SAGE.

Flyvbjerg, Bent. 2001. *Making Social Science Matter: Why Social Inquiry Fails and How It Can Succeed Again*. Cambridge: Cambridge University Press.

Foucault, Michel. 1975. *Discipline and Punish: The Birth of the Prison*. Translated by Alan Sheridan. New York: Vintage.

Fowler, Floyd J., Jr. 2014. *Survey Research Methods*, 5th ed. Thousand Oaks, CA: SAGE.

Fox, John. 1991. *Regression Diagnostics: An Introduction*. Thousand Oaks, CA: SAGE.

Franzosi, Roberto. 2010. *Quantitative Narrative Analysis*. Thousand Oaks, CA: SAGE.

Freire, Paulo. 2000 [1970]. *Pedagogy of the Oppressed*. 30th anniv. ed. Translated by Myra Berman Ramos. London: Bloomsbury.

Friedman, Milton. 1970. "The Social Responsibility of Business Is to Increase Its Profits." *New York Times Magazine*, September 13.

Friedman, Thomas L. 1999. *The Lexus and the Olive Tree*. New York: Picador.

Frühstück, Sabine. 2014. "Sexuality and Nation States." In *Global History of Sexuality*, edited by Robert Marshall Buffington, Eithne Luibheid, and Donna Guy, 17–56. London: Wiley-Blackwell.

Gandhi, Leela. 1998. *Postcolonial Theory: A Critical Introduction*. New York: Columbia University Press.

García Canclini, Néstor. 2014. *Imagined Globalization*. Translated and with an introduction by George Yúdice. Durham, NC: Duke University Press.

Gasper, Des. 2010. "Interdisciplinarity and Transdisciplinarity: Diverse Purposes of Research; Theory-Oriented, Situation-Oriented, Policy-Oriented." In *The Routledge Doctoral Student's Companion: Getting to Grips with Research in Education and the Social Sciences*, edited by Pat Thomson and Melanie Walker, 52–67. London: Routledge.

Gass, J. R. 1972. Preface to Apostel et al., *Interdisciplinarity*, 9–10.

Gaudelli, William. 2016. *Global Citizenship Education: Everyday Transcendence*. London: Routledge.

Gee, James Paul. 2014. *An Introduction to Discourse Analysis: Theory and Method*, 4th ed. London: Routledge.

Geertz, Clifford. 1973. *The Interpretation of Cultures: Selected Essays*. New York: Basic Books.

Gerring, John. 2012. *Social Science Methodology: A Unified Framework*, 2nd ed. Cambridge: Cambridge University Press.

Ghosh, Bishnupriya. 2011. *Global Icons: Apertures to the Popular*. Durham, NC: Duke University Press.

Giddens, Anthony. 1984. *The Constitution of Society: Outline of the Theory of Structuration*. Cambridge: Polity.

———. 1990. *The Consequences of Modernity*. Stanford, CA: Stanford University Press.

Gill, Stephen, ed. 2015. *Critical Perspectives on the Crisis of Global Governance: Reimagining the Future*. Basingstoke, UK: Palgrave Macmillan.

Gille, Zsuzsa, and Seán Ó Riain. 2002. "Global Ethnography." *Annual Review of Sociology* 28: 271–95.

Gilroy, Paul. 1993. *The Black Atlantic: Modernity and Double-Consciousness.* Cambridge: Cambridge University Press.

Given, Lisa M., ed. 2008. *The SAGE Encyclopedia of Qualitative Research Methods.* 2 vols. Thousand Oaks, CA: SAGE.

Glaser, Barney G., and Anselm L. Strauss. (1967) 1999. *The Discovery of Grounded Theory: Strategies for Qualitative Research.* New Brunswick, NJ: Transaction.

Glick Schiller, Nina. 2012. "Transnationality, Migrants and Cities." In *Beyond Methodological Nationalism: Research Methodologies for Cross-Border Studies,* edited by Anna Amelina, Devrimsel D. Nergiz, Thomas Faist, and Nina Glick Schiller, 23–40. London: Routledge.

Goebel, Michael. 2015. *Anti-Imperial Metropolis: Interwar Paris and the Seeds of Third World Nationalism.* Cambridge: Cambridge University Press.

Goldthorpe, John H., David Lockwood, Frank Bechhofer, and Jennifer Platt. 1969. *The Affluent Worker in the Class Structure.* Cambridge: Cambridge University Press.

Golledge, Reginald G., and Robert J. Stimson. 1996. *Spatial Behavior: A Geographic Perspective.* New York: Guilford.

Gould, Stephen Jay. 1996. *The Mismeasure of Man,* rev. and exp. ed. New York: Norton.

Grafton, Anthony, with April Shelford and Nancy Siraisi 1992. *New Worlds, Ancient Texts: The Power of Tradition and the Shock of Discovery.* Cambridge, MA: Belknap.

Grewal, Inderpal, and Caren Kaplan. 1994. "Introduction." In *Scattered Hegemonies: Postmodernity and Transnational Feminist Practices,* edited by Inderpal Grewal and Caren Kaplan, 1–33. Minneapolis: University of Minnesota Press.

Grosfoguel, Ramón. 2011. "Decolonizing Post-Colonial Studies and Paradigms of Political-Economy: Transmodernity, Decolonial Thinking and Global Coloniality." *Transmodernity* 1 (1): 1–37.

Grusin, Richard, ed. 2015. *The Nonhuman Turn.* Minneapolis: University of Minnesota Press.

Guha, Ranajit, and Gayatri Chakravorty Spivak, eds. 1988. *Selected Subaltern Studies.* Oxford: Oxford University Press.

Gunn, Giles. 2013. Introduction to *Ideas to Die For: The Cosmopolitan Challenge,* 1–13. London: Routledge.

Hacker, Karen. 2013. *Community-Based Participatory Research.* Thousand Oaks, CA: SAGE.

Hall, Anthony J. 2010. *Earth into Property: Colonization, Decolonization, and Capitalism.* Vol. 2, *The Bowl with One Spoon.* Montreal: McGill-Queen's University Press.

Hall, Marie Boas. (1962) 1994. *The Scientific Renaissance, 1450–1630*. New York: Dover.

Hall, Stuart. 1980. "Cultural Studies: Two Paradigms." *Media, Culture & Society* 2 (1): 57–72.

Halseth, Greg, Sean Markey, Laura Ryser, and Don Manson. 2016. *Doing Community-Based Research: Perspectives from the Field*. Montreal: McGill-Queen's University Press.

Hancock, Ange-Marie. 2016. *Intersectionality: An Intellectual History*. Oxford: Oxford University Press.

Harding, Sandra, ed. 1987. *Feminism and Methodology*. Bloomington: Indiana University Press.

———, ed. 2004. *The Feminist Standpoint Theory Reader: Intellectual and Political Controversies*. London: Routledge.

Hardt, Michael, and Antonio Negri. 2001. *Empire*. Cambridge, MA: Harvard University Press.

Harlow, John. 1848. "Passage of an Iron Rod through the Head." *Boston Medical and Surgical Journal* 39: 389–93.

Harpalani, Vinay. 2013. "DesiCrit: Theorizing the Racial Ambiguity of South Asian Americans." *NYU Annual Survey of American Law* 69 (1): 77–184.

Harris, Cheryl I. 1993. "Whiteness as Property." *Harvard Law Review* 106 (8): 1701–91.

Harris, Duchess. 2001. "From the Kennedy Commission to the Combahee Collective: Black Feminist Organizing, 1960–80." In *Sisters in the Struggle: African American Women in the Civil Rights–Black Power Movement*, edited by Bettye Collier-Thomas and V. P. Franklin, 280–305. New York: New York University Press.

Hartsock, Nancy C. M. 1999. *The Feminist Standpoint Revisited and Other Essays*. New York: Basic Books.

Harvey, David. 1990. *The Condition of Post-Modernity: An Enquiry into the Origins of Cultural Change*. Oxford: Blackwell.

———. 2007. *A Brief History of Neoliberalism*. Oxford: Oxford University Press.

Hayashi, Fumio. 2000. *Econometrics*. Princeton, NJ: Princeton University Press.

Haynes, Jeffrey. 2008. *Development Studies*. Cambridge: Polity.

Hedges, Chris. 2008. "The Best and the Brightest Led America Off a Cliff." *Truthdig*, December 8. http://www.truthdig.com/report/item/20081208_hedges_best_brightest.

Held, David. 2002. "Culture and Political Community: National, Global, and Cosmopolitan." In *Conceiving Cosmopolitanism: Theory, Context, and Practice*, edited by Steven Vertovec and Robin Cohen, 48–58. Oxford: Oxford University Press.

Held, David, Anthony McGrew, David Goldblatt, and Jonathan Perraton. 1999. *Global Transformations: Politics, Economics, and Culture*. Stanford, CA: Stanford University Press.

Helmers, Marguerite. 2005. *The Elements of Visual Analysis*. New York: Pearson Education.

Henry, Gary T. 1990. *Practical Sampling*. Thousand Oaks, CA: SAGE.

Herr, Kathryn, and Gary L. Anderson. 2015. *The Action Research Dissertation: A Guide for Students and Faculty*, 2nd ed. Thousand Oaks, CA: SAGE.

Herren, Madeleine, Martin Rüesch, Christiane Sibille. 2012. *Transcultural History: Theories, Methods, Sources*. New York: Springer.

Hesse-Biber, Sharlene Nagy, ed. 2014. *Feminist Research Practice: A Primer*, 2nd ed. Thousand Oaks, CA: SAGE.

Hinde, Andrew. 1998. *Demographic Methods*. London: Routledge.

Hobsbawm, Eric. 1994. *The Age of Extremes: A History of the World, 1914–1991*. New York: Random House.

———. 1997. *On History*. New York: New Press.

Hodgson, Geoffrey M. 2001. *How Economics Forgot History: The Problem of Historical Specificity in Social Science*. London: Routledge.

Hohn, Donovan. 2012. *Moby-Duck: The True Story of 28,800 Bath Toys Lost at Sea and of the Beachcombers, Oceanographers, Environmentalists & Fools Including the Author Who Went in Search of Them*. London: Penguin.

Holcomb, Zealure C. 1998. *Fundamentals of Descriptive Statistics*. Los Angeles: Pyrczak.

Hole, Rachelle D., Mike Evans, Lawrence D. Berg, Joan L. Bottorff, Carlene Dingwall, Carmella Alexis, Jessie Nyberg, and Michelle L. Smith. 2015. "Visibility and Voice: Aboriginal People Experience Culturally Safe and Unsafe Health Care." *Qualitative Health Research* 25 (12): 1662–74.

Howell, Martha, and Walter Prevenier. 2001. *From Reliable Sources: An Introduction to Historical Methods*. Ithaca, NY: Cornell University Press.

Howitt, Richard. 1993. "'A World in a Grain of Sand': Towards a Reconceptualization of Geographical Scale." *Australian Geographer* 24: 33–44.

Hughes-Warrington, Marnie, ed. 2005. *Palgrave Advances in World Histories*. Basingstoke, UK: Palgrave Macmillan.

Hutchings, Kimberly. 2008. *Time and World Politics: Thinking the Present*. Manchester: Manchester University Press.

Hutner, Gordon, and Feisal G. Mohamed, eds. 2015. *A New Deal for the Humanities: Liberal Arts and the Future of Higher Education*. New Brunswick, NJ: Rutgers University Press.

InterAcademy Partnership. 2016. *Doing Global Science: A Guide to Responsible Conduct in the Global Research Enterprise*. Princeton, NJ: Princeton University Press.

Iskander, Mai (Director). 2009. *Garbage Dreams*. Iskander Films. Documentary film available at http://www.garbagedreams.com.

Israel, Mark. 2015. *Research Ethics and Integrity for Social Scientists: Beyond Regulatory Compliance*, 2nd ed. Thousand Oaks, CA: SAGE.

Itard, Jean Marc Gaspard. 1802. *An Historical Account of the Discovery and Education of a Savage Man: Or, the First Developments, Physical and Moral, of the Young Savage Caught in the Woods Near Aveyron in the Year 1798*. London: Richard Phillips.

Iversen, Gudmund R., and Helmut Norpoth. 1987. *Analysis of Variance*, 2nd ed. Thousand Oaks, CA: SAGE.

Jackson, Matthew O. 2008. *Social and Economic Networks*. Princeton, NJ: Princeton University Press.

Jackson, Patrick Thaddeus. 2010. *The Conduct of Inquiry in International Relations: Philosophy of Science and Its Implications for the Study of World Politics*. London: Routledge.

Jacobs, Jerry A., and Scott Frickel. 2009. "Interdisciplinarity: A Critical Assessment." *Annual Review of Sociology* 35: 43–65.

Jasanoff, Shiela, ed. 2004. *States of Knowledge: The Co-Production of Science and Social Order*. London: Routledge.

Jensen, Klaus Bruhn. 2012. *A Handbook of Media and Communication Research: Qualitative and Quantitative Methodologies*. London: Routledge.

Jockers, Matthew L. 2014. *Text Analysis with R for Students of Literature*. New York: Springer.

Johnston, R. R. 2008. "On Connection and Community: Transdisciplinarity and the Arts." In Nicolescu, *Transdisciplinarity*, 223–36.

Johnstone, Barbara. 2008. *Discourse Analysis*, 2nd ed. Malden, MA: Blackwell.

Juergensmeyer, Mark. 2000. *Terror in the Mind of God: The Global Rise of Religious Violence*. Berkeley: University of California Press.

———. 2001. "Terror in the Name of God." *Current History* 100: 357–61.

———. 2011. "What Is Global Studies?" *global-e* 5: https://global-ejournal. org/2011/05/06/what-is-global-studies-3/.

———. 2013a. "What Is Global Studies?" *Religion and Social Change in a Global World* (blog), December 27. http://juergensmeyer.org/what-is-global-studies/.

———. 2013b. "What Is Global Studies?" *Globalizations* 10 (6): 765–69.

———, ed. 2014a. *Thinking Globally: A Global Studies Reader*. Berkeley: University of California Press.

———. 2014b. "The Origins of Global Studies." Interview by Manfred Steger and Paul James, *Globalizations* 11 (4): 539–47.

Juergensmeyer, Mark, Dinah Griego, and John Soboslai. 2015. *God in the Tumult of the Global Square: Religion in Global Civil Society*. Berkeley: University of California Press.

Kaldor, Mary. (1999) 2006. *New and Old Wars: Organized Violence in a Global Era*, 2nd ed. Stanford, CA: Stanford University Press.

Keim, Wiebke, Ercüment Çelik, Christian Ersche, and Veronika Wöhrer, eds. 2014. *Global Knowledge Production in the Social Sciences: Made in Circulation*. Farnham, UK: Ashgate.

Khagram, Sanjeev, and Peggy Levitt, eds. 2008. *The Transnational Studies Reader: Intersections and Innovations*. London: Routledge.

Kim, Jeong-Hee. 2016. *Understanding Narrative Inquiry: The Crafting and Analysis of Stories as Research*. Thousand Oaks, CA: SAGE.

Kirk, Andy. 2016. *Data Visualisation: A Handbook for Data Driven Design*. Thousand Oaks, CA: SAGE.

Kitzinger, Jenny. 1994. "The Methodology of Focus Groups: The Importance of Interaction between Research Participants." *Sociology of Health & Illness* 16 (1): 103–21.

Klein, Naomi. 2014. *This Changes Everything: Capitalism vs. the Climate*. London: Penguin.

Klotz, Audie, and Deepa Prakash, eds. 2009. *Qualitative Methods in International Relations: A Pluralist Guide*. Basingstoke, UK: Palgrave Macmillan.

Knights, David, and Hugh Willmott. 2011. *Organizational Analysis*. Boston: Cengage Learning.

Kovach, Margaret. 2009. *Indigenous Methodologies: Characteristics, Conversations, and Contexts*. Toronto: University of Toronto Press.

Krippendorff, Klaus, and Mary Angela Bock, eds. 2009. *The Content Analysis Reader*. Thousand Oaks, CA: SAGE.

Kuckartz, Udo. 2014. *Qualitative Text Analysis: A Guide to Methods, Practice and Using Software*. Thousand Oaks, CA: SAGE.

Kuhn, Thomas. 1962. *The Structure of Scientific Revolutions*. Chicago: University of Chicago Press.

Kupchan, Charles A. 2012. *No One's World: the West, the Rising Rest, and the Coming Global Turn*. Oxford: Oxford University Press.

Lagemann, Ellen Condliffe. 1989. *The Politics of Knowledge: The Carnegie Corporation, Philanthropy, and Public Policy*. Chicago: University of Chicago Press.

Lake, Marilyn, and Henry Reynolds. 2008. *Drawing the Global Colour Line: White Men's Countries and the International Challenge of Racial Equality*. Cambridge: Cambridge University Press.

Lambert, Lori. 2014. *Research for Indigenous Survival: Indigenous Research Methodologies in the Behavioral Sciences*. Pablo, MT: Salish Kootenai College Press.

Lamont, Christopher. 2015. *Research Methods in International Relations*. Thousand Oaks, CA: SAGE.

Lange, Matthew. 2012. *Comparative-Historical Methods*. Thousand Oaks, CA: SAGE.

Laslitt, Barbara, Ruth-Ellen B. Joeres, Mary Jo Maynes, Evelyn Brooks Higginbotham, and Jeanne Barker-Nunn, eds. 1997. *History and Theory: Feminist Research, Debates, Contestations*. Chicago: University of Chicago Press.

Latour, Bruno. 1988. *Science in Action: How to Follow Scientists and Engineers Through Society*. Cambridge, MA: Harvard University Press.

Lazarsfeld, Paul F., and Robert K. Merton. 1948. "Mass Communication, Popular Taste, and Organized Social Action." In *The Communication of Ideas: A Series of Addresses*, edited by Lyman Bryson, 95–118. New York: Harper.

Leavy, Patricia. 2011. *Essentials of Transdisciplinary Research: Using Problem-Centered Methodologies*. Walnut Creek, CA: Left Coast.

Le Play, Frédéric. (1855) 1878. *Les Ouvriers Europeens: Etude Sur Les Travaux, La Vie Domestique*. Paris: Alfred Mame et fils.

Lepore, Jill. 2015. "Politics and the New Machine: What the Turn from Polls to Data Science Means for Democracy." *New Yorker*, November 16. http://www.newyorker.com/magazine/2015/11/16/politics-and-the-new-machine.

Lewis-Beck, Michael S., Alan Bryman, and Tim Futing Liao. 2004. *The SAGE Encyclopedia of Social Science Research Methods*. 3 vols. Thousand Oaks, CA: SAGE.

Lezra, Esther. 2014. *The Colonial Art of Demonizing Others: A Global Perspective*. London: Routledge.

Lim, Jie-Hyun. 2017. "What is Critical in Critical Global Studies?" *global-e*. http://www.21global.ucsb.edu/global-e/march-2017/what-critical-critical-global-studies. Accessed March 18, 2017.

Lipsitz, George. 2010. "Ethnic Studies at the Crossroads." *Kalfou*: 11–15.

Lloyd, G. E. R. 1999. *Magic, Reason, and Experience: Studies in the Origin and Development of Greek Science*. Cambridge, MA: Hackett.

Loeke, Konstanze, and Matthias Middell, eds. forthcoming. *The Many Facets of Global Studies. Perspectives from the Erasmus Mundus Global Studies Programme*. Leipzig: Leipzig University Press.

Loomba, Ania. 2005. *Colonialism/Postcolonialism*, 2nd ed. London: Routledge.

Loomba, Ania, Suvir Kaul, Matti Bunzi, Antoinette Burton, and Jed Esty, eds. 2005. *Postcolonial Studies and Beyond*. Durham, NC: Duke University Press.

Lorde, Audre. 1984. "The Master's Tools Will Never Dismantle the Master's House." In *Sister Outsider: Essays and Speeches*, 110–14. Berkeley, CA: Crossing.

Lowe, Lisa. 2015. *The Intimacies of Four Continents*. Durham, NC: Duke University Press.

Ludden, David. 2000. "Area Studies in the Age of Globalization." *Frontiers: The Interdisciplinary Journal of Study Abroad* 6: 1–22.

Luhmann, Niklas. (2002) 2013. *Introduction to Systems Theory.* Translated by Peter Gilgen. Cambridge: Polity.

Lundborg, Tom. 2012. *Politics of the Event: Time, Movement, Becoming.* London: Routledge.

Lunn, Jenny, ed. 2014. *Fieldwork in the Global South: Ethical Challenges and Dilemmas.* London: Routledge.

Lynd, Robert S., and Helen Merrell Lynd. (1929) 1956. *Middletown: A Study in American Culture.* New York: Harcourt, Brace.

Lynn, Laurence E., Jr. 1998. *Teaching and Learning with Cases: A Guidebook.* New York: Chatham House.

Madison, D. Soyini, and Judith Hamera, eds. 2006. *The SAGE Handbook of Performance Studies.* Thousand Oaks, CA: SAGE.

Magnusson, Warren, and Karena Shaw, eds. 2003. *A Political Space: Reading the Global through Clayoquot Sound.* Minneapolis: University of Minnesota Press.

Mahoney, James, and Dietrich Rueschemeyer, eds. 2003. *Comparative Historical Analysis in the Social Sciences.* Cambridge: Cambridge University Press.

Mahoney, James, and Kathleen Thelen, eds. 2015. *Advances in Comparative-Historical Analysis.* Cambridge: Cambridge University Press.

Malagon, Maria C., Lindsay Pérez Huber, and Verónica N. Vélez. 2009. "Our Experiences, Our Methods: Using Grounded Theory to Inform a Critical Race Theory Methodology." *Seattle Journal for Social Justice* 8 (1): 253–72.

Malinowski, Bronislaw. (1922) 1984. *Argonauts of the Western Pacific.* Prospect Heights, IL: Waveland.

Marcus, George. 1995. "Ethnography in/of the World System: The Emergence of Multi-Sited Ethnography." *Annual Review of Anthropology* 24: 95–117.

Margolis, Eric, and Luc Pauwels. 2011. *The SAGE Handbook of Visual Research Methods.* Thousand Oaks, CA: SAGE.

Marshall, Catherine, and Gretchen B. Rossman. 1989. *Designing Qualitative Research.* Thousand Oaks, CA: SAGE.

Martell, Luke. 2007. "The Third Wave in Globalization Theory." *International Studies Review* 9 (2): 173–96.

Martin, William E., and Krista D. Bridgmon. 2012. *Quantitative and Statistical Research Methods: From Hypothesis to Results.* San Francisco: Jossey-Bass.

Martin, William G., ed. 2008. *Making Waves: Worldwide Social Movements, 1750–2005.* Boulder, CO: Paradigm.

Massey, Doreen. 1994. *Space, Place, and Gender.* Minneapolis: University of Minnesota Press.

Matsuda, Mari J. 1987. "Looking to the Bottom: Critical Legal Studies and Reparations." *Harvard Civil Rights-Civil Liberties Law Review* 22 (2): 323–99.

Mazlish, Bruce. 1993. "An Introduction to Global History." In *Conceptualizing Global History*, edited by Bruce Mazlish and Ralph Buultjens, 1–26. Boulder, CO: Westview.

McCann, Carole R., and Seung-kyung Kim, eds. 2013. *Feminist Theory Reader: Local and Global Perspectives*. London: Routledge.

McCarty, Philip. 2014a. *Integrated Perspectives in Global Studies*. Rev. first ed. San Diego: Cognella.

———. 2014b. "Globalizing Legal History." *Rechtsgeschichte—Legal History* 22: 283–91.

———. 2014c. "Communicating Global Perspectives." *Global Europe—Basel Papers on Europe in a Global Perspective* 105: 27–37.

McCullagh, C. Behan. 1984. *Justifying Historical Descriptions*. Cambridge: Cambridge University Press.

McGarry, Aidan, and James Jasper, eds. 2015. *The Identity Dilemma: Social Movements and Collective Identity*. Philadelphia, PA: Temple University Press.

McIntyre, Alice. 2008. *Participatory Action Research*. Thousand Oaks, CA: SAGE.

McLuhan, Marshall. 1964. *Understanding Media: The Extensions of Man*. New York: McGraw-Hill.

Merriam-Webster Dictionary. 2015. http://www.merriam-webster.com /dictionary/decenter.

Merrigan, Gerianne, and Carole L. Huston. 2014. *Communication Research Methods*. Oxford: Oxford University Press.

Merry, Sally Engle. 2006. *Human Rights and Gender Violence: Translating International Law into Local Justice*. Chicago: University of Chicago Press.

Mertens, Donna M., and Pauline E. Ginsberg. 2008. *The Handbook of Social Research Ethics*. Thousand Oaks, CA: SAGE.

Middell, Matthias. 2014. "What Is Global Studies All About?" *Global Europe – Basel Papers on Europe in a Global Perspective* 105: 45–49.

Miles, Matthew B., A. Michael Huberman, and Johnny Saldaña. 2014. *Qualitative Data Analysis: A Methods Sourcebook*, 3rd ed. Thousand Oaks, CA: SAGE Publications.

Milgram, Stanley. (1974) 2009. *Obedience to Authority: An Experimental View*. New York: HarperCollins.

Millman, Marcia, and Rosabeth Moss Kanter. 1987. "Introduction to Another Voice: Feminist Perspectives on Social Life and Social Science." In *Feminism and Methodology*, edited by Sandra Harding, 29–36. Bloomington: Indiana University Press.

Mills, Albert J., Gabrielle Eurepos, and Elden Wiebe, eds. 2010. *Encyclopedia of Case Study Research*. 2 vols. Thousand Oaks, CA: SAGE Publications.

Mills, C. Wright. 1959. *The Sociological Imagination*. Oxford: Oxford University Press.

Mintz, Sidney W. 1985. *Sweetness and Power: The Place of Sugar in Modern History*. London: Penguin.

Mitchell, Elizabeth. 2014. *Liberty's Torch: The Great Adventure to Build the Statue of Liberty*. New York: Atlantic Monthly.

Miyoshi, Masao, and Harry Harootunian, eds. 2002. *Learning Places: The Afterlives of Area Studies*. Durham, NC: Duke University Press.

Mongia, Padmini, ed. 1996. *Contemporary Postcolonial Theory: A Reader*. London: Arnold.

Moore, MariJo. 2003. *Genocide of the Mind: New Native American Writing*. New York: Nation Books.

Moraru, Christian. 2001. "The Global Turn in Critical Theory." *Symplokē* 9 (1/2): 74–82.

Morgan, David L. 1997. *Focus Groups as Qualitative Research*, 2nd ed. Thousand Oaks, CA: SAGE.

Morrison, Toni. 1992. *Playing in the Dark: Whiteness and the Literary Imagination*. New York: Vintage.

Morrow, Raymond A., with David D. Brown. 1994. *Critical Theory and Methodology*. Thousand Oaks. CA: SAGE.

Mulnix, Jennifer Wilson. 2012. "Thinking Critically about Critical Thinking." *Educational Philosophy and Theory* 44 (5): 464–79.

Mutua, Kagendo, and Beth Blue Swadener, eds. 2004. *Decolonizing Research in Cross-Cultural Contexts: Critical Personal Narratives*. Albany: State University of New York Press.

Naples, Nancy A. 2003. *Feminism and Methods: Ethnography, Discourse Analysis, and Activist Research*. London: Routledge.

Nederveen Pieterse, Jan. 2009. *Globalization & Culture: Global Mélange*, 2nd ed. Lanham, MD: Rowman & Littlefield.

———. 2012. "Periodizing Globalization: Histories of Globalization." *New Global Studies* 6 (2).

———. 2013. "What Is Global Studies?" special issue, *Globalizations* 10 (4): 499–514.

Newman, M. E. J. 2010. *Networks: An Introduction*. Oxford: Oxford University Press.

Ngũgĩ, wa Thiong'o. 1986. *Writing against Neo-Colonialism*. London: Vita.

Nicolescu, Basarab. 2008. "In Vitro and In Vivo Knowledge—Methodology of Transdisciplinarity." In *Transdisciplinarity: Theory and Practice*, edited by Basarab Nicolescu, 1–22. New York: Hampton.

Nixon, Rob. 2013. *Slow Violence and the Environmentalism of the Poor*. Cambridge, MA: Harvard University Press.

Nkrumah, Kwame. 1966. *Neo-Colonialism: The Last Stage of Imperialism*. New York: International.

Nowicka, Magdalena, and Anna Cieslik. 2014. "Beyond Methodological Nationalism in Insider Research with Migrants." *Migration Studies* 2: 1–15.

O'Byrne, Darren, and Alexander Hensby. 2011. *Theorizing Global Studies*. New York: Palgrave Macmillan.

Ogle, Vanessa. 2015. *The Global Transformation of Time: 1870–1950*. Cambridge, MA: Harvard University Press.

O'Hanlon, Rosalind, and David Washbrook. 1992. "After Orientalism: Culture, Criticism, and Politics in the Third World." *Comparative Studies in Society and History* 34 (1): 141–67.

Omi, Michael, and Howard Winant. 2015. *Racial Formation in the United States*, 3rd ed. London: Routledge.

Ong, Aihwa, and Stephen J. Collier, eds. 2004. *Global Assemblages: Technology, Politics, and Ethics as Anthropological Problems*. Malden, MA: Wiley-Blackwell.

O'Reilly, Karen. 2012. *Ethnographic Methods*, 2nd ed. London: Routledge.

O'Sullivan, David, and David J. Unwin. 2010. *Geographic Information Analysis*, 2nd ed. Hoboken, NJ: Wiley.

Ott, Brian L., and Robert L. Mack. 2014. *Critical Media Studies: An Introduction*. Malden, MA: Wiley-Blackwell.

Parker, Laurence, and Marvin Lynn. 2002. "What's Race Got to Do with It? Critical Race Theory's Conflicts with and Connections to Qualitative Research Methodology and Epistemology." *Qualitative Inquiry* 8 (1): 7–22.

Parker, Robert Dale. 2015. *How to Interpret Literature: Critical Theory for Literary and Cultural Studies*. Oxford: Oxford University Press.

Patterson, Philip, and Lee Wilkins. 2013. *Media Ethics: Issues and Cases*, 8th ed. New York: McGraw-Hill Education.

Patton, Carl, David Sawicki, and Jennifer Clark. 2012. *Basic Methods of Policy Analysis and Planning*, 3rd ed. London: Routledge.

Pernau, Margrit, and Dominic Sachsenmaier. 2016. "History of Concepts and Global History." In *Global Conceptual History: A Reader*, edited by Margrit Pernau and Dominic Sachsenmaier, 1–17. London: Bloomsbury.

Piaget, Jean. 1972. "The Epistemology of Interdisciplinary Relationships." In Apostel et al., *Interdisciplinarity*, 127–39.

Pierce, Sydney J. 1991. "Subject Areas, Disciplines and the Concept of Authority." *Library and Information Science Research* 13 (1): 21–35.

Plano Clark, Vicki L., and Nataliya V. Ivankova. 2016. *Mixed Methods Research: A Guide to the Field*. Thousand Oaks, CA: SAGE.

Powell, Walter W., and Paul J. DiMaggio, eds. 1991. *The New Institutionalism in Organizational Analysis*. Chicago: University of Chicago Press.

Prakash, Gyan. 1990. "Writing Post-Orientalist Histories of the Third World:

Perspectives from Indian Historiography." *Comparative Studies in Society and History* 32 (2): 383–408.

———. 1992. "Can the 'Subaltern' Ride? A Reply to O'Hanlon and Washbrook." *Comparative Studies in Society and History* 34 (1): 168–84.

Prashad, Vijay. 2012. *The Poorer Nations: A Possible History of the Global South*. London: Verso.

Pred, Allan. 1984. "Place as Historically Contingent Process: Structuration and the Time-Geography of Becoming Places." *Annals of the Association of American Geographers* 74 (2): 279–97.

Prestholdt, Jeremy. 2012. Review of *Global Icons: Apertures to the Popular*, by Bishnupriya Ghosh. *Indian Economic and Social History Review* 49 (4): 596–98.

Pries, Ludger. 2008. "Transnational Societal Spaces: Which Units of Analysis, Reference and Measurement?" In *Rethinking Transnationalism: The Meso-Link of Organizations*, edited by Ludger Pries, 1–20. London: Routledge.

Purkayastha, Bandana. 2012. "Intersectionality in a Transnational World." *Gender & Society* 26 (1): 55–66.

Ragin, Charles C. 2008. *Redesigning Social Inquiry: Fuzzy Sets and Beyond*. Chicago: University of Chicago Press.

Ramazanoğlu, Caroline, with Janet Holland. 2002. *Feminist Methodology: Challenges and Choices*. Thousand Oaks, CA: SAGE.

Reason, Peter, and Hilary Bradbury-Huang, eds. 2008. *The SAGE Handbook of Action Research: Participative Inquiry and Practice*. Thousand Oaks, CA: SAGE.

Rehbein, Boike. 2014. "Epistemology in a Multicentric World." In Keim et al., *Global Knowledge Production in the Social Sciences*, 217–22.

Reinharz, Shulamit. 1992. *Feminist Methods in Social Research*. Oxford: Oxford University Press.

Ridder-Symoens, Hilde de, ed. 1992. *A History of the University in Europe*. Vol. 2, *Universities in Early Modern Europe*. Cambridge: Cambridge University Press.

Rivoli, Pietra. 2005. *The Travels of a T-Shirt in the Global Economy: An Economist Examines the Markets, Power, and Politics of World Trade*. Hoboken, NJ: Wiley.

Robinson, Cedric J. (1983) 2000. *Black Marxism: The Making of the Black Radical Tradition*. Chapel Hill: University of North Carolina Press.

Robertson, Roland. 1992. *Globalization: Social Theory and Global Culture*. Thousand Oaks, CA: SAGE.

Rose, Gillian. 2016. *Visual Methodologies: An Introduction to Researching with Visual Materials*, 4th ed. Thousand Oaks, CA: SAGE.

Rose, Nikolas. 1990. *Governing the Soul: The Shaping of the Private Self*. London: Routledge.

Rosenzweig, Roy, and David Thelen. 1998. *The Presence of the Past: Popular Uses of History in American Life*. New York: Columbia University Press.

Rossman, Gretchen B., and Sharon F. Rallis. 2017. *An Introduction to Qualitative Research: Learning in the Field*, 4th ed. Thousand Oaks, CA: SAGE.

Roth, Michael S. 2015. *Beyond the University: Why Liberal Education Matters*. New Haven, CT: Yale University Press.

Rowland, Donald T. 2003. *Demographic Methods and Concepts*. Oxford: Oxford University Press.

Roy, Ananya, and Emma Shaw Crane, eds. 2015. *Territories of Poverty: Rethinking North and South*. Athens: University of Georgia Press.

Roy, Ananya, and Aihwa Ong, eds. 2011. *Worlding Cities: Asian Experiments and the Art of Being Global*. Malden, MA: Wiley-Blackwell.

Royse, David, Bruce A. Thyer, and Deborah K. Padgett. 2016. *Program Evaluation: An Introduction to an Evidence-Based Approach*. Boston: Cengage Learning.

Rudy, Willis. 1984. *The Universities of Europe, 1100–1914*. Rutherford, NJ: Fairleigh Dickinson University Press.

Sachsenmaier, Dominic. 2006. "Global History and Critiques of Western Perspectives." "Comparative Methodologies in the Social Sciences: Cross-Disciplinary Inspirations," edited by Jürgen Schriewer, special issue, *Comparative Education* 42 (3): 451–70.

———. 2011. *Global Perspectives on Global History: Theories and Approaches in a Connected World*. Cambridge: Cambridge University Press.

Sacks, Oliver. 1973. *Awakenings*. London: Duckworth.

Said, Edward. 1979. *Orientalism*. New York: Vintage.

———. 1983. "Opponents, Audiences, Constituencies, and Community." In *The Politics of Interpretation*, edited by W. J. T. Mitchell, 1–26. Chicago: University of Chicago Press.

———. 1993. *Culture and Imperialism*. New York: Random House.

Salevouris, Michael J., with Conal Furay. 2015. *The Methods and Skills of History: A Practical Guide*, 4th ed. Malden, MA: Wiley.

Samuel, Lawrence R. 2007. *The End of the Innocence: The 1964–1965 New York World's Fair*. Syracuse, NY: Syracuse University Press.

Sandoval, Chela. 2000. *Methodology of the Oppressed*. Minneapolis: University of Minnesota Press.

Santos, Boaventura de Sousa, ed. 2007. *Another Knowledge Is Possible: Beyond Northern Epistemologies*. London: Verso.

———. 2014. *Epistemologies of the South: Justice against Epistemicide*. Boulder, CO: Paradigm.

Sassen, Saskia. 1991. *The Global City: New York, London, Tokyo*. Princeton, NJ: Princeton University Press.

———. 2008. *Territory, Authority, Rights: From Medieval to Global Assemblages.* Princeton, NJ: Princeton University Press.

———. 2011. "The Global Street: Making the Political." *Globalizations* 8 (5): 573–79.

———. 2014. *Expulsions: Brutality and Complexity in the Global Economy.* Cambridge, MA: Belknap Press.

Saussure, Ferdinand de. (1916) 1983. *Course in General Linguistics.* Translated and annotated by Roy Harris. London: Duckworth.

Schäfer, Wolf. 2010. "Reconfiguring Area Studies for the Global Age." *Globality Studies Journal* 22: 1–18.

Schechner, Richard. 2013. *Performance Studies: An Introduction*, 3rd ed. London: Routledge.

Schensul, Stephen L., Jean J. Schensul, and Margaret D. LeCompte. 1999. *Essential Ethnographic Methods: Observations, Interviews, and Questionnaires.* Book 2, *Ethnographer's Toolkit.* Lanham, MD: AltaMira.

Schiffrin, Deborah, Deborah Tannen, and Heidi E. Hamilton, eds. 2001. *The Handbook of Discourse Analysis.* Malden, MA: Blackwell.

Schroeder, Larry D., David L. Sjoquist, and Paula E. Stephan. 1986. *Understanding Regression Analysis: An Introductory Guide.* Thousand Oaks, CA: SAGE.

Schwartz, Seth J., Koen Luyckx, and Vivian L. Vignoles, eds. 2011. *Handbook of Identity Theory and Research.* New York: Springer.

Schwarz, Henry, and Sangeeta Ray, eds. 2000. *A Companion to Postcolonial Studies.* Hoboken, NJ: Wiley-Blackwell.

Scriven, Michael, and Richard Paul. 1987. Statement presented at the 8th Annual International Conference on Critical Thinking and Education Reform, Summer 1987. http://www.criticalthinking.org/pages/defining-critical-thinking/766. Accessed February 1, 2016.

Seidman, Irving. 2013. *Interviewing as Qualitative Research: A Guide for Researchers in Education and the Social Sciences*, 4th ed. New York: Teachers College Press.

Sen, Gita, and Marina Durano, eds. 2014. *The Remaking of Social Contracts: Feminists in a Fierce New World.* London: Zed.

Shapin, Steven. 1994. *A Social History of Truth: Civility and Science in Seventeenth-Century England.* Chicago: Chicago University Press.

Shionoya, Yuichi, ed. 2001. *The German Historical School: The Historical and Ethical Approach to Economics.* London: Routledge.

Sikes, Gini. 1997. *8 Ball Chicks: A Year in the Violent World of Girl Gangs.* New York: Random House.

Silva, Denise Ferreira da. 2007. *Toward a Global Idea of Race.* Minneapolis: University of Minnesota Press.

Silverman, Hugh J. 1980. *Piaget, Philosophy, and the Human Sciences*. Evanston, IL: Northwestern University Press.

Simon, Carl P., and Lawrence Blume. 1994. *Mathematics for Economists*. New York: Norton.

Smith, Bonnie G. 2013. *Women's Studies: The Basics*. London: Routledge.

Smith, Dorothy E. 1977. *Feminism and Marxism: A Place to Begin, A Way to Go*. Vancouver: New Star.

Smith, Linda Tuhiwai. 2012. *Decolonizing Methodologies: Research and Indigenous Peoples*, 2nd ed. London: Zed.

Sobel, Dava. (1995) 2007. *Longitude: The True Story of a Lone Genius Who Solved the Greatest Scientific Problem of His Time*. London: Walker.

Solórzano, Daniel G., and Tara J. Yosso. 2002. "Critical Race Methodology: Counter-Storytelling as an Analytical Framework for Education Research." *Qualitative Inquiry* 8 (1): 23–44.

Sparke, Matthew. 2013. *Introducing Globalization: Ties, Tensions, and Uneven Integration*. Hoboken, NJ: Wiley-Blackwell.

Spivak, Gayatri Chakarvorty. 2003. *Death of a Discipline*. New York: Columbia University Press.

Spretnak, Charlene, and Fritjof Kapra. 1986. *Green Politics*. Rochester, VT: Bear & Co.

Stake, Robert E. 1995. *The Art of Case Study Research*. Thousand Oaks, CA: SAGE.

Steger, Manfred B. 2008. *The Rise of the Global Imaginary: Political Ideologies from the French Revolution to the Global War on Terror*. Oxford: Oxford University Press.

———, ed. 2015. *The Global Studies Reader*. 2nd ed. Oxford: Oxford University Press.

———. 2016. "Globalizing Political Theory: Benjamin Barber's Contribution to Global Studies." In *Strong Democracy in Crisis: Promise or Peril?*, edited by Trevor Norris, 233–52. Lanham, MD: Lexington.

Steger, Manfred B., and Paul James, eds. 2014. "Globalization: The Career of a Concept," special issue, *Globalizations* 11 (4).

Steger, Manfred B., and Amentahru Wahlrab. 2016. *What Is Global Studies? Theory and Practice*. London: Routledge.

Steinberg, Sheila Lakshmi, and Steven J. Steinberg. 2015. *GIS Research Methods: Incorporating Spatial Perspectives*. Redlands, CA: Esri.

Stichweh, Rudolf. 2001. "Scientific Disciplines, History of." In *International Encyclopedia of the Social and Behavioral Sciences*, edited by Neil J. Smelser and Paul B. Baltes, 13727–31. Oxford: Elsevier Science.

Stiglitz, Joseph E. 2002. *Globalization and Its Discontents*. New York: Norton.

Stiglitz, Joseph E., Amartya Sen, and Jean-Paul Fitoussi. 2010. *Mismeasuring Our Lives: Why GDP Doesn't Add Up; The Report by the Commission on the*

Measurement of Economic Performance and Social Progress. New York: New Press.

Stoecker, Randy. 2013. *Research Methods for Community Change: A Project-Based Approach*, 2nd ed. Thousand Oaks, CA: SAGE.

Storey, William Kelleher. 2009. *Writing History: A Guide for Students*. Oxford: Oxford University Press.

Strathern, Marilyn. 2005. "Experiments in Interdisciplinarity." *Social Anthropology* 13 (1): 75–90.

Stringer, Ernest. 2014. *Action Research*, 4th ed. Thousand Oaks, CA: SAGE.

Stubbs, Michael. 1983. *Discourse Analysis: The Sociolinguistic Analysis of Natural Language*. Chicago: University of Chicago Press.

Sumner, Andy, and Michael Tribe. 2008. *International Development Studies: Theories and Methods in Research and Practice*. Thousand Oaks, CA: SAGE.

Swyngedouw, Erik. 1997. "Neither Global Nor Local: 'Glocalization' and the Politics of Scale." In *Spaces of Globalization: Reasserting the Power of the Local*, edited by Kevin R. Cox, 137–66. New York: Guilford.

Szanton, David, ed. 2004. *The Politics of Knowledge: Area Studies and the Disciplines*. Berkeley: University of California Press.

Tally, Robert T., Jr. 2013. *Spatiality*. London: Routledge.

Tirella, Joseph. 2014. *Tomorrow-Land: The 1964–65 World's Fair and the Transformation of America*. Guilford, CT: Lyons.

Tobin, Brendan. 2014. *Indigenous Peoples, Customary Law and Human Rights—Why Living Law Matters*. London: Routledge.

Tong, Rosemarie. 2014. *Feminist Thought: A More Comprehensive Introduction*, 4th ed. Boulder, CO: Westview.

Tosh, John. 2015. *The Pursuit of History: Aims, Methods, and New Directions in the Study of History*, 6th ed. London: Routledge.

Treiman, Donald J. 2009. *Quantitative Data Analysis: Doing Social Research to Test Ideas*. San Francisco: Jossey-Bass.

Trouillot, Michel-Rolph. 1995. *Silencing the Past: Power and the Production of History*. Boston: Beacon.

———. 2003. *Global Transformations: Anthropology and the Modern World*. New York: Palgrave Macmillan.

Tsing, Anna Lowenhaupt. 2005. *Friction: An Ethnography of Global Connection*. Princeton, NJ: Princeton University Press.

Uglow, Jenny. 2002. *The Lunar Men: The Friends Who Made the Future*. London: Faber and Faber.

Urry, John. 2003. *Global Complexity*. Cambridge: Polity.

Valado, Trenna, and Randall Amster. 2012. *Professional Lives, Personal Struggles: Ethics and Advocacy in Research on Homelessness*. Lanham, MD: Lexington.

Van Leeuwen, Theo, and Carey Jewitt. 2001. *The Handbook of Visual Analysis*. Thousand Oaks, CA: SAGE.

Vaughan, Diane. 1996. *The Challenger Launch Decision: Risky Technology, Culture, and Deviance at NASA*. Chicago: University of Chicago Press.

Vogt, W. Paul, and R. Burke Johnson. 2016. *The SAGE Dictionary of Statistics and Methodology: A Nontechnical Guide for the Social Sciences*, 5th ed. Thousand Oaks, CA: SAGE.

Wachter, Kenneth W. 2014. *Essential Demographic Methods*. Cambridge, MA: Harvard University Press.

Wall, Derek. 2010. *The No-Nonsense Guide to Green Politics*. Oxford: New Internationalist.

Wallerstein, Immanuel. 1974. *Capitalist Agriculture and the Origins of the European World-Economy in the Sixteenth Century*. Vol. 1, *The Modern World-System*. New York: Academic Press.

———, ed. 1996. *Open the Social Sciences: Report of the Gulbenkian Commmision on the Restructuring of the Social Sciences*. Stanford, CA: Stanford University Press.

———. 2004. *World-Systems Analysis: An Introduction*. Durham, NC: Duke University Press.

Waltz, Kenneth N. 1959. *Man, the State, and War*. New York: Columbia University Press.

Wasserman, Stanley, and Katherine Faust. 1994. *Social Network Analysis: Methods and Applications*. Cambridge: Cambridge University Press.

Weimer, David L., and Aidan R. Vining. 2016. *Policy Analysis: Concepts and Practice*, 5th ed. London: Routledge.

Weiss, Robert. 1994. *Learning from Strangers: The Art and Method of Qualitative Interview Studies*. New York: Free Press.

Weiwei, Ai. 2012. *Weiwei-isms*. Edited by Larry Warsh. Princeton, NJ: Princeton University Press.

Weldemichael, Awet Tewelde. 2012. *Third World Colonialism and Strategies of Liberation: Eritrea and East Timor Compared*. Cambridge: Cambridge University Press.

Wertz, Frederick J., Kathy Charmaz, Linda M. McMullen, Ruthellen Josselson, Rosemarie Anderson, and Emalinda McSpadden. 2011. *Five Ways of Doing Qualitative Analysis: Phenomenological Psychology, Grounded Theory, Discourse Analysis, Narrative Research, and Intuitive Inquiry*. New York: Guilford.

West, Roianne, Lee Stewart, Kim Foster, and Kim Usher. 2012. "Through a Critical Lens: Indigenist Research and the Dadirri Method." *Qualitative Health Research* 22 (11): 1582–90.

Whyte, William Foote. (1943) 1955. *Street Corner Society: The Social Structure of an Italian Slum*. Chicago: University of Chicago Press.

Wibben, Annick T. R., ed. 2016. *Researching War: Feminist Methods, Ethics, and Politics*. London: Routledge.

Williams, Patricia J. 1992. *The Alchemy of Race and Rights: Diary of a Law Professor*. Cambridge, MA: Harvard University Press.

Williams, Patrick, and Laura Chrisman, eds. 1994. *Colonial Discourse and Post-Colonial Theory: A Reader*. New York: Columbia University Press.

Williams, Raymond. 1958. *Culture and Society*. London: Chatto and Windus.

Willig, Carla. 2008. *Introducing Qualitative Research in Psychology: Adventures in Theory and Method*. London: Open University Press.

Wimmer, Andreas, and Nina Glick Schiller. 2002. "Methodological Nationalism and Beyond: Nation-State Building, Migration, and the Social Sciences." *Global Networks* 2 (4): 301–34.

Winant, Howard. 2004. *New Politics of Race: Globalism, Difference, Justice*. Minneapolis: University of Minnesota Press.

Wing, Adrien Katherine, ed. 2000. *Global Critical Race Feminism: An International Reader*. With a foreword by Angela Y. Davis. New York: New York University Press.

Wolf, Eric. 1982. *Europe and the People without History*. Berkeley: University of California Press.

Wolf, Fredric M. 2013. *Meta-Analysis: Quantitative Methods for Research Synthesis*, 2nd ed. Thousand Oaks, CA: SAGE.

Yang, Mayfair Mei-hui. ed. 2008. *Chinese Religiosities: Afflictions of Modernity and State Formation*. Berkeley: University of California Press.

Yin, Robert K. 2014. *Case Study Research: Design and Methods*. Thousand Oaks, CA: SAGE.

Yetiv, Steve A. and Patrick James, eds. 2017. *Advancing Interdisciplinary Approaches to IR*. Basingstoke, UK: Palgrave Macmillan.

Yusuf, Farhat, Jo M. Martins, and David A. Swanson. 2014. *Methods of Demographic Analysis*. New York: Springer.

Zakaria, Fareed. 2016. *In Defense of a Liberal Education*. New York: Norton.

Zimbardo, Philip. 2007. *The Lucifer Effect: Understanding How Good People Turn Evil*. New York: Random House.

Zimmermann, Jens. 2015. *Hermeneutics: A Very Short Introduction*. Oxford: Oxford University Press.

Zürn, Michael. 2013. "Globalization and Global Governance." In Walter Carlsnaes, Thomas Risse, and Beth A. Simmons, eds. *Handbook of International Relations*, 401–25. Thousand Oaks, CA: SAGE.

Index

Amar, Paul, 157. *See* summary of *Security Archipelago*, 215–219
analysis, methods of, 141–148; content, 144; selective analysis, 204–205; statistical, 145–146. *See also* 147t
Anderson, Benedict, 36, 69

case study methodology, 178–182. *See also* global case study methodology
class, 64–65. *See also* critical theory, inequality and intersectional theory
cosmopolitanism, 39, 126, 152, 175. *See also* ethics
critical methodologies, 129, 151–177
critical theory, 39, 68–69, 73. *See also* class, hegemony, inequality, structure
critical thinking, 34–37, 50, 57–58, 89–90, 101, 206, 226
critical race methodologies, 162–165
critical race theory, 160–165
cultural studies, 17, 36, 62, 67–68, 215
cultural turn, 67–68, 72

Darian-Smith, Eve. *See* summary of *Bridging Divides*, 207–211
decenter: defined, 7–8
decentered processes, 45–47

decentering the nation-state, 6, 70–71, 154–158
decentering knowledge production, 7–9, 126–127, 153, 225–230
decolonize, 6, 54, 230
decolonization, 13, 16, 52, 69, 71, 166–167, 171–173, 195, 216
disciplinary/interdisciplinary debate, 10–12, 56–58

empirical research: foundations of, 78–84
epistemicide, 227
epistemology, 3, 151; non-Western, 7, 17–18, 37–39, 54, 56, 69, 167, 175, 227; triangulation of, 112, 230
ethics, 90, 112–124, 140, 162, 173, 176; global research ethics 39–40, 124–125, 183, 197–200, 230. *See also* cosmopolitanism
ethical pluralism, 40, 125–127

focal point, 185–191
feminist methodologies, 158–162
feminist theory, 158–162. *See also* summary of *Global Icons*, 211–215
Flyvbjerg, Bent, 153

gender, 24, 65–66, 96–97, 152, 158. *See also* feminist methodologies, feminist theory

Geertz, Clifford, 68, 153, 158
Ghosh, Bishnupriya. *See* summary of *Global Icons*, 211–215
global case study methodology, 178–205, 231. *See also* examples of global case studies research, 206–224
global case study outline, 231
global contexts, 2, 106, 109, 125–126, 161, 178, 183–184, 190, 193, 199–200, 229
global citizenship, 34, 53
global dimensions, 4, 7, 45, 75, 148, 183–185, 189, 193–198, 207. *See* 186*f,* 202*f,* 203*f*
global history, 23, 47–49
global imaginary, 3–7, 12–19, 45
global intersectional solidarity, 32
global knowledge production, 7–9, 11, 23, 27, 37–39, 53, 56, 60, 76, 112, 125–127, 171, 176, 198, 227–230
global methodologies, 129–130, 157, 174, 226
global perspectives, 4–5, 10, 32–34, 43–44, 193–198, 225, 227
global-scale, 3–4, 43–45, 183–184
global-scale issues, 11, 26, 30, 43–45, 47, 53, 192–3, 196
global standpoint theory, 175, 226
global studies: characteristics of, 40–54; emergence of the field 21–28; importance 29–40
global transdisciplinary framework, 10–11, 26–27, 55–77, 225–227
global turn, 2, 72
globalization, 1–2, 9–13, 18–22, 58, 70, 74, 152, 155, 166, 174, 195, 227
Griego, Dinah, 219–224

hegemony, 64, 68

imperialism: modern, 32, 61, 65, 68, 69, 162, 165, 169–170, 174, 227–230; cultural, 68; intellectual, 8, 51, 109. *See also* neoimperialism
indigenous methodologies, 169–174
inequality, 19, 32, 41, 50, 64–65, 161, 200, 227
interdisciplinary, 10, 17–18, 21–27, 42, 53, 57–58, 62–63, 73, 86. *See also* disciplinary/interdisciplinary debate
interdisciplinarity/transdisciplinarity: distinguishing between, 59–63
intersectional theory, 65–66, 123, 151–152, 160–162, 174–175, 196–197, 226. *See also* feminist theory , global intersectional solidarity

Juergensmeyer, Mark, 23n3, 25–26, 193. *See also* global-scale issues, global studies, thinking globally, summary of *God in the Tumult of the Global Square,* 219–224

Kuhn, Thomas, 66, 80–81, 90

linguistic turn, 67, 72
local-global continuum, 12, 32, 43–45, 64, 73, 89, 138, 150, 152, 178–179, 183, 188, 191–192, 194–195, 197, 207, 225–226

methods, 129–177; basic data collection, 133; content analysis, 144–145; focus group, 138–139; historical archival, 133–136; interview, 137–138; observation and participant observation, 136–137; statistics, 145–146; survey, 139–141. *See also* analysis, methods of, 141–148, 142*t*
methodologies, 130, 141–177; case study methodology, 142, 178–182; comparing multidimensional cases, 200–204; critical methodologies, 129, 151–177; critical race methodologies, 162–165; feminist methodologies, 158–162; global case study methodology, 183–205; global methodologies, 174–177; indigenous methodologies, 169–174; methodological nationalism, 154–158; mixed methods, 77, 133, 148–151, 154, 176, 193, 207; multidimensional methodology, 191–198; multi-methods, 149; postcolonial methodologies, 165–169; selective analysis, 204–205. *See also* examples of global case studies research, 206–224, global case study outline, 231–232
methodological nationalism, 71, 154–158
mixed methods, 77, 133, 148–151, 154, 176, 193, 207
nationalism, 20, 32, 34, 36, 53, 69–71, 157, 228. *See also* Benedict Anderson, decentering the nation-state, methodological nationalism
neoimperialism, 16–17, 32, 37, 166, 168. *See also* imperialism
non-state actors, 3, 18, 31, 43, 70, 152, 156–157

orientalism, 68, 72. *See also* Edward Said

paradigm shift, 66, 80, 90. *See also* Thomas
    Kuhn
Piaget, Jean, 8, 18, 55, 59, 180. *See also*
    decenter, transdisciplinary
postcolonial methodologies, 165–169
postcolonial studies, 23, 68–69, 163, 165–169
postcolonial theory, 9, 17, 19, 36, 39, 68–69,
    152, 159–161, 167, 211
poststructural theory, 66–67

race, 64. *See also* critical race methodologies,
    critical race theory
research design, 76–128
conceptual triangulation, 111, 226; descriptive
    research designs, 98–100; empirical
    research, 78–84; epistemological
    triangulation, 17–18, 26, 37–39, 54, 56,
    69, 112, 167, 175–176, 227–230;
    explanatory research designs, 94–96;
    exploratory research designs, 96–98;
    focal point, 185–191; global research
    question, 89–92; global sampling logics,
    105–106; policy and applied research
    designs, 100–101; primary and secondary
    research, 131–133; reliability and validity,
    106–109; research ethics, 112–127;
    research question, 87–89; reflexivity, 104,
    151, 213; sampling logic, 101–105;
    triangulation, 109–112, 226

Said, Edward, 9, 68, 162, 227
Santos, Boaventura de Sousa, 227
Sassen, Saskia, 5, 9, 30, 51, 72, 228–229
sexuality, 24, 65–66, 96–97, 152, 158. *See*
    summary of *Security Archipelago*,
    215–219
Soboslai, John, 219–224
social constructionism, 66–67
spatial turn, 72

standpoint theory, 65, 126, 151, 159–160, 162.
    See also global standpoint theory
Steger, Manfred, 3, 13, 19, 23
structure, 36, 41, 49–50, 64, 67, 160;
    racialized, 163–165, 174, 207
subaltern studies, 17, 23, 36, 69, 167

thinking globally, 2, 56, 193–4, 207, 229
theory, 85–87; critical race theory, 160;
    critical theory, 39, 68–69, 73; feminist
    theory, 158–162; global transdisciplinary
    framework, 10–11, 26–27, 55–77,
    225–227; gender, 24, 65–66, 96–97,
    152, 158; postcolonial theory, 9, 17, 19,
    36, 39, 68–69, 152, 159–161, 167, 211;
    poststructural theory, 66–67; race
    theory, 64; social constructionism,
    66–67; standpoint theory, 65, 126, 151,
    159–160, 162; systems theory, 72;
    world-systems, 36, 51, 216. *See also*
    class, critical race methodologies,
    critical race theory, hegemony, global
    standpoint theory
transdisciplinary, 10–13, 18, 55, 58–63, 180.
    See also global transdisciplinary
    framework
triangulation, 109–112, 226; conceptual,
    111, 226; epistemological, 17–18, 26,
    37–39, 54, 56, 69, 112, 167, 175–176,
    227–230

United Nations, 3, 13, 15, 132

validity, 106–112; global validity, 109, 127,
    150, 193, 229

Wallerstein, Immanuel, 16–17, 51
world-systems, 36, 51, 216
Wolf, Eric, 10